New York State Museum Bulletin

Application pending for admission as second-class matter at the Post Office at Albany, N. Y.
under the act of August 24, 1912

Published monthly by The University of the State of New York

No. 184   ALBANY, N. Y.   APRIL 1, 1916

The University of the State of New York

New York State Museum

JOHN M. CLARKE, Director

THE CONSTITUTION OF TF⎯ ⎯

OR

THE IROQUOIS BOOK OF

BY

ARTHUR C. PARKER

ALBANY
THE UNIVERSITY OF THE STATE OF NEW YORK
1916

Reprint Series Editor — Wm. Guy Spittal

The University of the State of New York
Science Department, July 12, 1915

Dr John H. Finley
    President of the University

SIR: I beg to communicate to you herewith and to recommend for publication as a bulletin of the State Museum, a manuscript with accompanying illustrations, entitled *The Constitution of the Five Nations,* which has been prepared by Arthur C. Parker, the Archeologist of the State Museum.

Very respectfully

JOHN M. CLARKE
Director

THE UNIVERSITY OF THE STATE OF NEW YORK
OFFICE OF THE PRESIDENT

Approved for publication this 15th day of March 1915

President of the University

Plate I

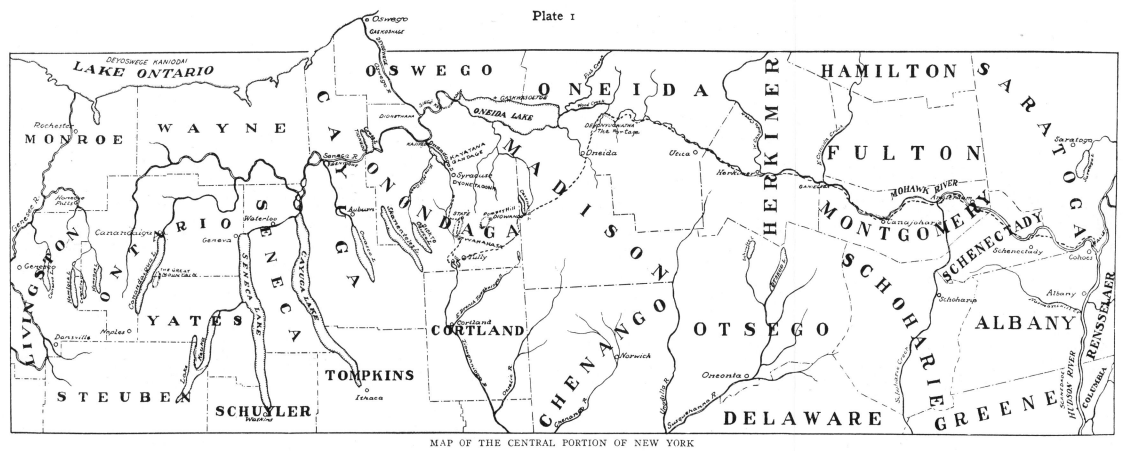

MAP OF THE CENTRAL PORTION OF NEW YORK

THE LONG HOUSE COUNTRY

This area covers the principal region traversed by Dekanawida and Hiawatha in their efforts to effect the formation of the Five Nations' Confederacy. The dotted lines from Onondaga lake through the Mohawk valley shows approximately the route taken by Hiawatha in his journey to meet Dekanawida.

9. THE CENTRAL FIRE OF THE CONFEDERACY, Onondaga, NY
   This composite photo shows the three buildings on the Longhouse grounds, June 30, 1991. The 19th Century frame Longhouse is to the left. It now serves as a recreational building. The "Fire" was moved from the old Longhouse to the new log Longhouse, centre, in 1984. The cemetary is behind this building. To the right is a portion of the "Mud House", a kitchen and dining hall.

New York State Museum Bulletin

Application pending for entry as second-class matter at the Post Office at Albany, N. Y.,
under the act of August 24, 1912

Published monthly by The University of the State of New York

No. 184   ALBANY, N. Y.   APRIL 1, 1916

The University of the State of New York
New York State Museum
JOHN M. CLARKE, Director

THE CONSTITUTION OF THE FIVE NATIONS

OR

THE IROQUOIS BOOK OF THE GREAT LAW

BY

ARTHUR C. PARKER

THE IROQUOIS CONSTITUTION

The constitution of the Iroquois League is known to the Iroquois as the Great Binding Law, or the Great Immutable Law. Their term for it is Ne" Gayänĕshä"gowā. It was transmitted orally from one generation to another through certain of the lords or sachems of the confederacy who had made it their business to learn it. Not until recently have the Iroquois attempted to put their code in written form. For many generations its knowledge has been preserved by a collection of wampum belts and strings, each of which served to recall each law or regulation. Many of the belts and strings became lost or destroyed, and fearing a total destruction of their ancient archives, the Six Nations[1] of New York Indians in 1898 elected The University of the State of New York the official custodian of their wampums. The University accepted the charge and the Legislature passed suitable laws governing the custody of the wampums. In 1908 the Director of the State Museum was proclaimed the keeper of the wampums by Sa-ha-whi, president of the Six Nations.

---

[1] The Five Nations became the Six Nations, with the admission of the Tuscarora in 1724.

The Iroquois constitution is mentioned by both Morgan and Hale, but neither seems to have been able to make a transcript and translation of it. All the Iroquois nations were acquainted with it and extracts from the law are found in many of the speeches of their sachems, as recorded by historians, notably the French explorers and Colden.

The version of the constitution now held authentic by the Iroquois of New York and Ontario, embraces a narrative of the events in the lives of Hiawatha and Dekanawida that lead up to its foundation. Its special interest lies in the fact that it is an attempt of the Iroquois themselves to explain their own civic and social system. It is therefore an invaluable guide to many interesting branches of Iroquois ethnology. Many of the facts contained in this document are familiar to students, but that they formed a part of a definite system of law will perhaps be new. Several of the wampum belts in the New York State Museum are constitutional belts or memorials.

Originally the Five Nations of Iroquois were similar to other Indian tribes or bands — independent bodies with similar dialects and similar customs but with no political coherence. Each man and each tribe to itself, was the rule. Often the individual nations warred with one another, and with external enemies pressing them from all quarters they found themselves in a precarious situation. The very peril in which they lived developed their strategic ability and fostered diplomacy. It likewise produced leaders and finally the great lawgiver who should bring about peace and unity and make the Iroquois the "Indians of Indian," the "Romans of the New World." Hale referred to Hiawatha as the "lawgiver of the Stone age"[1] but Hiawatha does not deserve the title. He was only the spokesman of a greater mind. The Mohawk nation recognizes in Dekanawida its great culture hero and the founder of its civic system, giving Haiyentwatha (Hiawatha) a second place. Nearly all authorities among the other nations of the five agree in this and attribute to Dekanawida the establishment of the Great Peace. The prefatory articles of the Great Immutable Law recognize him as such and represent him as saying:

> I am Dekanawideh and with the Five Nations' confederate lords I plant the Tree of the Great Peace. I plant it in your territory Adodarhoh and the Onondaga Nation, in the territory of you who are fire keepers.
> I name the tree the Tree of the Great Long Leaves. Under the shade of this Tree of the Great Peace we spread the soft, white, feathery down of the globe thistle as seats for you, Adodarhoh and your cousin lords.

---

[1] Proc. Amer. Ass'n. Adv. Sci., 30:324. 1881.

. . . There shall you sit and watch the council fire of the Confederacy of the Five Nations.

Roots have spread out from the Tree of the Great Peace . . . and the name of these roots is the Great White Roots of Peace. If any man of any nation outside of the Five Nations shall show a desire to obey the laws of the Great Peace . . . they may trace the roots to their source . . . and they shall be welcomed to take shelter beneath the Tree of the Long Leaves.

The smoke of the confederate council fire shall ever ascend and shall pierce the sky so that all nations may discover the central council fire of the Great Peace.

I, Dekanawideh, and the confederate lords now uproot the tallest pine tree and into the cavity thereby made we cast all weapons of war. Into the depths of the earth, down into the deep underearth currents of water flowing into unknown regions, we cast all weapons of strife. We bury them from sight forever and plant again the tree. Thus shall all Great Peace be established and hostilities shall no longer be known between the Five Nations but only peace to a united people.

As one goes further into the unique document, the method by which universal peace is to be established is revealed. All nations were to sit beneath the peace tree and acknowledge the imperial regency of the Five Nations' council. To the Five Nations this seemed a very simple thing for they called themselves Ongweoweh, Original Men, a term that implied their racial superiority. Thus to them it seemed quite natural that other nations should acknowledge their right to rule. They never doubted the justness of their claim or saw that it possibly could be disputed. With them it was the basis for universal action. Other nations were inclined to dispute that the Iroquois were inherently superior and naturally rebelled at the idea of submission, even though it might be for their own ultimate benefit.

From tribe to tribe, tradition shows,[1] the emissaries of the Great Peace went carrying with them the messages in their wampum strands, and inviting delegates to sit beneath the Peace Tree and "clasp their arms about it" and to discuss the advantages of an alliance.

The political success of the Iroquois as a result of their system gave them phenomenal strength and likewise excited widespread jealousy. Thus the Iroquois found themselves plunged in a war for existence and without friends to call upon.

How a government calling itself the Great Peace provided for war is shown in the part of the great immutable law called " Skanawatih's Laws of Peace and War." Extracts from these laws follow :

When the proposition to establish the Great Peace is made to a foreign nation it shall be done in mutual council. The nation is to be persuaded

---

[1] See, for example, The Passamaquoddy Wampum Records by J. D. Prince, page 483. Proc. Amer. Phil. Soc., v. 36. Also Appendix, page 119 of this bulletin.

by reason and urged to come into the Great Peace. If the Five Nations fail . . . after a third council . . . the war captain of the Five Nations shall address the head chief of the rebellious nation and request him three times to accept the Great Peace. If refusal steadfastly follows the war captain shall let a bunch of white lake shells fall from his outstretched hand and shall bound quickly forward and club the offending chief to death. War shall thereby be declared and the war captain shall have his men at his back to support him in any emergency. War shall continue until won by the Five Nations. . . . Then shall the Five Nations seek to establish the Great Peace by a conquest of the rebellious nation.

When peace shall have been established by the termination of the war . . . then the war captain shall cause all weapons of war to be taken from the nation. Then shall the Great Peace be established and the nation shall observe all the rules of the Great Peace for all time to come.

Whenever a foreign nation is conquered or has by their own free will accepted the Great Peace, their own system of internal government may continue so far as is consistent but they must cease all strife with other nations.

In this manner and under these provisions and others every rebellious tribe or nation, almost without exception, was either exterminated or absorbed. The Erie, the Neutral, the Huron, the Andaste and other cognate tribes of the Iroquoian stock were broken up and the scattered bands or survivors settled in the numerous Iroquois towns to forget in time their birth nation and to be known forever after only as Iroquois. The law read, " Henceforth let no one so adopted mention the name of his birth nation. To do so will hasten the end of the Great Peace." The Lenni Lenape or Delaware, the Nanticoke, the broken bands of the Minsi and the Shawne, the Brothertown and other Algonquian tribes yielded to the armed persuasions to accept the Great Peace; likewise did the Tutelo and Catawba of the eastern Siouan stock, and the Choctaw of the Muskoghean yield, and to that action is due the fact that they have descendants today.

The Iroquois policy of adopting captives led to the mixture of widely scattered stocks. The Iroquois therefore became an ethnic group of composite elements. Thus from the ideas of universal peace and brotherhood grew universal intermarriage, modified of course by clan laws.

According to the great immutable law the Iroquois confederate council was to consist of fifty rodiyaner (civil chiefs) and was to be divided into three bodies, namely, the older brothers, the Mohawk and the Seneca ; the younger brothers, the Cayuga and the Oneida ; and the fire keepers, the Onondaga. Each brotherhood debated a question separately and reported to the fire keepers, who referred the matter back and ordered a unanimous report. If the two brotherhoods still disagreed the fire keepers had the casting vote.

If, however, the brotherhoods agreed and their decision was not in accord with the wishes of the fire keepers, the fire keepers could only confirm the decision, for absolute unanimity was the law and required for the passage of any question. Provisions to break speedily any deadlock were provided. All the work of the council was done without an executive head, save a temporary speaker appointed by acclamation. Adodarhoh, in spite of his high title, was only the moderator of the fire keepers.

These "lords" or civil chiefs were nominated by certain noble women in whose families the titles were hereditary; the nominations were confirmed by popular councils both of men and of women and finally by the confederate council. Women thus had great power for not only could they nominate their rulers but also depose them for incompetency in office. Here, then, we find the right of popular nomination, the right of recall and of woman suffrage, all flourishing in the old America of the Red Man and centuries before it became the clamor of the new America of the white invader. Who now shall call Indians and Iroquois savages!

Not only were there popular councils to check an overambitious government, but both the men and the women had in their "war chief" a sort of aboriginal public service commissioner who had authority to voice their will before the council. Men of worth who had won their way into the hearts of the people were elected pine tree chiefs with voice but no vote in the governing body. The rights of every man were provided for and all things done for the promotion of the Great Peace.

Among the interesting things in this Iroquois constitution are the provisions for the official symbols. Many of these symbols, such as the point within a circle, the bundle of arrows, the watchful eagle, are described in detail. The fifteenth string of the Tree of the Long Leaves section, for example, reads:

"Five arrows shall be bound together very strongly and each arrow shall represent one nation. As the five arrows are strongly bound, this shall symbolize the union of the nations. . . ."

This reference to the arrows bound together was quoted by King Hendrick in 1755 in his talk with Sir William Johnson.

Perhaps a more striking paragraph to students of Indian history will be the reference to a certain wampum belt:

"A broad, dark belt of wampum . . . having a white heart in the center on either side of which are two white squares all connected with the heart by white rows shall be the emblem of the unity of the Five Nations. The white heart in the middle . . .

means the Onondaga nation . . . and it also means that the heart of the Five Nations is single in its loyalty to the Great Peace. . . ."

This belt is sometimes called the Hiawatha belt and is one of the most valuable Iroquois belts now extant. It is now on exhibition in the Congressional Library.

The Great Peace as a governmental system was an almost ideal one for the stage of culture with which it was designed to cope. I think it will be found to be the greatest ever devised by barbaric man on any continent. By adhering to it the Five Nations became the dominant native power east of the Mississippi and during the colonial times exercised an immense influence in determining the fate of English civilization on the continent. They, as allies of the British, fought for it and destroyed all French hopes for colonization.

The authors of the great immutable law gave the Iroquois two great culture heroes, heroes almost without equal in American Indian annals. Through the law as a guiding force and through the heroes as ideals the Iroquois have persisted as a people, preserved their national identity and much of their native culture and lore. Today in their various bodies they number more than 16,000 souls. This is a remarkable fact when it is considered that they are entirely surrounded by a dominant culture whose encroachments are persistent and unrelenting in the very nature of things.

The Canadian Iroquois indeed govern themselves by the laws contained in these codes, proving their utility even in modern days.

The two principal manuscripts that form the basis of this work were found in the Six Nations Reservation, Ontario, Canada, in 1910.

The first manuscript was a lengthy account of the Dekanawida legend and an account of the Confederate Iroquois laws. This material has been brought together by Seth Newhouse, a Mohawk, who has expended a large amount of time and given the subject a lengthy study. His account written in Indian English was submitted to Albert Cusick, a New York Onondaga-Tuscarora, for review and criticism. Mr Cusick had long been an authority on Iroquois law and civic rites, and had been a chief informant for Horatio Hale, William M. Beauchamp and in several instances for the present writer. Mr Cusick was employed for more than a month in correcting the Newhouse manuscript until he believed the form in which it is now presented fairly correct and at least as accurate as a free translation could be made.

The second manuscript was compiled by the chiefs of the Six Nations council and in the form here published has been reviewed and corrected by several of their own number, including Chiefs John Gibson, Jacob Johnson and John William Elliott. The official copy was made by Hilton Hill, a Seneca, then employed by the Dominion superintendent for the Six Nations. It has been reviewed and changes were suggested by Albert Cusick.

The Newhouse code was divided into three sections. These were, " The Tree of the Long Leaves," " The Emblematical Union Compact," and " Skanawatih's Law of Peace and War." Each law was associated with a wampum belt or string of wampum beads. The string number and the section of the code from which it is extracted is indicated after each law, as given in the text.

In examining this code of Iroquois law it will be noted that no reference is made in the Canadian codes to the " Long House of the Five Nations." Various reasons are assigned for this. Mr Newhouse cut out all reference to it from his original manuscript because some of the older chiefs said that Handsome Lake, the destroyer of the old religious system, had successfully associated his religious teachings with the Long House. The force of this fact is apparent when we learn that a follower of the Handsome Lake religion is called among other names, Gānūñ'sisnē'ha, " Long House Lover." Another reason is that the historic Long House territory is in New York State, and that the Ontario Iroquois who left New York after the Revolution to cling to the British, dislike any reference to their former habitation that seems to bind them to it. The Dekanawida code provides a refuge for the confederacy in distress, and in Canada they believe they have found " the great elm " under which they may gather in safety to continue their national existence.

In presenting these documents the original orthography has been retained. The only attempt to record Iroquois names and words phonetically is in the notes. This will account for some variations in spelling. The Mohawk and Onondaga writers in their manuscripts used Ayonhwatha and Hayonhwatha interchangeably and there are other variations.

THE DEKANAWIDA LEGEND[1]
DEKANAWIDA'S BIRTH AND JOURNEY

North of the beautiful lake (Ontario) in the land of the Crooked Tongues, was a long winding bay and at a certain spot was the Huron town, Ka-ha-nah-yenh. Near by was the great hill, Ti-ro-nat-ha-ra-da-donh. In the village lived a good woman who had a virgin daughter. Now strangely this virgin conceived and her mother knew that she was about to bear a child. The daughter about this time went into a long sleep and dreamed that her child should be a son whom she should name Dekanawida. The messenger in the dream told her that he should become a great man and that he should go among the Flint people to live and that he should also go to the Many Hill Nation and there raise up the Great Tree of Peace. It was true as had been said the virgin gave birth to a boy and the grandmother greatly disliked him and she rebuked her daughter.

"You refuse to tell me the father of the child," she said, "and now how do you know that great calamity will not befall us, and our nation? You must drown the child."

So then the mother took the child to the bay and chopped a hole in the ice where she customarily drew water and thrust him in, but when night came the child was found at his mother's bosom. So then the mother took the child again and threw him in the bay but at night the child returned. Then the third time the grandmother herself took the child and drowned him but in the morning the child nestled as before on its mother's own bosom.

So the grandmother marveled that the child, her grandson, could not be drowned. Then she said to her daughter:

"Mother, now nurse your child for he may become an important man. He can not be drowned, we know, and you have borne him without having marriage with any man. Now I have never heard of such an occurrence nor has the world known of it before."

Beginning with that time the mother took great care of her child and nursed him. She named him Dekanawida in accord with the instruction of her dream.

The child rapidly grew and was remarkably strong and healthy. His appearance was noticed for its good aspect and his face was most handsome.

When Dekanawida had grown to manhood he was greatly abused

---

[1] From the Newhouse version.

by the Huron people because of his handsome face and his good mind. He was always honest and always told what he believed was right. Nevertheless he was a peculiar man and his people did not understand him.

Many things conspired to drive him away for the Crooked Tongues had no love for such a man. Their hearts were bitter against a man who loved not war better than all things.

After a journey by canoe across the lake he came into the hunting territory of the Flint Nation. He journeyed on to the lower fall of the river of the Flint Nation and made a camp a short way from the fall on the flat land above it. He sat beneath a tall tree and smoked his pipe in quiet meditation.

A man of the Flints passed by and seeing the fire and the stranger approached him cautiously to discover what weapon he bore, if any. Carefully the man of the Flint reconnoitered but saw no weapon, but only the stranger quietly smoking. Returning to the town a short distance away the presence of the odd stranger was reported. Then the chiefs and their men went out and assembled about the man who smoked. One of the head men was delegated to question the stranger and so he asked " From whence came you?"

" I am from Ka-ka-na-yenh," the stranger replied.

" I am of the Wyandots, whom you call the Crooked Tongues because our speech is slightly different," answered the stranger, " My·mother is a virgin woman."

" Then," said the speaker, " By what name are you known?"

" I am Dekanawidah, so named because my virgin mother dreamed that it should be so and no one else shall ever be named by this name."

" What brought you here to us," asked the speaker.

So then Dekanawidah answered, " The Great Creator from whom we all are descended sent me to establish the Great Peace among you. No longer shall you kill one another and nations shall cease warring upon each other. Such things are entirely evil and he, your Maker, forbids it. Peace and comfort are better than war and misery for a nation's welfare."

Then answered the speaker of the Flints, "All that you say is surely true and we are not able to contradict it. We must have proof, however, before we submit ourselves to you whereby we may know that you indeed possess rightful power to establish the Great Peace."

So answered Dekanawida, " I am able to demonstrate my power for I am the messenger of the Creator and he truly has given me my choice of the manner of my death."

" Choose then," said the speaker, " a manner of destruction for we are ready to destroy you." Dekanawida replied, " By the side of the falls at the edge of a precipice stands a tall tree. I will climb the tree and seat myself in the topmost branches. Then shall you cut down the tree and I shall fall into the depths below. Will not that destroy me?"

Then said the speaker, " Let us proceed at once."

Dekanawida ascended the tree and it was chopped down. A multitude of people saw him fall into the chasm and plunge into the water. So they were satisfied that he was surely drowned. Night came but Dekanawida did not appear and thus were the people sure of his death, and then were they satisfied.

The next morning the warriors saw strange smoke arising from the smoke hole of an empty cabin. They approached cautiously and peering in the side of the wall where the bark was loosened they saw Dekanawidah. He was alive and was not a ghost and he was cooking his morning meal.

So the watchers reported their discovery and then were the chiefs and people truly convinced that indeed Dekanawidah might establish the Great Peace.

THE TROUBLED NATIONS

The Ongwe-oweh had fought long and bravely. So long had they fought that they became lustful for war and many times Endeka-Gakwa, the Sun, came out of the east to find them fighting. It was thus because the Ongwe-oweh were so successful that they said the Sun loved war and gave them power.

All the Ongwe-oweh fought other nations sometimes together and sometimes singly and, ah-gi! ofttimes they fought among themselves. The nation of the Flint had little sympathy for the Nation of the Great Hill, and sometimes they raided one another's settlements. Thus did brothers and Ongwe-oweh fight. The nation of the Sunken Pole fought the Nation of the Flint and hated them, and the Nation of the Sunken Pole was Ongwe.

Because of bitter jealousy and love of bloodshed sometimes towns would send their young men against the young men of another town to practise them in fighting.

Even in his own town a warrior's own neighbor might be his enemy and it was not safe to roam about at night when Soi-ka-Gakwa, our Grandmother, the Moon, was hidden.

Everywhere there was peril and everywhere mourning. Men were ragged with sacrifice and the women scarred with the flints, so everywhere there was misery. Feuds with outer nations, feuds with brother nations, feuds of sister towns and feuds of families and of clans made every warrior a stealthy man who liked to kill.

Then in those days there was no great law. Our founder had not yet come to create peace and give united strength to the Real Men, the Ongwe-oweh.

In those same days the Onondagas had no peace. A man's life was valued as nothing. For any slight offence a man or woman was killed by his enemy and in this manner feuds started between families and clans. At night none dared leave their doorways lest they be struck down by an enemy's war club. Such was the condition when there was no Great Law.

South of the Onondaga town lived an evil-minded man. His lodge was in a swale and his nest was made of bulrushes. His body was distorted by seven crooks and his long tangled locks were adorned by writhing living serpents. Moreover, this monster was a devourer of raw meat, even of human flesh. He was also a master of wizardry and by his magic he destroyed men but he could not be destroyed. Adodarhoh was the name of the evil man.

Notwithstanding the evil character of Adadarhoh the people of Onondaga, the Nation of Many Hills, obeyed his commands and though it cost many lives they satisfied his insane whims, so much did they fear him for his sorcery.

The time came, however, when the Onondaga people could endure him no longer. A council was called to devise a way to pacify him and to entreat him to cease his evil ways. Hayonwatha called the council for he had many times sought to clear the mind of Adodarhoh and straighten his crooked body. So then the council was held in the house of Hayontawatha. It was decided that half the people should go by boat across the creek where it widens and that others should skirt the shore. Adodarhoh was not in his nest in the swale but in a new spot across the wide place in the creek.

The boats started and the people walked. From the bushes that overhung the shore a loud voice sounded. " Stand quickly and look behind you for a storm will overwhelm you."

In dismay the people arose in their canoes and turned about. As they did so the canoes overturned and the men were plunged into the water and many were drowned. A few escaped and then all survivors returned to the village. So had Adodarhoh frustrated the attempt to meet with him.

Again the people prepared to conciliate Adodarho. Three times they agreed to attempt the undertaking. So on the second occasion they go by canoe and by land, those who go by canoe follow the shore and those who go by land walk on the pebbles close to the water's edge.

Again the cunning Adodarho sees them and calling down Hagoks he shook him, and the people in a wild rush scramble for the feathers, for the plumes of Hagoks are most beautiful and men are proud when their heads are adorned with them. There is a tumult and blows are struck. Evil feelings arise and in anger the people return to the village still contending. The mission of conciliation is forgotten.

The next day Ayonhwatha called the people to their promise and for the third time to attempt a council with Adodarho. Moreover, they promised to obey every instruction and listen neither to a voice outside nor an omen nor any commotion.

Another council was held in the lodge of a certain great dreamer. He said, " I have dreamed that another shall prevail. He shall come from the north and pass to the east. Hayonwhatha shall meet him there in the Mohawk country and the two together shall prevail. Hayonwhatha must not remain with us but must go from us to the Flint land people."

So when the journey across the lake was attempted there was a division and the dreamer's council prevailed.

Then the dreamer held two councils and those who believed in him conspired to employ Ohsinoh, a famous shaman.

Hayonwhatha had seven daughters whom he loved and in whom he took great pride. While they lived the conspirators knew he would not depart. With the daughters dead they knew the crushing sorrow would sever every tie that bound him to Onondaga. Then would he be free to leave and in thinking of the welfare of the people forget his own sorrow.

Hayonwhatha could not call the people together for they refused further to listen to his voice. The dreamer's council had prevailed.

At night Osinoh climbed a tree overlooking his lodge and sat on a large limb. Filling his mouth with clay he imitated the sound of a screech owl. Calling the name of the youngest daughter he sang:

> " Unless you marry Osinoh
> You will surely die, -whoo-hoo!"

Then he came down and went to his own home.

In three days the maiden strangely died. Hayonwhatha was disconsolate and sat sitting with his head bowed in his hands. He mourned, but none came to comfort him.

In like manner five other daughters passed away and the grief of Hayonwhatha was extreme.

Clansmen of the daughters then went to the lodge of Hayonwhatha to watch, for they knew nothing of Osinoh's sorcery. They gathered close against the large trees and in the shadows of bushes. The clansmen suspected some evil treachery and were there to discover it.

There was no moon in the sky when Osinoh came. Cautiously he came from habit but he was not afraid. He drove his staff in the ground, he breathed loud like a magic totem animal snorting and then he climbed the tree. He spat the clay about the tree to imitate the screech owl and as he did he said: " Si-twit, si-twit, si-twit." Then he sang:

> " Unless you marry Osinoh
> You shall surely die, whoo-hoo! "

The morning came and Osinoh descended. As he touched the ground a clansman shot an arrow and transfixed him. Prostrate fell Osinoh and the clansman rushed at him with a club.

Osinoh looked up. " You are unable to club me," he said. " Your arm has no power at all. It weakens. Today I shall recover from this wound. It is of no purpose to injure me."

It was true indeed; the clansman could not lift the club to kill Osinoh. Then Osinoh arose and went home and in three days the daughter died. So perished all by the evil magic arts of Osinoh.

The grief of Hayonwhatha was terrible. He threw himself about as if tortured and yielding to the pain. No one came near him so awful was his sorrow. Nothing would console him and his mind was shadowed with the thoughts of his heavy sorrow.

" I shall cast myself away, I shall bury myself in the forest, I shall become a woodland wanderer," he said. Thus he expressed his desire to depart. Then it was known that he would go to another nation.

Hayonwhatha " split the heavens," Watanwhakacia, when he departed and his skies were rent asunder.

Toward the south he went and at night he camped on the mountain. This was the first day of his journey. On the second day he descended and camped at the base of the hill. On the third day he journeyed onward and when evening came he camped in a hickory grove. This he named O-nea-no-ka-res-geh, and it was on the morning he came to a place where round jointed rushes grew. He paused as he saw them and made three strings of them and when he had built a fire he said: "This would I do if I found anyone burdened with grief even as I am. I would console them for they would be covered with night and wrapped in darkness. This would I lift with words of condolence and these strands of beads would become words with which I would address them."

So at this place he stayed that night and he called the spot O-hon-do-gon-wa, meaning Rush-land.

When daylight came he wandered on again and altering the course of his journey turned to the east. At night he came to a group of small lakes and upon one he saw a flock of ducks. So many were there and so closely together did they swim that they seemed like a raft.

"If I am to be truly royaneh (noble)," he said aloud to himself, "I shall here discover my power." So then he spoke aloud and said: "Oh you who are 'floats' lift up the water and permit me to pass over the bottom of the lake dryshod."

In a compact body the ducks flew upward suddenly and swiftly, lifting the water with them. Thus did he walk down the shore and upon the bottom of the lake. There he noticed lying in layers the empty shells of the water snail, some shells white, and others purple. Stooping down he filled a pouch of deer skin with them, and then passed on to the other shore. Then did the ducks descend and replace the water.

It was here that Hayonwhatha desired for the first time to eat. He then killed three ducks and roasted them. This was the evening of the fifth day.

In the morning he ate the cold meat of the roasted ducks and resumed his journey. This was the sixth day and on that day he hunted for small game and slept.

On the morning of the seventh day he ate again and turned his way to the south. Late in the evening he came to a clearing and found a bark field hut. There he found a shelter and there he erected two poles, placed another across the tops and suspended three shell strings. Looking at them he said: "Men boast what they would do in extremity but they do not do what they say. If I should see anyone in deep grief I would remove these shell strings from the pole and console them. The strings would become words and lift away the darkness with which they are covered. Moreover what I say I would surely do." This he repeated.

A little girl discovered smoke arising from the field lodge and she crept up and listened. She advanced and peered in a chink in the bark. Then she ran homeward and told her father of the strange man.

"The stranger must be Hayonwhatha," said the father, "I have heard that he has departed from Onondaga. Return, my daughter, and invite him to our house."

The girl-child obeyed and Hayonwhatha went to her house. "We are about to hold a council," the father said. "Sit in that place on one side of the fire and I will acquaint you with our decisions."

The council was convened and there was a great discussion. Before darkness every evening the council dissolved and at no time was Hayonwhatha called upon for advice nor was anything officially reported to him.

On the tenth day of his journey during the debate in the council Hayonwhatha quietly left and resumed his wandering. Nothing had been asked of him and he felt himself not needed by the people. Late in the evening he came to the edge of another settlement and as was his custom he kindled a fire and erected a horizontal pole on two upright poles. On this he placed three strings of the wampum shells. Then he sat down and repeated his saying: "Men boast what they would do in extremity but they do not do what they promise. If I should see any one in deep grief I would remove these shells from this pole and console him. The shells would become words and lift away the darkness with which they are covered. Moreover, I truly would do as I say." This he repeated.

The chief man of the village saw the smoke at the edge of the forest and sent a messenger to discover who the stranger might be. Now when the messenger reached the spot he saw a man seated before a fire and a horizontal pole from which three strings of small shells were suspended. He also heard the words spoken as the stranger looked at the strings. So then when he had seen all he returned and reported what he had seen and heard.

Then said the chief man, "The person whom you describe must truly be Hayonwhatha whom we have heard left his home at Onondaga. He it is who shall meet the great man foretold by the dreamer. We have heard that this man should work with the man who talks of the establishment of peace."

So then the chiefs sent a messenger who should say, "Our principal chief sent me to greet you. Now then I wish you would come into our village with me."

Hayonwhatha heard the messenger and gathered up his goods and went into the village and when he had entered the chief's house the chief said, " Seat yourself on the opposite side of the fire so that you may have an understanding of all that we do here in this place."

Then Hayonhwatha sat there for seven days and the chiefs and people talked without arriving at any decision. No word was asked Hayonhwatha and he was not consulted. No report was made officially to him. So he did not hear what they talked about.

On the eighteenth night a runner came from the south. He was from the nation residing on the seashore. He told the chiefs of the eminent man who had now come to the town on the Mohawk river at the lower falls. Then the messenger said: " We have heard of the dream of Onodaga which told of the great man who came from the north. Now another great man who shall now go forward in haste to meet him shall change his course and go eastward to meet in the Flinty land village (Kanyakahake), the great man. There shall the two council together and establish the Great Peace." So said the messenger from the salt water seashore, who came to tell Hayonwhatha to journey east.

So the chiefs of the town where Hayonhwatha was staying chose five men as an escort for Hayonhwatha. They must go with him until he reached the house where Dekanawida was present. So then on the next day the chief himself went with the party and watched carefully the health of Hayonhwatha. The journey lasted five days and on the fifth day the party stopped on the outskirts of the town where Dekanawida was staying and then they built a fire. This was the custom, to make a smoke so that the town might know that visitors were approaching and send word that they might enter without danger to their lives. The smoke was the signal of friends approaching.[1] The Mohawks (People of the Flinty Country) knew the meaning of the signal so they sent messengers and invited the party into the village.

When Hayonhwatha had entered the house where the people had gathered the chief asked him whom he would like to see most. Then Ayonhwatha answered, " I came to see a very great man who lately came from the north." The chief said, " I have with you two men who shall escort you to the house where Dekanawida is

---

[1] In those days it was necessary to build a fire on the outskirts of a village about to be entered. If necessary to kill an animal for food, its pelt must be hung on a tree in plain sight because it is the property of the nation in whose territory it is killed. This information was given to me by Albert Cusick and Seth Newhouse.

present." Then the people went out and the two men escorted Hayonhwatha to Dekanawida. This was on the twenty-third day. Then Dekanawida arose when Hayonhwatha had entered and he said: " My younger brother I perceive that you have suffered from some deep grief. You are a chief among your people and yet you are wandering about."

Hayonhwatha answered, " That person skilled in sorcery, Osinoh, has destroyed my family of seven daughters. It was truly a great calamity and I am now very miserable. My sorrow and my rage have been bitter. I can only rove about since now I have cast myself away from my people. I am only a wanderer. I split the heavens when I went away from my house and my nation."

Dekanawida replied, " Dwell here with me. I will represent your sorrow to the people here dwelling."

So Hayonhwatha had found some one who considered his distress and he did stay. Then Dekanawida told of his suffering and the people listened.

The five escorts were then dismissed and Hayonhwatha gave thanks to them and told them to return to their own region again. Then the escorts said, " Now today it has happened as was foretold in a dream. The two are now together. Let them now arrange the Great Peace." Then they returned home.

When Dekanawida laid the trouble before the council he promised to let Hayonhwatha know their decision. The chiefs deliberated over the sad events and then decided to do as Dekanawida should say. He then should remedy the trouble. Then Dekanawida went in perplexity to his lodge and as he came to it he heard Hayonhwatha say, " It is useless, for the people only boast what they will do, saying ' I would do this way,' but they do nothing at all. If what has befallen me should happen to them I would take down the three shell strings from the upright pole and I would address them and I would console them because they would be covered by heavy darkness." Dekanawida stood outside the door and heard all these words. So then Dekanawida went forward into the house and he went up to the pole, then he said: " My younger brother, it has now become very plain to my eyes that your sorrow must be removed. Your griefs and your rage have been great. I shall now undertake to remove your sorrow so that your mind may be rested. Have you no more shell strings on your pole ? "

Hayonhwatha replied, " I have no more strings but I have many shells in a tanned deer's skin." So he opened his bundle and a great

quantity of shells fell out. So then Dekanawida said, "My younger
brother, I shall string eight more strands because there must be
eight parts to my address to you." So then Hayonhwatha permitted the stringing of the shells and Dekanawida made the strings
so that in all there were thirteen strings and bound them in four
bunches. These must be used to console the one who has lost by
death a near relative. "My younger brother, the thirteen strings
are now ready on this horizontal pole. I shall use them. I shall
address you. This is all that is necessary in your case."

So then he took one bunch off the pole and held it in his hand
while he talked. While he talked one after another he took them
down and gave one to Hayonhwatha after each part of his address.

The words that he spoke when he addressed Hayonhwatha were
eight of the thirteen condolences.

When the eight ceremonial addresses had been made by Dekana
wida the mind of Hayonhwatha was made clear. He was then satisfied and once more saw things rightly.

Dekanawida then said, "My younger brother, these thirteen
strings of shell are now completed. In the future they shall be used
in this way: They shall be held in the hand to remind the speaker
of each part of his address, and as each part is finished a string
shall be given to the bereaved chief (Royaneh) on the other side of
the fire. Then shall the Royaneh hand them back one by one as he
addresses a reply; it then can be said, ' I have now become even
with you.' "

Dekanawida then said, " My junior brother, your mind being
cleared and you being competent to judge, we now shall make our
laws and when all are made we shall call the organization we have
formed the Great Peace. It shall be the power to abolish war and
robbery between brothers and bring peace and quietness.

"As emblems of our Royoneh titles we shall wear deer antlers
and place them on the heads of Royaneh men."

Hayonhwatha then said, " What you have said is good, I do
agree."

Dekanawida said, " My younger brother, since you have agreed
I now propose that we compose our Peace song. We shall use it
on our journey to pacify Adodarhoh. When he hears it his mind
shall be made straight. His mind shall then be like that of other
men. This will be true if the singer remembers and makes no error
in his singing from the beginning to the end, as he walks before
Adodarhoh."

Hayonhwatha said, "I do agree, I truly believe the truth of what you say."

Then Dekanawida said, "My younger brother, we shall now propose to the Mohawk council the plan we have made. We shall tell our plan for a confederation and the building of a house of peace. It will be necessary for us to know its opinion and have its consent to proceed."

The plan was talked about in the council and Dekanawida spoke of establishing a union of all the nations. He told them that all the chiefs must be virtuous men and be very patient. These should wear deer horns as emblems of their position, because as he told them their strength came from the meat of the deer. Then Hayonhwatha confirmed all that Dekanawida had said.

Then the speaker of the Mohawk council said, " You two, Dekanawida and Hayonhwatha, shall send messengers to the Oneida (People of the Stone) and they shall ask Odatshedeh if he will consider the plan."

When Odatshedeh had been asked he replied, " I will consider this plan and answer you tomorrow."

When the tomorrow of the next year had come, there came the answer of the Oneida council, " We will join the confederation."

So then the Mohawks (Kanyenga) sent two messengers to Onondaga asking that the nation consider the proposals of Dekanawida. It was a midsummer day when the message went forth and the Onondaga council answered, "Return tomorrow at high sun." So the two great men returned home and waited until the next midsummer. Then the midday came and the Onondaga council sent messengers who said, " We have decided that it would be a good plan to build the fire and set about it with you." Dekanawida and Hayonhwatha heard this answer.

So then at the same time Dekanawida and Hayonhwatha sent messengers to the Cayuga nation and the answer was sent back. The Cayugas said they would send word of their decision tomorrow, upon the midsummer day. The next year at midsummer the Cayugas sent their answer and they said, "We do agree with Dekanawida and Hayonhwatha."

Now the People of the Great Hill were divided and were not agreed because there had been trouble between their war chiefs, but messengers were sent to them but the Senecas could not agree to listen and requested the messengers to return the next year. So when the messengers returned the councils did listen and considered the proposals. After a year had passed they sent messengers to say that they had agreed to enter into the confederacy.

Then Dekanawida said, " I now will report to the Mohawk council the result of my work of five years." Hayonhwatha then said, " I do agree to the report."

THE ESTABLISHMENT OF THE GREAT PEACE

Dekanawida requested some of the Mohawk chiefs to call a council, so messengers were sent out among the people and the council was convened.

Dekanawida said, " I, with my co-worker, have a desire to now report what we have done on five successive midsummer days, of five successive years. We have obtained the consent of five nations. These are the Mohawks, the Oneidas, the Onondagas, the Cayugas and the Senecas. Our desire is to form a compact for a union of our nations. Our next step is to seek out Adodarhoh. It is he who has always set at naught all plans for the establishment of the Great Peace. We must seek his fire and look for his smoke."

The chief speaker of the council then said, " We do agree and confirm all you have said and we wish to appoint two spies who shall volunteer to seek out the smoke of Adodarhoh."

Two men then eagerly volunteered and Dekanawida asked them if they were able to transform themselves into birds or animals, for such must be the ability of the messengers who approached Adodarhoh. The two men replied, " We are able to transform ourselves into herons and cranes."

" Then you will not do for you will pause at the first creek or swamp and look for frogs and fish."

Two men then said, " We have magic that will transform us into humming birds. They fly very swiftly."

" Then you will not do because you are always hungry and are looking for flowers."

Two other men then said, " We can become the Dare, the white crane."

" Then you will not do because you are very wild and easily frightened. You would be afraid when the clouds move. You would become hungry and fly to the ground looking about for ground nuts."

Then two men who were crows by magic volunteered but they were told that crows talked too loudly, boasted and were full of mischief.

So then in the end two men who were powerful by the magic of the deer and the bear stepped before the council and were chosen. The speaker for the council then reported to Dekanawida that the spies were ready to go. Then they went.

Now Dekanawida addressed the council and he said, " I am Dekanawida and with me is my younger brother. We two now lay before you the laws by which to frame the Ka-ya-neh-renh-ko-wa. The emblems of the chief rulers shall be the antlers of deer. The titles shall be vested in certain women and the names shall be held in their maternal families forever." All the laws were then recited and Hayonhwatha confirmed them.

Dekanawida then sang the song to be used when conferring titles. So in this way all the work and the plans were reported to the Mohawk council and Hayonhwatha confirmed it all. Therefore the council adopted the plan.

When the spies returned the speaker of the council said, " Ska-non-donh, our ears are erected." Then the spies spoke and they said, "At great danger to ourselves we have seen Adodarhoh. We have returned and tell you that the body of Adodarhoh has seven crooked parts, his hair is infested with snakes and he is a cannibal."

The council heard the message and decided to go to Onondaga at midsummer.

Then Dekanawida taught the people the Hymn of Peace and the other songs. He stood before the door of the longhouse and walked before it singing the new songs. Many came and learned them so that many were strong by the magic of them when it was time to carry the Great Peace to Onondaga.

When the time had come, Dekanawida summoned the chiefs and people together and chose one man to sing the songs before Adodar-hoh. Soon then this singer led the company through the forest and he preceded all, singing the Peace songs as he walked. Many old villages and camping places were passed as they went and the names were lifted to give the clan name holders. Now the party passed through these places:

Old Clearing
Overgrown with bushes
A temporary place
Protruding rocks
Between two places
Parties opposite at the council fire
In the Valley

Drooping Wing
On the Hillside
Man Standing
I have daubed it
Lake Bridge
Between two side hills
Lake Outlet
At the forks
Long Hill
Broken Branches Lying
The Spring
White
Corn Stalks on both sides
Two Hillsides
The Old Beast

All these places were in the Mohawk country.

Now they entered the Oneida country and the great chief Odat-shedeh with his chiefs met them. Then all of them marched onward to Onondaga, the singer of the Peace Hymn going on ahead.

The frontier of the Onondaga country was reached and the expedition halted to kindle a fire, as was customary. Then the chiefs of the Onondagas with their head men welcomed them and a great throng marched to the fireside of Adodarhoh, the singer of the Peace Hymn leading the multitude.

The lodge of Adodarhoh was reached and a new singer was appointed to sing the Peace Hymn. So he walked before the door of the house singing to cure the mind of Adodarhoh. He knew that if he made a single error or hesitated his power would be weakened and the crooked body of Adodarhoh remain misshapen. Then he hesitated and made an error. So another singer was appointed and he too made an error by hesitating.

Then Dekanawida himself sang and walked before the door of Adodarhoh's house. When he finished his song he walked toward Adodarhoh and held out his hand to rub it on his body and to know its inherent strength and life. Then Adodarhoh was made straight and his mind became healthy.

When Adodarhoh was made strong in rightful powers and his body had been healed, Dekanawida addressed the three nations. He said, " We have now overcome a great obstacle. It has long stood in the way of peace. The mind of Adodarhoh is now made

right and his crooked parts are made straight. Now indeed may
we establish the Great Peace.

"Before we do firmly establish our union each nation must appoint a certain number of its wisest and purest men who shall be
rulers, Rodiyaner. They shall be the advisers of the people and
make the new rules that may be needful. These men shall be selected and confirmed by their female relations in whose lines the
titles shall be hereditary. When these are named they shall be
crowned, emblematically, with deer antlers."

So then the women of the Mohawks brought forward nine chiefs
who should become Rodiyaner and one man, Ayenwaehs, as war
chief.

So then the women of the Oneidas brought forward nine chiefs
who should become Rodiyaner, and one man, Kahonwadironh, who
should be war chief.

So then the Onondaga women brought forward fourteen chiefs
who should become Rodiyaner, and one man, Ayendes, who should
be war chief.

Each chief then delivered to Dekanawida a string of lake shell
wampum a span in length as a pledge of truth.

Dekanawida then said: "Now, today in the presence of this
great multitude I disrobe you and you are not now covered by
your old names. I now give you names much greater." Then
calling each chief to him he said: "I now place antlers on your
head as an emblem of your power. Your old garments are torn
off and better robes are given you. Now you are Royaner, each
of you. You will receive many scratches and the thickness of
your skins shall be seven spans. You must be patient and henceforth work in unity. Never consider your own interests but work
to benefit the people and for the generations not yet born. You
have pledged yourselves to govern yourselves by the laws of the
Great Peace. All your authority shall come from it.

"I do now order that Skanawateh shall in one-half of his being
be a Royaneh of the Great Peace, and in his other half a war
chief, for the Rodiyaner must have an ear to hear and a hand to
feel the coming of wars."

Then did Dekanawida repeat all the rules which he with
Ayonhwatha had devised for the establishment of the Great Peace.

Then in the councils of all the Five Nations he repeated them
and the Confederacy was established.

THE COUNCIL OF THE GREAT PEACE

THE GREAT BINDING LAW, GAYANASHAGOWA

1 I am Dekanawidah and with the Five Nations' Confederate Lords[1] I plant the Tree of the Great Peace. I plant it in your territory, Adodarhoh, and the Onondaga Nation, in the territory of you who are Firekeepers.

I name the tree the Tree of the Great Long Leaves. Under the shade of this Tree of the Great Peace we spread the soft white feathery down of the globe thistle as seats for you, Adodarhoh, and your cousin Lords.

We place you upon those seats, spread soft with the feathery down of the globe thistle, there beneath the shade of the spreading branches of the Tree of Peace. There shall you sit and watch the Council Fire of the Confederacy of the Five Nations, and all the affairs of the Five Nations shall be transacted at this place before you, Adodarhoh, and your cousin Lords, by the Confederate Lords of the Five Nations. (1–I, TLL).[2]

2 Roots have spread out from the Tree of the Great Peace, one to the north, one to the east, one to the south and one to the west. The name of these roots is The Great White Roots and their nature is Peace and Strength.

If any man or any nation outside the Five Nations shall obey the laws of the Great Peace and make known their disposition to the Lords of the Confederacy, they may trace the Roots to the Tree and if their minds are clean and they are obedient and promise to obey the wishes of the Confederate Council, they shall be welcomed to take shelter beneath the Tree of the Long Leaves.

We place at the top of the Tree of the Long Leaves an Eagle who is able to see afar. If he sees in the distance any evil approaching or any danger threatening he will at once warn the people of the Confederacy. (2–II, TLL).

3 To you Adodarhoh, the Onondaga cousin Lords, I and the other Confederate Lords have entrusted the caretaking and the watching of the Five Nations Council Fire.

When there is any business to be transacted and the Confederate Council is not in session, a messenger shall be dispatched either to

---

[1] Royaneh is always translated "lord."
[2] The abbreviations after each law refer to the sections in the original code and their numbers. TLL, means Tree of the Long Leaves; EUC, Emblematical Union Compact, and LPW, Skanawita's Laws of Peace and War. The first number in Roman numerals refers to the original number of the law, the second number, in Arabic numerals, to the section number in the division of the law named by the abbreviation following.

Adodarhoh, Hononwirehtonh or Skanawatih, Fire Keepers, or to their War Chiefs with a full statement of the case desired to be considered. Then shall Adodarho call his cousin (associate) Lords together and consider whether or not the case is of sufficient importance to demand the attention of the Confederate Council. If so, Adodarhoh shall dispatch messengers to summon all the Confederate Lords to assemble beneath the Tree of the Long Leaves.

When the Lords are assembled the Council Fire shall be kindled, but not with chestnut wood,[1] and Adodarhoh shall formally open the Council.

Then shall Adodarhoh and his cousin Lords, the Fire Keepers, announce the subject for discussion.

The Smoke of the Confederate Council Fire shall ever ascend and pierce the sky so that other nations who may be allies may see the Council Fire of the Great Peace.

Adodarho and his cousin Lords are entrusted with the Keeping of the Council Fire. (4-IV, TLL).

4 You, Adodarho, and your thirteen cousin Lords, shall faithfully keep the space about the Council Fire clean and you shall allow neither dust nor dirt to accumulate. I lay a Long Wing before you as a broom. As a weapon against a crawling creature I lay a staff with you so that you may thrust it away from the Council Fire. If you fail to cast it out then call the rest of the United Lords to your aid. (3-III, TLL).

5 The Council of the Mohawk shall be divided into three parties as follows: Tekarihoken, Ayonhwhathah and Shadekariwade are the first party; Sharenhowaneh, Deyoenhegwenh and Oghrenghrehgowah are the second party, and Dehennakrineh, Aghstawenserenthah and Shoskoharowaneh are the third party. The third party is to listen only to the discussion of the first and second parties and if an error is made or the proceeding is irregular they are to call attention to it, and when the case is right and properly decided by the two parties they shall confirm the decision of the two parties and refer the case to the Seneca Lords for their decision. When the Seneca Lords have decided in accord with the Mohawk Lords, the case or question shall be referred to the Cayuga and Oneida Lords on the opposite side of the house. (5-V, TLL).

6 I, Dekanawidah, appoint the Mohawk Lords the heads and the leaders of the Five Nations Confederacy. The Mohawk Lords are

---

[1] Because chestnut wood in burning throws out sparks, thereby creating a disturbance in the council.

the foundation of the Great Peace and it shall, therefore, be against the Great Binding Law to pass measures in the Confederate Council after the Mohawk Lords have protested against them. (6–VI, TLL).

No council of the Confederate Lords shall be legal unless all the Mohawk Lords are present. (13–XIII, TLL).

7 Whenever the Confederate Lords shall assemble for the purpose of holding a council, the Onondaga Lords shall open it by expressing their gratitude to their cousin Lords and greeting them, and they shall make an address and offer thanks to the earth where men dwell, to the streams of water, the pools, the springs and the lakes, to the maize and the fruits, to the medicinal herbs and trees, to the forest trees for their usefulness, to the animals that serve as food and give their pelts for clothing, to the great winds and the lesser winds, to the Thunderers, to the Sun, the mighty warrior, to the moon, to the messengers of the Creator who reveal his wishes and to the Great Creator[1] who dwells in the heavens above, who gives all the things useful to men, and who is the source and the ruler of health and life.

Then shall the Onondaga Lords declare the council open.

The council shall not sit after darkness has set in. (7–VII, TLL).

8 The Firekeepers shall formally open and close all councils of the Confederate Lords, they shall pass upon all matters deliberated upon by the two sides and render their decision.

Every Onondaga Lord (or his deputy) must be present at every Confederate Council and must agree with the majority without unwarrantable dissent, so that a unanimous decision may be rendered. (8–VIII, TLL).

If Adodarho or any of his cousin Lords are absent from a Confederate Council, any other Firekeeper may open and close the Council, but the Firekeepers present may not give any decisions, unless the matter is of small importance. (9–IX, TLL).

9 All the business of the Five Nations Confederate Council shall be conducted by the two combined bodies of Confederate Lords. First the question shall be passed upon by the Mohawk and Seneca Lords, then it shall be discussed and passed by the Oneida and Cayuga Lords. Their decisions shall then be referred to the Onondaga Lords, (Fire Keepers) for final judgment. (10–X, TLL).

The same process shall obtain when a question is brought before the council by an individual or a War Chief. (11–XI, TLL).

---

[1] Hodiänok'doon Hĕdiohe' (Seneca).

10 In all cases the procedure must be as follows: when the Mohawk and Seneca Lords have unanimously agreed upon a question, they shall report their decision to the Cayuga and Oneida Lords who shall deliberate upon the question and report a unanimous decision to the Mohawk Lords. The Mohawk Lords will then report the standing of the case to the Firekeepers, who shall render a decision (17–XVII, TLL) as they see fit in case of a disagreement by the two bodies, or confirm the decisions of the two bodies if they are identical. The Fire Keepers shall then report their decision to the Mohawk Lords who shall announce it to the open council. (12–XII, TLL).

11 If through any misunderstanding or obstinacy on the part of the Fire Keepers, they render a decision at variance with that of the Two Sides, the Two Sides shall reconsider the matter and if their decisions are jointly the same as before they shall report to the Fire Keepers who are then compelled to confirm their joint decision. (18–XVIII, TLL).

12 When a case comes before the Onondaga Lords (Fire Keepers) for discussion and decision, Adodarho shall introduce the matter to his comrade Lords who shall then discuss it in their two bodies. Every Onondaga Lord except Hononwiretonh shall deliberate and he shall listen only. When a unanimous decision shall have been reached by the two bodies of Fire Keepers, Adodarho shall notify Hononwiretonh of the fact when he shall confirm it. He shall refuse to confirm a decision if it is not unanimously agreed upon by both sides of the Fire Keepers. (19–XIX, TLL).

13 No Lord shall ask a question of the body of Confederate Lords when they are discussing a case, question or proposition. He may only deliberate in a low tone with the separate body of which he is a member. (21–XXI, TLL).

14 When the Council of the Five Nation Lords shall convene they shall appoint a speaker for the day. He shall be a Lord of either the Mohawk, Onondaga or Seneca Nation.

The next day the Council shall appoint another speaker, but the first speaker may be reappointed if there is no objection, but a speaker's term shall not be regarded more than for the day. (35–XXXV, TLL).

15 No individual or foreign nation interested in a case, question or proposition shall have any voice in the Confederate Council except to answer a question put to him or them by the speaker for the Lords. (41–XLI, TLL).

16 If the conditions which shall arise at any future time call for an addition to or change of this law, the case shall be carefully considered and if a new beam seems necessary or beneficial, the proposed change shall be voted upon and if adopted it shall be called, "Added to the Rafters." (48–XLVII, TLL).

Rights, duties and qualifications of Lords

17 A bunch of a certain number of shell (wampum) strings each two spans in length shall be given to each of the female families in which the Lordship titles are vested. The right of bestowing the title shall be hereditary in the family of females legally possessing the bunch of shell strings and the strings shall be the token that the females of the family have the proprietary right to the Lordship title for all time to come, subject to certain restrictions hereinafter mentioned. (59–LIX, TLL).

18 If any Confederate Lord neglects or refuses to attend the Confederate Council, the other Lords of the Nation of which he is a member shall require their War Chief to request the female sponsors of the Lord so guilty of defection to demand his attendance of the Council. If he refuses, the women holding the title shall immediately select another candidate for the title.

No Lord shall be asked more than once to attend the Confederate Council. (30–XXX, TLL).

19 If at any time it shall be manifest that a Confederate Lord has not in mind the welfare of the people or disobeys the rules of this Great Law, the men or the women of the Confederacy, or both jointly,[1] shall come to the Council and upbraid the erring Lord through his War Chief. If the complaint of the people through the War Chief is not heeded the first time it shall be uttered again and then if no attention is given a third complaint and warning shall be given. If the Lord is still contumacious the matter shall go to the council of War Chiefs. (66–LXVI, TLL). The War Chiefs shall then divest the erring Lord of his title by order of the women in whom the titleship is vested. When the Lord is deposed the women shall notify the Confederate Lords through their War Chief, and the Confederate Lords shall sanction the act. The women will then select another of their sons as a candidate and the Lords shall elect him. Then shall the chosen one be installed by the Installation Ceremony. (123–XLI, EUC), (Cf. 42–XLII).

---

[1] See sections 94 and 95 for right of popular councils.

When a Lord is to be deposed, his War Chief shall address him as follows:

" So you, —————————, disregard and set at naught the warnings of your women relatives. So you fling the warnings over your shoulder to cast them behind you.

" Behold the brightness of the Sun and in the brightness of the Sun's light I depose you of your title and remove the sacred emblem of your Lordship title. I remove from your brow the deer's antlers, which was the emblem of your position and token of your nobility. I now depose you and return the antlers to the women whose heritage they are."

The War Chief shall now address the women of the deposed Lord and say:

" Mothers, as I have now deposed your Lord, I now return to you the emblem and the title of Lordship, therefore repossess them."

Again addressing himself to the deposed Lord he shall say:

" As I have now deposed and discharged you so you are now no longer Lord. You shall now go your way alone, the rest of the people of the Confederacy will not go with you, for we know not the kind of mind that possesses you. As the Creator has nothing to do with wrong so he will not come to res ue you from the precipice of destruction in which you have cast yourself. You shall never be restored to the position which you once occupied."

Then shall the War Chief address himself to the Lords of the Nation to which the deposed Lord belongs and say:

" Know you, my Lords, that I have taken the deer's antlers from the brow of —————————, the emblem of his position and token of his greatness."

The Lords of the Confederacy shall then have no other alternative than to sanction the discharge of the offending Lord. (42–XLII, TLL).

20 If a Lord of the Confederacy of the Five Nations should commit murder the other Lords of the Nation shall assemble at the place where the corpse lies and prepare to depose the criminal Lord. If it is impossible to meet at the scene of the crime the Lords shall discuss the matter at the next Council of their nation and request their War Chief to depose the Lord guilty of crime, to " bury " his women relatives and to transfer the Lordship title to a sister family.

2

The War Chief shall address the Lord guilty of murder and say:
" So you, ————————— (giving his name) did kill ——————
(naming the slain man), with your own hands! You have committed
a grave sin in the eyes of the Creator. Behold the bright light of
the Sun, and in the brightness of the Sun's light I depose you of
your title and remove the horns, the sacred emblems of your Lordship title. I remove from your brow the deer's antlers, which was
the emblem of your position and token of your nobility. I now
depose you and expel you and you shall depart at once from the
territory of the Five Nations Confederacy and nevermore return
again. ·We, the Five Nations Confederacy, moreover, bury your
women relatives because the ancient Lordship title was never intended to have any union with bloodshed. Henceforth it shall not
be their heritage. By the evil deed that you have done they have
forfeited it forever."

The War Chief shall then hand the title to a sister family and he
shall address it and say:
" Our mothers, ————————, listen attentively while I address
you on a solemn and important subject. I hereby transfer to you
an ancient Lordship title for a great calamity has befallen it in
the hands of the family of a former Lord. We trust that you, our
mothers, will always guard it, and that you will warn your Lord
always to be dutiful and to advise his people to ever live in love,
peace and harmony that a great calamity may never happen again."
(47–XLVII, TLL).

21 Certain physical defects in a Confederate Lord make him ineligible to sit in the Confederate Council. Such defects are infancy, idiocy, blindness, deafness, dumbness and impotency. When
a Confederate Lord is restricted by any of these conditions, a
deputy shall be appointed by his sponsors to act for him, but in
case of extreme necessity the restricted Lord may exercise his
rights. (29–XXIX, TLL).

22 If a Confederate Lord desires to resign his title he shall
notify the Lords of the Nation of which he is a member of his intention. If his coactive Lords refuse to accept his resignation he
may not resign his title.

A Lord in proposing to resign may recommend any proper candidate which recommendation shall be received by the Lords, but
unless confirmed and nominated by the women who hold the title
the candidate so named shall not be considered. (31–XXXI,
TLL).

23 Any Lord of the Five Nations Confederacy may construct shell strings (or wampum belts) of any size or length as pledges or records of matters of national or international importance.

When it is necessary to dispatch a shell string by a War Chief or other messenger as the token of a summons, the messenger shall recite the contents of the string to the party to whom it is sent. That party shall repeat the message and return the shell string and if there has been a summons he shall make ready for the journey.

Any of the people of the Five Nations may use shells (or wampum) as the record of a pledge, contract or an agreement entered into and the same shall be binding as soon as shell strings shall have been exchanged by both parties. (32–XXXII, TLL).

24 The Lords of the Confederacy of the Five Nations shall be mentors of the people for all time. The thickness of their skin shall be seven spans — which is to say that they shall be proof against anger, offensive actions and criticism. Their hearts shall be full of peace and good will and their minds filled with a yearning for the welfare of the people of the Confederacy. With endless patience they shall carry out their duty and their firmness shall be tempered with a tenderness for their people. Neither anger nor fury shall find lodgement in their minds and all their words and actions shall be marked by calm deliberation. (33–XXXIII, TLL).

25 If a Lord of the Confederacy should seek to establish any authority independent of the jurisdiction of the Confederacy of the Great Peace, which is the Five Nations, he shall be warned three times in open council, first by the women relatives, second by the men relatives and finally by the Lords of the Confederacy of the Nation to which he belongs. If the offending Lord is still obdurate he shall be dismissed by the War Chief of his nation for refusing to conform to the laws of the Great Peace. His nation shall then install the candidate nominated by the female name holders of his family. (34–XXXIV, TLL).

26 It shall be the duty of all of the Five Nations Confederate Lords, from time to time as occasion demands, to act as mentors and spiritual guides of their people and remind them of their Creator's will and words. They shall say:

" Hearken, that peace may continue unto future days!

"Always listen to the words of the Great Creator, for he has spoken.

" United People, let not evil find lodging in your minds

" For the Great Creator has spoken and the cause of Peace shall not become old.

" The cause of peace shall not die if you remember the Great Creator."

Every Confederate Lord shall speak words such as these to promote peace. (37–XXXVII, TLL).

27 All Lords of the Five Nations Confederacy must be honest in all things. They must not idle or gossip, but be men possessing those honorable qualities that make true royaneh. It shall be a serious wrong for anyone to lead a Lord into trivial affairs, for the people must ever hold their Lords high in estimation out of respect to their honorable positions. (45–XLV, TLL).

28 When a candidate Lord is to be installed he shall furnish four strings of shells (or wampum) one span in length bound together at one end. Such will constitute the evidence of his pledge to the Confederate Lords that he will live according to the constitution of the Great Peace and exercise justice in all affairs.

When the pledge is furnished the Speaker of the Council must hold the shell strings in his hand and address the opposite side of the Council Fire and he shall commence his address saying: " Now behold him. He has now become a Confederate Lord. See how splendid he looks." An address may then follow. At the end of it he shall send the bunch of shell strings to the opposite side and they shall be received as evidence of the pledge. Then shall the opposite side say:

" We now do crown you with the sacred emblem of the deer's antlers, the emblem of your Lordship. You shall now become a mentor of the people of the Five Nations. The thickness of your skin shall be seven spans — which is to say that you shall be proof against anger, offensive actions and criticism. Your heart shall be filled with peace and good will and your mind filled with a yearning for the welfare of the people of the Confederacy. With endless patience you shall carry out your duty and your firmness shall be tempered with tenderness for your people. Neither anger nor fury shall find lodgement in your mind and all your words and actions shall be marked with calm deliberation. In all of your deliberations in the Confederate Council, in your efforts at law making, in all your official acts, self interest shall be cast into oblivion. Cast not over your shoulder behind you the warnings of the nephews and nieces should they chide you for any error or wrong you may do, but return to the way of the Great Law which is just and right. Look and listen for the welfare of the whole people and have always in view not only the present but also the coming generations, even those whose faces are yet beneath the surface of the ground — the unborn of the future Nation." (51–LI, TLL).

29 When a Lordship title is to be conferred, the candidate Lord shall furnish the cooked venison, the corn bread and the corn soup, together with other necessary things and the labor for the Conferring of Titles Festival. (50–L, TLL).

30 The Lords of the Confederacy may confer the Lordship title upon a candidate whenever the Great Law is recited, if there be a candidate, for the Great Law speaks all the rules. (XLIV–44, TLL).

31 If a lord of the Confederacy should become seriously ill and be thought near death, the women who are heirs of his title shall go to his house and lift his crown of deer antlers, the emblem of his Lordship, and place them at one side. If the Creator spares him and he rises from his bed of sickness he may rise with the antlers on his brow.

The following words shall be used to temporarily remove the antlers:

"Now our comrade Lord (or our relative Lord) the time has come when we must approach you in your illness. We remove for a time the deer's antlers from your brow, we remove the emblem of your Lordship title. The Great Law has decreed that no Lord should end his life with the antlers on his brow. We therefore lay them aside in the room. If the Creator spares you and you recover from your illness you shall rise from your bed with the antlers on your brow as before and you shall resume your duties as Lord of the Confederacy and you may labor again for the Confederate people." (XXVII–27, TLL).

32 If a Lord of the Confederacy should die while the Council of the Five Nations is in session the Council shall adjourn for ten days. No Confederate Council shall sit within ten days of the death of a Lord of the Confederacy.

If the Three Brothers (the Mohawk, the Onondaga and the Seneca) should lose one of their Lords by death, the Younger Brothers (the Oneida and the Cayuga) shall come to the surviving Lords of the Three Brothers on the tenth day and console them. If the Younger Brothers lose one of their Lords then the Three Brothers shall come to them and console them. And the consolation shall be the reading of the contents of the thirteen shell (wampum) strings of Ayonhwhathah. At the termination of this rite a successor shall be appointed, to be appointed by the women heirs of the Lordship title. If the women are not yet ready to place their nominee before the Lords the Speaker shall say, "Come let us go out." All shall then leave the Council or the place of gathering. The installation shall then wait until such a time as the women are ready. The Speaker shall lead the way from the house by saying, "Let us depart to the edge of the woods and lie in waiting on our bellies."

When the women title holders shall have chosen one of their sons the Confederate Lords will assemble in two places, the Younger Brothers in one place and the Three Older Brothers in another. The Lords who are to console the mourning Lords shall choose one of their number to sing the Pacification Hymn as they journey to the sorrowing Lords. The singer shall lead the way and the Lords and the people shall follow. When they reach the sorrowing Lords they shall hail the candidate Lord and perform the rite of Conferring the Lordship Title. (22–XXII, TLL).

33 When a Confederate Lord dies, the surviving relatives shall immediately dispatch a messenger, a member of another clan, to the Lords in another locality. When the runner comes within hailing distance of the locality he shall utter a sad wail, thus: "Kwa-ah, Kwa-ah, Kwa-ah!" The sound shall be repeated three times and then again and again at intervals as many times as the distance may require. When the runner arrives at the settlement the people shall assemble and one must ask him the nature of his sad message. He shall then say, "Let us consider." Then he shall tell them of the death of the Lord. He shall deliver to them a string of shells (wampum) and say "Here is the testimony, you have heard the message." He may then return home.

It now becomes the duty of the Lords of the locality to send runners to other localities and each locality shall send other messengers until all Lords are notified. Runners shall travel day and night. (23–XXIII, TLL).

34 If a Lord dies and there is no candidate qualified for the office in the family of the women title holders, the Lords of the Nation shall give the title into the hands of a sister family in the clan until such a time as the original family produces a candidate, when the title shall be restored to the rightful owners.

No Lordship title may be carried into the grave. The Lords of the Confederacy may dispossess a dead Lord of his title even at the grave. (24–XXIV, TLL).

Election of Pine Tree chiefs

35 Should any man of the Nation assist with special ability or show great interest in the affairs of the Nation, if he proves himself wise, honest and worthy of confidence, the Confederate Lords may elect him to a seat with them and he may sit in the Confederate Council. He shall be proclaimed a *Pine Tree sprung up for the Nation* and be installed as such at the next assembly for the installation of Lords. Should he ever do anything contrary to the rules of the Great Peace, he may not be deposed from office — no one shall cut him down[1]— but thereafter everyone shall be deaf to his voice and his advice. Should he resign his seat and title no one shall prevent him. A Pine Tree chief has no authority to name a successor nor is his title hereditary. (LXVIII–68, TLL).

Names, duties and rights of war chiefs

36 The title names of the Chief Confederate Lords' War Chiefs shall be:

Ayonwaehs, War Chief under Lord Takarihoken (Mohawk)
Kahonwahdironh, War Chief under Lord Odatshedeh (Oneida)
Ayendes, War Chief under Lord Adodarhoh (Onondaga)
Wenenhs, War Chief under Lord Dekaenyonh (Cayuga)
Shoneradowaneh, War Chief under Lord Skanyadariyo (Seneca)

The women heirs of each head Lord's title shall be the heirs of the War Chief's title of their respective Lord. (52–LII, TLL).

The War Chiefs shall be selected from the eligible sons of the female families holding the head Lordship titles. (53–LIII, TLL).

37 There shall be one War Chief for each Nation and their duties shall be to carry messages for their Lords and to take up the arms of war in case of emergency. They shall not participate in the proceedings of the Confederate Council but shall watch its progress and in case of an erroneous action by a Lord they shall receive the complaints of the people and convey the warnings of the women to him. The people who wish to convey messages to the Lords in the Confederate Council shall do so through the War Chief of their Nation. It shall ever be his duty to lay the cases, questions and propositions of the people before the Confederate Council. (54–LIV, TLL).

38 When a War Chief dies another shall be installed by the same rite as that by which a Lord is installed. (56–LVI, TLL).

---

[1] Because, "his top branches pierce the sky and if his roots are cut he will not fall but hang upright before the people."

39 If a War Chief acts contrary to instructions or against the provisions of the Laws of the Great Peace, doing so in the capacity of his office, he shall be deposed by his women relatives and by his men relatives. Either the women or the men alone or jointly may act in such case. The women title holders shall then choose another candidate. (55–LV, TLL).

40 When the Lords of the Confederacy take occasion to dispatch a messenger in behalf of the Confederate Council, they shall wrap up any matter they may send and instruct the messenger to remember his errand, to turn not aside but to proceed faithfully to his destination and deliver his message according to every instruction. (57–XLVII, TLL).

41 If a message borne by a runner is the warning of an invasion he shall whoop, " Kwa-ah, Kwa-ah," twice and repeat at short intervals; then again at a longer interval.

If a human being is found dead, the finder shall not touch the body but return home immediately shouting at short intervals, " Koo-weh! " (23–XXIII, TLL).

Clans and consanguinity

42 Among the Five Nations and their posterity there shall be the following original clans: Great Name Bearer, Ancient Name Bearer, Great Bear, Ancient Bear, Turtle, Painted Turtle, Standing Rock, Large Plover, Little Plover, Deer, Pigeon Hawk, Eel, Ball, Opposite-Side-of-the-Hand, and Wild Potatoes. These clans distributed through their respective Nations, shall be the sole owners and holders of the soil of the country and in them is it vested as a birthright. (94–XI, EUC).

43 People of the Five Nations members of a certain clan shall recognize every other member of that clan, irrespective of the Nation, as relatives. Men and women, therefore, members of the same clan are forbidden to marry. (98–XV, EUC).

44 The lineal descent of the people of the Five Nations shall run in the female line. Women shall be considered the progenitors of the Nation. They shall own the land and the soil. Men and women shall follow the status of the mother. (60–LX, TLL).

45 The women heirs of the Confederate Lordship titles shall be called Royaneh (Noble) for all time to come. (61–LXI, TLL).

46 The women of the Forty Eight (now fifty) Royaneh families shall be the heirs of the Authorized Names for all time to come.

When an infant of the Five Nations is given an Authorized Name at the Midwinter Festival or at the Ripe Corn Festival, one in the cousinhood of which the infant is a member shall be appointed a speaker. He shall then announce to the opposite cousinhood the names of the father and the mother of the child together with the clan of the mother. Then the speaker shall announce the child's name twice. The uncle of the child shall then take the child in his arms and walking up and down the room shall sing: " My head is firm, I am of the Confederacy." As he sings the opposite cousinhood shall respond by chanting, " Hyenh, Hyenh, Hyenh, Hyenh," until the song is ended. (95–XII, EUC).

47 If the female heirs of a Confederate Lord's title become extinct, the title right shall be given by the Lords of the Confederacy to the sister family whom they shall elect and that family shall hold the name and transmit it to their (female) heirs, but they shall not appoint any of their sons as a candidate for a title until all the eligible men of the former family shall have died or otherwise have become ineligible. (25–XXV, TLL).

48 If all the heirs of a Lordship title become extinct, and all the families in the clan, then the title shall be given by the Lords of the Confederacy to the family in a sister clan whom they shall elect. (26–XXVI, TLL).

49 If any of the Royaneh women, heirs of a titleship, shall wilfully withhold a Lordship or other title and refuse to bestow it, or if such heirs abandon, forsake or despise their heritage, then shall such women be deemed buried and their family extinct. The titleship shall then revert to a sister family or clan upon application and complaint. The Lords of the Confederacy shall elect the family or clan which shall in future hold the title. (28–XXVIII, TLL).

50 The Royaneh women of the Confederacy heirs of the Lordship titles shall elect two women of their family as cooks for the Lord when the people shall assemble at his house for business or other purposes.

It is not good nor honorable for a Confederate Lord to allow his people whom he has called to go hungry. (62–LXII, TLL).

51 When a Lord holds a conference in his home, his wife, if she wishes, may prepare the food for the Union Lords who assemble with him. This is an honorable right which she may exercise and an expression of her esteem. (38–XXXVIII, TLL).

52 The Royaneh women, heirs of the Lordship titles, shall, should it be necessary, correct and admonish the holders of their titles. Those only who attend the Council may do this and those

who do not shall not object to what has been said nor strive to undo the action. (63–LXIII, TLL).

53 When the Royaneh women, holders of a Lordship title, select one of their sons as a candidate, they shall select one who is trustworthy, of good character, of honest disposition, one who manages his own affairs, supports his own family, if any, and who has proven a faithful man to his Nation. (64–LXIV, TLL).

54 When a Lordship title becomes vacant through death or other cause, the Royaneh women of the clan in which the title is hereditary shall hold a council and shall choose one from among their sons to fill the office made vacant. Such a candidate shall not be the father of any Confederate Lord. If the choice is unanimous the name is referred to the men relatives of the clan. If they should disapprove it shall be their duty to select a candidate from among their own number. If then the men and women are unable to decide which of the two candidates shall be named, then the matter shall be referred to the Confederate Lords in the Clan. They shall decide which candidate shall be named. If the men and the women agree to a candidate his name shall be referred to the sister clans for confirmation. If the sister clans confirm the choice, they shall refer their action to their Confederate Lords who shall ratify the choice and present it to their cousin Lords, and if the cousin Lords confirm the name then the candidate shall be installed by the proper ceremony for the conferring of Lordship titles. (65–LXV, TLL).

Official symbolism

55 A large bunch of shell strings, in the making of which the Five Nations Confederate Lords have equally contributed, shall symbolize the completeness of the union and certify the pledge of the nations represented by the Confederate Lords of the Mohawk, the Oneida, the Onondaga, the Cayuga and the Seneca, that all are united and formed into one body or union called the Union of the Great Law, which they have established.

A bunch of shell strings is to be the symbol of the council fire of the Five Nations Confederacy. And the Lord whom the Council of Fire Keepers shall appoint to speak for them in opening the council shall hold the strands of shells in his hands when speaking. When he finishes speaking he shall deposit the strings on an elevated place (or pole) so that all the assembled Lords and the people may see it and know that the council is open and in progress.

When the council adjourns the Lord who has been appointed by his comrade Lords to close it shall take the strands of shells in his hands and address the assembled Lords. Thus will the council adjourn until such a time and place as appointed by the council. Then shall the shell strings be placed in a place for safekeeping.

Every five years the Five Nations Confederate Lords and the people shall assemble together and shall ask one another if their minds are still in the same spirit of unity for the Great Binding Law and if any of the Five Nations shall not pledge continuance and steadfastness to the pledge of unity then the Great Binding Law shall dissolve. (14–XIV, TLL).

56 Five strings of shell tied together as one shall represent the Five Nations. Each string shall represent one territory and the whole a completely united territory known as the Five Nations Confederate territory. (108–XXV, EUC).

57 Five arrows shall be bound together very strong and each arrow shall represent one nation. As the five arrows are strongly bound this shall symbolize the complete union of the nations. Thus are the Five Nations united completely and enfolded together, united into one head, one body and one mind. Therefore they shall labor, legislate and council together for the interest of future generations.

The Lords of the Confederacy shall eat together from one bowl the feast of cooked beaver's tail. While they are eating they are to use no sharp utensils for if they should they might accidentally cut one another and bloodshed would follow. All measures must be taken to prevent the spilling of blood in any way. (15–XV, TLL).

58 There are now the Five Nations Confederate Lords standing with joined hands in a circle. This signifies and provides that should any one of the Confederate Lords leave the council and this Confederacy his crown of deer's horns, the emblem of his Lordship title, together with his birthright, shall lodge on the arms of the Union Lords whose hands are so joined. He forfeits his title and the crown falls from his brow but it shall remain in the Confederacy.

A further meaning of this is that if any time any one of the Confederate Lords choose to submit to the law of a foreign people he is no longer in but out of the Confederacy, and persons of this class shall be called " They have alienated themselves." Likewise such persons who submit to laws of foreign nations shall forfeit all birthrights and claims on the Five Nations Confederacy and territory.

You, the Five Nations Confederate Lords, be firm so that if a tree falls upon your joined arms it shall not separate you or weaken your hold. So shall the strength of the union be preserved. (16–XIV, TLL).

59 A bunch of wampum shells on strings, three spans of the hand in length, the upper half of the bunch being white and the lower half black, and formed from equal contributions of the men of the Five Nations, shall be a token that the men have combined themselves into one head, one body and one thought, and it shall also symbolize their ratification of the peace pact of the Confederacy, whereby the Lords of the Five Nations have established the Great Peace.

The white portion of the shell strings represent the women and the black portion the men. The black portion, furthermore, is a token of power and authority vested in the men of the Five Nations.

This string of wampum vests the people with the right to correct their erring Lords. In case a part or all the Lords pursue a course not vouched for by the people and heed not the third warning of their women relatives, then the matter shall be taken to the General Council of the women of the Five Nations. If the Lords notified and warned three times fail to heed, then the case falls into the hands of the men of the Five Nations. The War Chiefs shall then, by right of such power and authority, enter the open council to warn the Lord or Lords to return from their wrong course. If the Lords heed the warning they shall say, " we will reply to-morrow." If then an answer is returned in favor of justice and in accord with this Great Law, then the Lords shall individually pledge themselves again by again furnishing the necessary shells for the pledge. Then shall the War Chief or Chiefs exhort the Lords urging them to be just and true.

Should it happen that the Lords refuse to heed the third warning, then two courses are open: either the men may decide in their council to depose the Lord or Lords or to club them to death with war clubs. Should they in their council decide to take the first course the War Chief shall address the Lord or Lords, saying: " Since you the Lords of the Five Nations have refused to return to the procedure of the Constitution, we now declare your seats vacant, we take off your horns, the token of your Lordship, and others shall be chosen and installed in your seats, therefore vacate your seats."

Should the men in their council adopt the second course, the War Chief shall order his men to enter the council, to take positions beside the Lords, sitting between them wherever possible. When this is accomplished the War Chief holding in his outstretched hand a bunch of black wampum strings shall say to the erring Lords: " So now, Lords of the Five United Nations, harken to these last words from your men. You have not heeded the warnings of the women relatives, you have not heeded the warnings of the General Council of women and you have not heeded the warnings of the men of the nations, all urging you to return to the right course of action. Since you are determined to resist and to withhold justice from your people there is only one course for us to adopt." At this point the War Chief shall let drop the bunch of black wampum and the men shall spring to their feet and club the erring Lords to death. Any erring Lord may submit before the War Chief lets fall the black wampum. Then his execution is withheld.

The black wampum here used symbolizes that the power to execute is buried but that it may be raised up again by the men. It is buried but when occasion arises they may pull it up and derive their power and authority to act as here described. (SPW 81 XII).

60 A broad dark belt of wampum of thirty-eight rows, having a white heart in the center, on either side of which are two white squares all connected with the heart by white rows of beads shall be the emblem of the unity of the Five Nations.[1]

The first of the squares on the left represents the Mohawk nation and its territory; the second square on the left and the one near the heart, represents the Oneida nation and its territory; the white heart in the middle represents the Onondaga nation and its territory, and it also means that the heart of the Five Nations is single in its loyalty to the Great Peace, that the Great Peace is lodged in the heart (meaning with Onondaga Confederate Lords), and that the Council Fire is to burn there for the Five Nations, and further, it means that the authority is given to advance the cause of peace whereby hostile nations out of the Confederacy shall cease warfare; the white square to the right of the heart represents the Cayuga nation and its territory and the fourth and last white square represents the Seneca nation and its territory.

White shall here symbolize that no evil or jealous thoughts shall creep into the minds of the Lords while in council under the Great

---

[1] This is the " Hiawatha Belt " purchased by John Boyd Thatcher of Albany and now in the Congressional Library.

Peace. White, the emblem of peace, love, charity and equity surrounds and guards the Five Nations. (84–EUC, 1).

61 Should a great calamity threaten the generations rising and living of the Five United Nations, then he who is able to climb to the top of the Tree of the Great Long Leaves may do so. When, then, he reaches the top of the Tree he shall look about in all directions, and, should he see that evil things indeed are approaching, then he shall call to the people of the Five United Nations assembled beneath the Tree of the Great Long Leaves and say: "A calamity threatens your happiness."

Then shall the Lords convene in council and discuss the impending evil.

When all the truths relating to the trouble shall be fully known and found to be truths, then shall the people seek out a Tree of Ka-hon-ka-ah-go-nah,[1] and when they shall find it they shall assemble their heads together and lodge for a time between its roots. Then, their labors being finished, they may hope for happiness for many days after. (II-85, EUC).

62 When the Confederate Council of the Five Nations declares for a reading of the belts of shell calling to mind these laws, they shall provide for the reader a specially made mat woven of the fibers of wild hemp. The mat shall not be used again, for such formality is called the honoring of the importance of the law. (XXXVI-36, TLL).

63 Should two sons of opposite sides of the council fire agree in a desire to hear the reciting of the laws of the Great Peace and so refresh their memories in the way ordained by the founder of the Confederacy, they shall notify Adodarho. He then shall consult with five of his coactive Lords and they in turn shall consult their eight brethren. Then should they decide to accede to the request of the two sons from opposite sides of the Council Fire, Adodarhoh shall send messengers to notify the Chief Lords of each of the Five Nations. Then they shall despatch their War Chiefs to notify their brother and cousin Lords of the meeting and its time and place.

When all have come and have assembled, Adodarhoh, in conjunction with his cousin Lords, shall appoint one Lord who shall repeat the laws of the Great Peace. Then shall they announce who they have chosen to repeat the laws of the Great Peace to the two sons. Then shall the chosen one repeat the laws of the Great Peace. (XLIII-43, TLL).

---

[1] A great swamp Elm.

64 At the ceremony of the installation of Lords if there is only one expert speaker and singer of the law and the Pacification Hymn to stand at the council fire, then when this speaker and singer has finished addressing one side of the fire he shall go to the opposite side and reply to his own speech and song. He shall thus act for both sides of the fire until the entire ceremony has been completed. Such a speaker and singer shall be termed the " Two Faced" because he speaks and sings for both sides of the fire. (XLIX--49, TLL).

65 I, Dekanawida, and the Union Lords, now uproot the tallest pine tree and into the cavity thereby made we cast all weapons of war. Into the depths of the earth, down into the deep underearth currents of water flowing to unknown regions we cast all the weapons of strife. We bury them from sight and we plant again the tree. Thus shall the Great Peace be established and hostilities shall no longer be known between the Five Nations but peace to the United People.

Laws of adoption

66 The father of a child of great comliness, learning, ability or specially loved because of some circumstance may, at the will of the child's clan, select a name from his own (the father's) clan and bestow it by ceremony, such as is provided. This naming shall be only temporary and shall be called, "A name hung about the neck." (XII–96, EUC).

67 Should any person, a member of the Five Nations' Confederacy, specially esteem a man or a woman of another clan or of a foreign nation, he may choose a name and bestow it upon that person so esteemed. The naming shall be in accord with the ceremony of bestowing names. Such a name is only a temporary one and shall be called "A name hung about the neck." A short string of shells shall be delivered with the name as a record and a pledge. (XIV–97, EUC).

68 Should any member of the Five Nations, a family or person belonging to a foreign nation submit a proposal for adoption into a clan of one of the Five Nations, he or they shall furnish a string of shells, a span in length, as a pledge to the clan into which he or they wish to be adopted. The Lords of the nation shall then consider the proposal and submit a decision. (XXI–104, EUC).

69 Any member of the Five Nations who through esteem or other feeling wishes to adopt an individual, a family or number of families may offer adoption to him or them and if accepted the

matter shall be brought to the attention of the Lords for confirmation and the Lords must confirm the adoption. (XXII–105, EUC).

70 When the adoption of anyone shall have been confirmed by the Lords of the Nation, the Lords shall address the people of their nation and say: " Now you of our nation, be informed that such a person, such a family or such families have ceased forever to bear their birth nation's name and have buried it in the depths of the earth. Henceforth let no one of our nation ever mention the original name or nation of their birth. To do so will be to hasten the end of our peace. (XXIII–106, EUC).

Laws of emigration

71 When any person or family belonging to the Five Nations desires to abandon their birth nation and the territory of the Five Nations, they shall inform the Lords of their nation and the Confederate Council of the Five Nations shall take cognizance of it. (XXXIX–39, TLL).

72 When any person or any of the people of the Five Nations emigrate and reside in a region distant from the territory of the Five Nations Confederacy, the Lords of the Five Nations at will may send a messenger carrying a broad belt of black shells and when the messenger arrives he shall call the people together or address them personally displaying the belt of shells and they shall know that this is an order for them to return to their original homes and to their council fires. (XL–40, TLL).

Rights of foreign nations

73 The soil of the earth from one end of the land to the other is the property of the people who inhabit it. By birthright the Oñgwehonweh (Original beings) are the owners of the soil which they own and occupy and none other may hold it. The same law has been held from the oldest times.

The Great Creator has made us of the one blood and of the same soil he made us and as only different tongues constitute different nations he established different hunting grounds and territories and made boundary lines between them. (LXIX–69, TLL).

74 When any alien nation or individual is admitted into the Five Nations the admission shall be understood only to be a temporary one. Should the person or nation create loss, do wrong or cause suffering of any kind to endanger the peace of the Confederacy,

the Confederate Lords shall order one of their war chiefs to repri-
mand him or them and if a similar offence is again committed the
offending party or parties shall be expelled from the territory of
the Five United Nations. (XXVI–119, EUC).

75 When a member of an alien nation comes to the territory
of the Five Nations and seeks refuge and permanent residence, the
Lords of the Nation to which he comes shall extend hospitality and
make him a member of the nation. Then shall he be accorded equal
rights and privileges in all matters except as after mentioned.
(XXXVII–120, EUC).

76 No body of alien people who have been adopted temporarily
shall have a vote in the council of the Lords of the Confederacy,
for only they who have been invested with Lordship titles may
vote in the Council. Aliens have nothing by blood to make claim
to a vote and should they have it, not knowing all the traditions
of the Confederacy, might go against its Great Peace. In this
manner the Great Peace would be endangered and perhaps be
destroyed. (XXXVIII–121, EUC).

77 When the Lords of the Confederacy decide to admit a foreign
nation and an adoption is made, the Lords shall inform the adopted
nation that its admission is only temporary. They shall also say
to the nation that it must never try to control, to interfere with
or to injure the Five Nations nor disregard the Great Peace or
any of its rules or customs. That in no way should they cause
disturbance or injury. Then should the adopted nation disregard
these injunctions, their adoption shall be annulled and they shall
be expelled.

The expulsion shall be in the following manner: The council
shall appoint one of their War Chiefs to convey the message of
annulment and he shall say, "You (naming the nation) listen to
me while I speak. I am here to inform you again of the will of the
Five Nations' Council. It was clearly made known to you at a
former time. Now the Lords of the Five Nations have decided
to expel you and cast you out. We disown you now and annul
your adoption. Therefore you must look for a path in which to
go and lead away all your people. It was you, not we, who committed wrong and caused this sentence of annulment. So then
go your way and depart from the territory of the Five Nations
and from the Confederacy." (XXXIX–122, EUC).

78 Whenever a foreign nation enters the Confederacy or accepts
the Great Peace, the Five Nations and the foreign nation shall

enter into an agreement and compact by which the foreign nation shall endeavor to pursuade other nations to accept the Great Peace. (XLVI–46, TLL).

Rights and powers of war

79 Skanawatih shall be vested with a double office, duty and with double authority. One-half of his being shall hold the Lordship title and the other half shall hold the title of War Chief. In the event of war he shall notify the five War Chiefs of the Confederacy and command them to prepare for war and have their men ready at the appointed time and place for engagement with the enemy of the Great Peace. (I–70, SPW).

80 When the Confederate Council of the Five Nations has for its object the establishment of the Great Peace among the people of an outside nation and that nation refuses to accept the Great Peace, then by such refusal they bring a declaration of war upon themselves from the Five Nations. Then shall the Five Nations seek to establish the Great Peace by a conquest of the rebellious nation. (II–71, SPW).

81 When the men of the Five Nations, now called forth to become warriors, are ready for battle with an obstinate opposing nation that has refused to accept the Great Peace, then one of the five War Chiefs shall be chosen by the warriors of the Five Nations to lead the army into battle. It shall be the duty of the War Chief so chosen to come before his warriors and address them. His aim shall be to impress upon them the necessity of good behavior and strict obedience to all the commands of the War Chiefs. He shall deliver an oration exhorting them with great zeal to be brave and courageous and never to be guilty of cowardice. At the conclusion of his oration he shall march forward and commence the War Song and he shall sing:

> Now I am greatly surprised
> And, therefore, I shall use it,—
> The power of my War Song.
> I am of the Five Nations
> And I shall make supplication
> To the Almighty Creator.
> He has furnished this army.
> My warriors shall be mighty

In the strength of the Creator.[1]
Between him and my song they are
For it was he who gave the song
This war song that I sing!
(III–72, SPW).

82 When the warriors of the Five Nations are on an expedition against an enemy, the War Chief shall sing the War Song as he approaches the country of the enemy and not cease until his scouts have reported that the army is near the enemies' lines when the War Chief shall approach with great caution and prepare for the attack. (IV–73, SPW).

83 When peace shall have been established by the termination of the war against a foreign nation, then the War Chief shall cause all the weapons of war to be taken from the nation. Then shall the Great Peace be established and that nation shall observe all the rules of the Great Peace for all time to come. (V–74, SPW).

84 Whenever a foreign nation is conquered or has by their own will accepted the Great Peace their own system of internal government may continue, but they must cease all warfare against other nations. (VI–75, SPW).

85 Whenever a war against a foreign nation is pushed until that nation is about exterminated because of its refusal to accept the Great Peace and if that nation shall by its obstinacy become exterminated, all their rights, property and territory shall become the property of the Five Nations. (VII–76, SPW).

86 Whenever a foreign nation is conquered and the survivors are brought into the territory of the Five Nations' Confederacy and placed under the Great Peace the two shall be known as the Conqueror and the Conquered. A symbolic relationship shall be devised and be placed in some symbolic position. The conquered nation shall have no voice in the councils of the Confederacy in the body of the Lords. (VIII–77, SPW).

87 When the War of the Five Nations on a foreign rebellious nation is ended, peace shall be restored to that nation by a withdrawal of all their weapons of war by the War Chief of the Five Nations. When all the terms of peace shall have been agreed upon a state of friendship shall be established. (IX–78, SPW).

---

[1] It will be recalled that when the Eries demanded by what power the Five Nations demanded their surrender, the Iroquois replied "The Master of Life fights for us!"

88 When the proposition to establish the Great Peace is made to a foreign nation it shall be done in mutual council. The foreign nation is to be persuaded by reason and urged to come into the Great Peace. If the Five Nations fail to obtain the consent of the nation at the first council a second council shall be held and upon a second failure a third council shall be held and this third council shall end the peaceful methods of persuasion. At the third council the War Chief of the Five Nations shall address the Chief of the foreign nation and request him three times to accept the Great Peace. If refusal steadfastly follows the War Chief shall let the bunch of white lake shells drop from his outstretched hand to the ground and shall bound quickly forward and club the offending chief to death. War shall thereby be declared and the War Chief shall have his warriors at his back to meet any emergency. War must continue until the contest is won by the Five Nations (X–79, SPW).

89 When the Lords of the Five Nations propose to meet in conference with a foreign nation with proposals for an acceptance of the Great Peace, a large band of warriors shall conceal themselves in a secure place safe from the espionage of the foreign nation but as near at hand as possible. Two warriors shall accompany the Union Lord who carries the proposals and these warriors shall be especially cunning. Should the Lord be attacked, these warriors shall hasten back to the army of warriors with the news of the calamity which fell through the treachery of the foreign nation. (XI–80, SPW).

90 When the Five Nations' Council declares war any Lord of the Confederacy may enlist with the warriors by temporarily renouncing his sacred Lordship title which he holds through the election of his women relatives. The title then reverts to them and they may bestow it upon another temporarily until the war is over when the Lord, if living, may resume his title and seat in the Council. (XII–82, SPW).

91 A certain wampum belt of black beads shall be the emblem of the authority of the Five War Chiefs to take up the weapons of war and with their men to resist invasion. This shall be called a war in defense of the territory. (XIV–83, SPW).

Treason or secession of a nation

92 If a nation, part of a nation, or more than one nation within the Five Nations should in any way endeavor to destroy the Great Peace by neglect or violating its laws and resolve to dissolve the

Confederacy, such a nation or such nations shall be deemed guilty of treason and called enemies of the Confederacy and the Great Peace.

It shall then be the duty of the Lords of the Confederacy who remain faithful to resolve to warn the offending people. They shall be warned once and if a second warning is necessary they shall be driven from the territory of the Confederacy by the War Chiefs and his men. (III–86, EUC).

Rights of the people of the Five Nations

93 Whenever a specially important matter or a great emergency is presented before the Confederate Council and the nature of the matter affects the entire body of Five Nations, threatening their utter ruin, then the Lords of the Confederacy must submit the matter to the decision of their people and the decision of the people shall affect the decision of the Confederate Council. This decision shall be a confirmation of the voice of the people. (XV–84, SPW).

94 The men of every clan of the Five Nations shall have a Council Fire ever burning in readiness for a council of the clan. When it seems necessary for a council to be held to discuss the welfare of the clans, then the men may gather about the fire. This council shall have the same rights as the council of the women. (V–88, EUC).

95 The women of every clan of the Five Nations shall have a Council Fire ever burning in readiness for a council of the clan. When in their opinion it seems necessary for the interest of the people they shall hold a council and their decision and recommendation shall be introduced before the Council of Lords by the War Chief for its consideration. (IV–87, EUC).

96 All the Clan council fires of a nation or of the Five Nations may unite into one general council fire, or delegates from all the council fires may be appointed to unite in a general council for discussing the interests of the people. The people shall have the right to make appointments and to delegate their power to others of their number. When their council shall have come to a conclusion on any matter, their decision shall be reported to the Council of the Nation or to the Confederate Council (as the case may require) by the War Chief or the War Chiefs. (VI–89, EUC).

97 Before the real people united their nations, each nation had its council fires. Before the Great Peace their councils were held. The five Council Fires shall continue to burn as before and they

are not quenched. The Lords of each nation in future shall settle their nation's affairs at this council fire governed always by the laws and rules of the council of the Confederacy and by the Great Peace. (VII–90, EUC).

98 If either a nephew or a niece see an irregularity in the performance of the functions of the Great Peace and its laws, in the Confederate Council or in the conferring of Lordship titles in an improper way, through their War Chief they may demand that such actions become subject to correction and that the matter conform to the ways prescribed by the laws of the Great Peace. (LXVII–67, TLL).

Religious ceremonies protected

99 The rites and festivals of each nation shall remain undisturbed and shall continue as before because they were given by the people of old times as useful and necessary for the good of men. (XVI–99, EUC).

100 It shall be the duty of the Lords of each brotherhood to confer at the approach of the time of the Midwinter Thanksgiving and to notify their people of the approaching festival. They shall hold a council over the matter and arrange its details and begin the Thanksgiving five days after the moon of Dis-ko-nah is new. The people shall assemble at the appointed place and the nephews shall notify the people of the time and the place. From the beginning to the end the Lords shall preside over the Thanksgiving and address the people from time to time. (XVII–100, EUC).

101 It shall be the duty of the appointed managers of the Thanksgiving festivals to do all that is needful for carrying out the duties of the occasions.

The recognized festivals of Thanksgiving shall be the Midwinter Thanksgiving, the Maple or Sugar-making Thanksgiving, the Raspberry Thanksgiving, the Strawberry Thanksgiving, the Cornplanting Thanksgiving, the Corn Hoeing Thanksgiving, the Little Festival of Green Corn, the Great Festival of Ripe Corn and the complete Thanksgiving for the Harvest.

Each nation's festivals shall be held in their Long Houses. (XVIII–101, EUC).

102 When the Thanksgiving for the Green Corn comes the special managers, both the men and women, shall give it careful attention and do their duties properly. (XIX–102, EUC).

103 When the Ripe Corn Thanksgiving is celebrated the Lords of the Nation must give it the same attention as they give to the Midwinter Thanksgiving. (XX–103, EUC).

104 Whenever any man proves himself by his good life and his knowledge of good things, naturally fitted as a teacher of good things, he shall be recognized by the Lords as a teacher of peace and religion and the people shall hear him. (X–93, EUC).

The installation song

105 The song used in installing the new Lord of the Confederacy shall be sung by Adodarhoh and it shall be:

" Haii, haii Agwah wi-yoh
"   "   A-kon-he-watha,
"   "   Ska-we-ye-se-go-wah
"   "   Yon-gwa-wih
"   "   Ya-kon-he-wa-tha

Haii, haii, It is good indeed
"   "   (That) a broom,—
"   "   A great wing,
"   "   It is given me
"   "   For a sweeping
                 instrument.

(LVIII–58, TLL).

106 Whenever a person properly entitled desires to learn the Pacification Song he is privileged to do so but he must prepare a feast at which his teachers may sit with him and sing. The feast is provided that no misfortune may befall them for singing the song on an occasion when no chief is installed. (XXIV–107, EUC).

Protection of the house

107 A certain sign shall be known to all the people of the Five Nations which shall denote that the owner or occupant of a house is absent. A stick or pole in a slanting or leaning position shall indicate this and be the sign. Every person not entitled to enter the house by right of living within it upon seeing such a sign shall not approach the house either by day or by night but shall keep as far away as his business will permit. (IX–92, EUC).

Funeral addresses

108 At the funeral of a Lord of the Confederacy, say: " Now we become reconciled as you start away. You were once a Lord of the Five Nations' Confederacy and the United People trusted you. Now we release you for it is true that it is no longer possible for us to walk about together on the earth. Now, therefore, we lay it (the body) here. Here we lay it away. Now then we say to you, ' Persevere onward to the place where the Creator dwells in peace. Let not the things of the earth hinder you. Let nothing that transpired while yet you lived hinder you. In hunting you once took delight; in the game of Lacrosse you once took delight and in the feasts and pleasant occasions your mind was amused, but now do not allow thoughts of these things to give you trouble. Let not your relatives hinder you and also let not your friends and associates trouble your mind. Regard none of these things.'

" Now then, in turn, you here present who were related to this man and you who were his friends and associates, behold the path that is yours also! Soon we ourselves will be left in that place. For this reason hold yourselves in restraint as you go from place to place. In your actions and in your conversation do no idle thing. Speak not idle talk neither gossip. Be careful of this and speak not and do not give way to evil behavior. One year is the time that you must abstain from unseemly levity but if you can not do this for ceremony, ten days is the time to regard these things for respect."

109 At the funeral of a War Chief, say:

" Now we become reconciled as you start away. You were once a war chief of the Five Nations' Confederacy and the United People trusted you as their guard from the enemy. (The remainder is the same as the address at the funeral of a Lord). (XXVII-110, EUC).

110 At the funeral of a Warrior say:

" Now we become reconciled as you start away. Once you were a devoted provider and protector of your family and you were ever ready to take part in battles for the Five Nations' Confederacy. The United People trusted you. (The remainder is the same as the address at the funeral of a Lord). (XXVIII-111, EUC).

111 At the funeral of a young man, say:

" Now we become reconciled as you start away. In the beginning of your career you are taken away and the flower of your life is withered away. (The remainder is the same as the address at the funeral of a Lord). (XXIX-112, EUC).

112 At the funeral of a chief woman say:

" Now we become reconciled as you start away. You were once a chief woman in the Five Nations' Confederacy. You once were a mother of the nations. Now we release you for it is true that it is no longer possible for us to walk about together on the earth. Now, therefore, we lay it (the body) here. Here we lay it away. Now then we say to you, ' Persevere onward to the place where the Creator dwells in peace. Let not the things of the earth hinder you. Let nothing that transpired while you lived hinder you. Looking after your family was a sacred duty and you were faithful. You were one of the many joint heirs of the Lordship titles. Feastings were yours and you had pleasant occasions. . . .' (The remainder is the same as the address at the funeral of a Lord). (XXX–113, EUC).

113 At the funeral of a woman of the people, say:

" Now we become reconciled as you start away. You were once a woman in the flower of life and the bloom is now withered away. You once held a sacred position as a mother of the nation. (Etc.) Looking after your family was a sacred duty and you were faithful. Feastings . . . (Etc.) (The remainder is the same as the address at the funeral of a Lord.) (XXXI–114, EUC).

114 At the funeral of an infant or young woman say:

" Now we become reconciled as you start away. You were a tender bud and gladdened our hearts for only a few days. Now the bloom has withered away . . . (Etc.) Let none of the things that transpired on earth hinder you. Let nothing that happened while you lived hinder you. (The remainder is the same as the address at the funeral of a Lord).' (XXXII–115, EUC).

115 When an infant dies within three days, mourning shall continue only five days. Then shall you gather the little boys and girls at the house of mourning and at the funeral feast a speaker shall address the children and bid them be happy once more, though by a death, gloom has been cast over them. Then shall the black clouds roll away and the sky shall show blue once more. Then shall the children be again in sunshine. (XXXIII–116, EUC).

116 When a dead person is brought to the burial place, the speaker on the opposite side of the Council Fire shall bid the bereaved family cheer their minds once again and rekindle their hearth fires in peace, to put their house in order and once again be in brightness for darkness has covered them. He shall say that the black clouds shall roll away and that the bright blue sky is

visible once more. Therefore shall they be in peace in the sunshine again. (XXXIV–117, EUC).

117 Three strings of shell one span in length shall be employed in addressing the assemblage at the burial of the dead. The speaker shall say:

"Hearken you who are here, this body is to be covered. Assemble in this place again ten days hence for it is the decree of the Creator that mourning shall cease when ten days have expired. Then shall a feast be made."

Then at the expiration of ten days the Speaker shall say: "Continue to listen you who are here. The ten days of mourning have expired and your minds must now be freed of sorrow as before the loss of the relative. The relatives have decided to make a little compensation to those who have assisted at the funeral. It is a mere expression of thanks. This is to the one who did the cooking while the body was lying in the house. Let her come forward and receive this gift and be dismissed from the task. In substance this shall be repeated for every one who assisted in any way until all have been remembered. (XXXV–118, EUC).

THE CODE OF DEKANAHWIDEH

TOGETHER WITH

THE TRADITION OF THE ORIGIN OF THE FIVE NATIONS' LEAGUE

Prepared by the committee of chiefs appointed by the Six Nations' Council of Grand River, Canada, and adopted by Council of Chiefs, July 3, 1900.

The committee was as follows:

Chief Peter Powless	Mohawk
Chief J. W. M. Elliott	Mohawk
Chief Nicodemus Porter	Oneida
Chief Thomas William Echo	Onondaga
Chief William Wage	Cayuga
Chief Abram Charles	Cayuga
Chief John A. Gibson	Seneca
Chief Josiah Hill	Tuscarora
Chief John Danford	Oneida of the Thames
Chief Isiah Sickles	Oneida of the Thames

INTRODUCTORY

For several hundred years the Five Nations (since 1715 the Six Nations) have existed without a written history chronicled by themselves, of their ancient customs, rites and ceremonies, and of the formation of the Iroquois League. Books have been written by white men in the past, but these have been found to be too voluminous and inaccurate in some instances.

Of the existence of the Five Nations therefore, before the formation of the League of Great Peace by Dekanahwideh, living as they did apart from one another as separate nations and having nothing in common, much might be written, but at this juncture our object will only admit of the relation of the formation of the League of the Five Nations, which as far as can be ascertained took place about the year 1390.

The purpose for which this league or confederation of the Five Nations was organized was to enable them to protect themselves against the invasion of their vast domains by other nations who were hostile to them, and also the formation of a form of government among themselves. Ever since the birth of the league this government has existed with but very slight modifications.

The student of ethnology may find something which may be of interest to him in this record, compiled as it is by the elder ceremonial chiefs who are now among those who are ruling the people of the Six Nations as chiefs or lords, under the old régime of dynastical lords in perpetuation of that system of government by hereditary succession as it was constituted by Dekanahwideh and his associates at the time of the formation of the League of the Iroquois.

This account is not intended to be a concise history of this interesting people, but simply a record of those interesting traditions which have been for centuries handed down from father to son in connection with the formation of the league.

There is no doubt in the minds of the writers of this preface that many of the ancient traditions of the Six Nations have become much modified, and some have been long relegated to oblivion owing to the fact that in the earlier history of these peoples there were for a long time no members of the various nations capable of rendering these traditions in writing and thus preserving them intact to their posterity.

It is a noteworthy fact that the League of the Five Nations (now known as the Six Nations) as constituted centuries ago by Dekanahwideh and his associates, has been followed in accordance with the rules of the confederacy as laid down by this founder of the league, and that the installation of the lords (chiefs) as rulers of the people as laid down in these unwritten rules hundreds of years ago is still strictly observed and adhered to by the chiefs of the Six Nations and their people.

With reference to the origin or birth, character and doings of Dekanahwideh as herein chronicled, it will be observed that they present an analogy or similarity to Hebrew biblical history and teachings. This is portrayed strongly in the narration of the birth of Dekanahwideh and also in certain extraordinary powers which he is attributed to have possessed.

There is little doubt that some of this influence was brought about as a result of the labors and teachings of the Jesuit fathers among them. In the early discovery of the Five Nations the Jesuit fathers made an effort to christianize them.

These precepts as taught and inculcated in the minds of the people by these missionaries have been assimilated to some extent and wrought into their own religious belief, as well perhaps as into the story of the traditional nativity of this founder of the Iroquois Confederacy.

It was in recognition of the fact that all nations have a traditional history similar to this one (and some of them have long since become enlightened and educated to better things) which originated with these people while they were yet in a crude state (notably, for example, may be cited the English, Irish and Scotch legends and traditions) that this small fragment of Iroquois traditional history was written by the chiefs, so that they might preserve it as other nations have done.

It is only natural for a people undergoing a transition from a state of barbarism to that of civilization and christianity to evince a desire to have their past mythological legends and crude history preserved.

It was therefore at the request of, and by the authority of the Six Nations' Council, that that portion of the traditional history of this people relating to the formation of the League of the Five Nations, together with the condolence ceremonies, now used in the creation and induction into office of new chiefs as successors to deceased members of the council, was written from dictation by the ceremonial chiefs as follows: Chiefs Peter Powless, Mohawk; Nicodemus Porter, Oneida; William Wage and Abram Charles, Cayuga; John A. Gibson, Seneca; Thomas William Echo, Onondaga; and Josiah Hill, Tuscarora. Chiefs Josiah Hill and J. W. M. Elliott were appointed to act as secretaries, with the express purpose of having it published by the Department of Indian Affairs, so that the future generations of the people of the Six Nations may have preserved to them these traditions of their forefathers which otherwise in time would become lost.

Signed at Ohsweken Council House, Six Nations Reserve, Ontario, Canada, August 17, 1900.

Josiah Hill, *Secretary Six Nations' Council.*

J. W. M. Elliott, *Mohawk Chief, Secretary of the ceremonial committee of Indian rites and customs.*

Indian words

The meanings of some of the more difficult Indian words to be found in this work are as follows:

1 A-ka-rah-ji-ko-wah—A great swamp elm
2 Ska-reh-heh-se-go-wah—The great tall tree

3 Jo-neh-rah-de-se-go-wah—The great long leaves
4 Djok-de-he-sko-na—The great white roots
5 Ka-ya-neh-renh-ko-wah—The great peace
6 Karihwiyoh—Good tidings of peace and power
7 Rodiyanesho'o—Lords or chiefs
8 Hoyane (Royaneh) — Lord or chief
9 Ehkanehdodeh—A pine tree, applied to earned or self-made chiefs
10 Kwa-ah — The mourning cry used by a chief warrior to convey the news of the death of a lord or head chief
11 Kanekonketshwaserah — The condolence ceremony used upon the death of a lord or chief

THE TRADITIONAL NARRATIVE

OF THE

ORIGIN OF THE CONFEDERATION OF THE FIVE NATIONS

COMMONLY KNOWN AS THE IROQUOIS

Together with an account of the ancient customs, usages and ceremonies in use by these nations in the choice and installation into office of their Ro-de-ya-ner-shoh (lords or chiefs), including traditions relating to the lives and characters of Dekanahwideh, the framer of the league, Hay-yonh-wa-tha (Hiawatha), the lawgiver, Tha-do-da-ho and other leaders.

The peculiar beginning of the Great Peace,[1] or the Great League of the Five Nations at a time most ancient, is here told.

The name of the place mentioned as the birthplace of Dekanah-wideh[2] was called Kah-ha-nah-yenh,[3] somewhere in the neighborhood of the Bay of Quinte.

According to tradition, a woman[4] was living in that neighborhood who had one daughter of stainless character who did not travel away from home, but remained with her mother constantly, and when she had attained the age of womanhood she had held no manner of intercourse with any man. In the course of time, notwithstanding, she showed signs of conception and her mother was very much aggrieved. The mother, therefore, spoke to her daughter and said: "I am going to ask you a question and I want you to tell me the truth. What has happened to you and how is it that you are going to bear a child?" Then the daughter replied and said, "Mother I will tell you the truth, I do not know how I became with child."[5]

Then the mother said: "The reply you give me is not sufficient to remove my grief. I am sure that you did not tell me the full truth concerning what I asked you." Then the daughter replied: "I have indeed told you the whole truth concerning what you asked me." Then the sorrowing mother said: "Of a truth, my daughter, you have no love for me."

---

[1] Gaya"nässhägo, in Onondaga; Gayanĕs'shä"gowa, in Seneca. Derived from Gayanĕs'shä, *A compelling rule of virtue,* and gowa, *great, exalted.*

[2] Dekanäwi'da, *Two water currents flowing together.*

[3] Kanyĕn'gĕ (Onon.), *Among the flints, Flinty peace,* cf. Hadineyĕ"ge'gä, *They are flint people.*

[4] No father or husband; that is, no male is mentioned in this family until Dekanahwideh appears.

[5] A virgin (female) is called deyĕn'nowädon'; (masc.) dehaⁿnowä'doⁿ' meaning, *He is hidden;* from nowä'doⁿ', *hidden.* Ye'wayei' is the word for *pure.*

Then she began to ill-treat her daughter, and then the daughter also began to feel aggrieved because of this ill-treatment from her mother.

It so happened that as the time approached when the daughter would deliver the child, that the mother dreamed [1] that she saw a man whom she did not know, and that he said that he appeared as a messenger to her on account of her troubled mind, caused by the condition of her daughter who had in so mysterious a manner conceived a child.

"I am here to deliver to you a message and now I will ask you to cease your grieving and trouble of mind, and the ill-treatment of your daughter from day to day because it is indeed a fact that your daughter does not know how she became with child. I will tell you what has happened. It is the wish of the Creator that she should bear a child, and when you will see the male child you shall call him Dekanahwideh. The reason you shall give him that name is because this child will reveal to men-beings (Oñg'wĕoⁿwĕ'), the Good Tidings of Peace and Power [2] from Heaven, and the Great Peace shall rule and govern on earth, and I will charge you that you and your daughter should be kind to him becaues he has an important mission to perform in the world, and when he grows up to be a man do not prevent him from leaving home."

Then the old woman, (Iăgĕn'tci) asked the messenger, what office the child should hold.

The messenger answered and said: "His mission is for peace and life to the people both on earth and in heaven."

When the old woman woke up the next morning she spoke to her daughter and said: "My daughter, I ask you to pardon me for all the ill-treatment I have given you because I have now been satisfied that you told me the truth when you told me that you did not know how you got the child which you are about to deliver."

Then the daughter also was made glad, and when she was delivered of the child, it was as had been predicted; the child was a male child, and the grandmother called him Dekanahwideh.

The child grew up rapidly, and when he had become a young man he said: "The time has come when I should begin to perform my duty in this world. I will therefore begin to build my canoe and by tomorrow I must have it completed because there is work for me to do tomorrow when I go away to the eastward."

---

[1] *She dreamed,* waagoi'shĕⁿdŭksĕⁿá. To guess the meaning of a dream, third person, plural, present, Hodinowaiya'ha.

[2] Ne"gā'ihwiio'ne"skäñ'noⁿkhu (Seneca), literally, *The good message* (or edict), *the power.*

Then he began to build his canoe out of a white rock, and when he had completed it, Dekanahwideh said: "I am ready now to go away from home and I will tell you that there is a tree[1] on top of the hill and you shall have that for a sign whenever you wish to find out whether I shall be living or dead. You will take an axe and chop the tree and if the tree flows blood[2] from the cut, you will thereby know that I am beheaded and killed, but if you find no blood running from this tree after you have chopped a chip from it, then you may know that my mission was successful. The reason that this will happen is be.ause I came to stop forever the wanton shedding of blood among human beings."

Then Dekanahwideh also said: "Come to the shore of the lake and see me start away."

So his mother and his grandmother went together with him and helped to pull the boat to the lake and as they stood at the lake, Dekanahwideh said: "Good bye, my mothers, for I am about to leave you for I am to go for a long time. When I return I will not come this way."

Then the grandmother said "How are you going to travel since your canoe is made out of stone. It will not float."

Then Dekanahwideh said, "This will be the first sign of wonder that man will behold; a canoe made out of stone will float."

Then he bade them farewell, put his canoe in the lake and got in. Then he paddled away to the eastward and the grandmother and his mother with wonder beheld him and saw that his canoe was going swiftly. In a few moments he disappeared out of their sight.

It happened at that time a party of hunters had a camp on the south side of the lake now known as Ontario and one of the party went toward the lake and stood on the bank of the lake, and beheld the object coming toward him at a distance, and the man could not understand what it was that was approaching him; shortly afterwards he understood that it was a canoe, and saw a man in it, and the moving object was coming directly toward where he stood, and when the man (it was Dekanahwideh) reached the shore he came out of his boat and climbed up the bank.

Then Dekanahwideh asked the man what had caused them to be where they were, and the man answered and said: "We are here

---

[1] Djirhonathăradadon'.
[2] That men enter into or become trees is an old Iroquois conception. The sap of the tree becomes blood that flows when the tree is injured.

3

for a double object. We are here hunting game for our living and also because there is a great strife in our settlement."

Then Dekanahwideh said, "You will now return to the place from whence you came. The reason that this occurs is because the Good Tidings of Peace and Friendship have come to the people, and you will find all strife removed from your settlement when you go back to your home. And I want you to tell your chief that the Ka-rih-wi-yoh[1] (Good Tidings of Peace and Power) have come and if he asks you from whence came the Good Tidings of Peace and Power, you will say that the Messenger of the Good Tidings of Peace and Power will come in a few days.

Then the man said: "Who are you now speaking to me?"

Dekanahwideh answered: "It is I who came from the west and am going eastward and am called Dekanahwideh in the world."

Then the man wondered and beheld his canoe and saw that his canoe was made out of white stone.

Then Dekanahwideh said, "I will go and visit Tyo-den-he deh[2] first." Dekanahwideh then went down the bank and got into his boat, and passed on. Then the man also turned away and went home, and when he came back to the camp he said: "I saw a strange man coming from the lake with a canoe made out of white stone and when he landed he came up the bank and I had a conversation with him. First, he asked me where I came from and when I told him he understood everything.[3] Then he said: "You will all go home for there is now peace, and all strife has been removed from the settlement."

Then the party went home and as soon as they reached home, they went and told the Royaner[4] (lord) and said that the Good Tidings of Peace and Power had come. Then the lord asked the speaker who told him the message and then he said that he saw a man who was called Dekanahwideh in the world. Then the lord asked him from whence the Good Tidings of Peace and Strength were coming.

[1] Karhihwiio, or in Seneca, Ne"Gä'ihwiio, meaning a proclamation of good ... terally the word is interpreted, *A good message*. The mis-... use the word gä-i-hwi-io for *Gospel*. The power of the new civil government is called skĕñ'non', meaning *inherent potence*.

[2] Tiodenhe'dĕ, meaning He (having died) lives again, cf. Siga'hedŭs, *He resurrects,* used as a name for Christ.

[3] Dekanawida is reputed to have been a clairvoyant.

[4] Royaner is hoya'ne in Seneca. The Mohawk root-equivalent is Ya"nerhe. Royaner means *excellent, noble, good, exalted, pure*. Thus as a title the name is translated *Lord*. Missionaries so use the name, cf. Hale Book of Rites, p. 65.

Then the man said: " It is coming and will come soon."

Then the lord said: " Where did you see the man?" He replied, " I saw him in the lake with his canoe; he came from the west and he is going eastward."

Then the lord began to wonder and said that he thought the settlement should remain in silence, for all would be glad and satisfied.

Dekanahwideh continued his journey and came to where the great wizard Toh-do-dah-ho[1] lived. This man was possessed with great power as a wizard and no man could come to him without endangering his life and it is related that even the fowls of the air whenever they flew directly over his place of abode would die and fall down on his premises, and that if he saw a man approaching him he was sure to destroy him or kill him. This man was a cannibal, and had left the settlement to which he belonged for a long time and lived by himself in an isolated place.

Dekanahwideh came[2] and approached the abode of the cannibal and saw him carrying a human body into his house and shortly he saw him come out again and go down to the river and draw some water. Dekanahwideh went closer and when he had come to the house he went up onto the roof and from the chimney opening[3] he looked in and saw the owner come back with a pail of water, put up a kettle on the fireplace to cook his meal and after it was cooked he saw him take the kettle from the fire and place it at the end of the fireplace and say to himself, " I suppose it is now time for me to have my meal and after I am finished I will go where I am required on business."

Dekanahwideh moved still closer over the smoke hole and looked straight down into the kettle. The man Tah-do-dah-ho was then moving around the house and when he came back to take some of the meat from the kettle he looked into it and saw that a man was looking at him from out of the kettle. This was the reflection of Dekanahwideh. Then the man Tah-do-dah-ho moved back and sat down near the corner of the house and began to think seriously and he thought that it was a most wonderful thing which had happened. He said to himself that such a thing had never occurred before as long as he had been living in the house. " I did not

---

[1] Thadoda'ho.

[2] He came on a tour of inspection. The Onondaga version says it was Hiawatha.

[3] Albert Cusick, the Onondaga informant, says this incident is an interpolation.

know that I was so strange a man," he said. " My mode of living must be wrong." Then he said: " Let me look again and be sure that what I have seen is true." Then he arose, went to the kettle and looked into it again, and he saw the same object — the face of a great man and it was looking at him. Then he took the kettle and went out and went toward the hillside and he emptied it there.

Then Dekanahwideh came down from the roof and made great haste toward the hillside, and when Tha-do-dah-ho came up the hill he met Dekanahwideh.

Dekanahwideh asked Tah-do-dah-ho where he came from and he said, " I had cooked my meal and I took the kettle from the fire and placed it on the floor. I thought that I would take some of the meat out of the kettle and then I saw a man's face looking at me from the kettle. I do not know what had happened; I only know such a thing never occurred to me before as long as I have been living in this house. Now I have come to the conclusion that I must be wrong in the way I am and the way I have been living. That is why I carried the kettle out of my house and emptied it over there by the stump. I was returning when I met you." Then he said, " From whence did you come?"

Dekanahwideh answered, "I came from the west and am going eastward."

Then the man said, " Who are you that is thus speaking to me?"

Then Dekanahwideh said, " It is he who is called Dekanahwideh in this world." Dekanahwideh then asked: " From whence have you come?"

The man then said: " There is a settlement to which I belong but I left that settlement a long time ago."

Then Dekanahwideh said, " You will now return, for peace and friendship have come to you and your settlement and you have now repented the course of wrong doing which you pursued in times past. It shall now also occur that when you return to your settlement you, yourself, shall promote peace and friendship for it is a fact that peace is now ruling in your settlement and I want you to arrange and settle all matters." Then Dekanahwideh also said: " I shall arrive there early tomorrow morning. I shall visit the west first. I shall visit there the house of the woman, Ji-kon-sah-seh. The reason why I shall do this (go and visit this woman first) is because the path passes there which runs from the east to the west."

Then after saying these words Dekanahwideh went on his way and arrived at the house of Ji-kon-sah-seh and said to her that he had come on this path which passed her home and which led from the east to the west, and on which traveled the men of blood-thirsty and destructive nature. Then he said unto her, " It is your custom to feed these men when they are traveling on this path on their war expeditions." He then told her that she must desist from practising this custom. He then told her that the reason she was to stop this custom was that the Karihwiyoh[1] or Good Tidings of Peace and Power had come. He then said: " I shall, therefore, now change your disposition and practice." Then also, "I now charge you that you shall be the custodian of the Good Tidings of Peace and Power, so that the human race may live in peace in the future." Then Dekanahwideh also said, " You shall therefore now go east where I shall meet you at the place of danger (to Onondaga), where all matters shall be finally settled and you must not fail to be there on the third day. I shall now pass on in my journey."

Then he journeyed on a great way and went to another settlement. Here he inquired who their Royaner was and after he had ascertained his abode he went to his home and found him, and when they met, Dekanahwideh said, " Have you heard that the Good Tidings of Peace and Power are coming? " The lord then said: " I truly have heard of it."

Then Dekanahwideh asked him what he thought about it.

Then the lord said, " Since I have heard of the good news I have been thinking about it and since then I have not slept." Then Dekanhwideh said, " It is now at hand — that which has been the cause of your sleeplessness."

Then Dekanahwideh said, " You shall hereafter be called Hayyonh-wa-tha [2] (Hiawatha)."

Then the lord said, " To whom am I speaking? " Dekanahwideh answered and said: " I am the man who is called on earth by the name of Dekanahwideh, and I have just come from the west and am now going east for the purpose of propagating peace, so that the shedding of human blood might cease among you."

Then the Lord Hahyonhwatha asked, " Will you wait until I go and announce the news to my colleagues? " Dekanahwideh then

---

[1] Djikonsä'sĕ', *The wild cat* (fat faced), known as the "mother of nations." This was the most honored female title among the Huron Iroquois. She is sometimes call the Peace Queen. She was of the Neuter Nation and her lodge was on the east side of the Niagara, at Kai-a-nieu-ka. Often she was termed Ye-go-wa-neh, the great woman.

[2] Haiyonhwat'hä, meaning *He has misplaced something but knows where to find it.*

said that he could wait as he was on this good mission. Then the Lord Hahyonhwatha announced to his colleagues and people that they assemble to hear Dekanahwideh, and when they were assembled Hahyonhwatha asked Dekanahwideh what news he had for the people. Dekanahwideh answered that the proclamation of the Good Tidings of Peace and Power had arrived and that he had come on a mission to proclaim the Good News of Peace and Power that bloodshed might cease in the land, as the Creator, he had learned, never intended that such should ever be practised by human beings.

Lord Hahyonhwatha answered the people: " We have now heard the Good News of Peace and Power from this man Dekanahwideh." He then turned and asked his colleagues and all the people what answer they should give. Then one of the chief warriors asked: " What shall we do with the powerful tribes on the east and on the west[1] of our villages who are always hostile to us? "

Then Dekanahwideh answered and said that the hostile nations referred to had already accepted the Good News of Peace and Power.

Then the chief warrior answered and said: " I am still in doubt and I would propose (as a test of power) that this man (Dekanahwideh) climb up a big tree by the edge of a high cliff and that we then cut the tree down and let it fall with him over the cliff,[2] and then if he does not die I shall truly believe the message which he has brought us."

Then the deputy chief warrior said: " I also am of the same opinion and I approve of the suggestion of the chief warrior."

Then Dekanahwideh said: " I am ready and most willingly accede to your request, because the Good News of Peace and Power has come unto us, I now confidently place myself in your hands."

Then the lord said: " It has now been decided. We will therefore all go to where the tree stands." They then started to go there and when they arrived where the tree stood, the lord said: " We have now arrived where the tree that we have decided upon stands."

Then the chief warrior said to Dekanahwideh: " I made this proposal and therefore you will now climb this tree so that it will

---

[1] To the west of the Onondagas were the Seneca and Cayuga nations; to the east the Oneida and Mohawk. It is possible, however, that the New England Indians on the east and the Neuters on the west were meant by this paragraph. Consult J. D. Prince. Wampum Records of the Passamaquoddy Documents, Annals N. Y. Acad. Sci. No. 15, p. 369–77. 1898.

[2] The Newhouse version (q.v.) gives more details of this incident.

be a sign of proof, and the people may see your power. If you live to see tomorrow's sunrise then I will accept your message." Then Dekanahwideh said, " This shall tru'y be done and carried out." He then climbed the tree and when he had reached the top of the tree[1] he sat down on a branch, after which the tree was cut down, and it fell over the cliff with him. Then the people kept vigilant watch so that they might see him, but they failed to see any signs of him. Then the chief warrior said, " Now my proposition has been carried out and Dekenahwideh has disappeared and so now we will vigilantly watch at sunrise tomorrow morning. Then the Lord Hahyonhwatha said, " We shall now return home."

Now when the new day dawned one of the warriors arose before sunrise and at once went to the place where the tree had been cut and when he had arrived there he saw at a short distance a field of corn, and near by the smoke from a fire[2] toward which the warrior went. When he arrived there he saw a man sitting by the fire and after seeing the man he at once returned to the Lord Hahyonhwatha and when he arrived there he said that he had seen the man sitting by the fire, and that it was he who was on the tree which was cut the evening before.

Then Hahyonhwatha charged him to convey these tidings to his colleagues and all the people and in a short time all the people had assembled. Then the Lord Hahyonhwatha said, " We will now call Dekanahwideh," and he then commissioned the chief warrior and the deputy chief warrior to go after him and they went to where Dekanahwideh had his fire and when they arrived they told him that the Lord Hahyonhwatha had sent them to bring him and that they would escort him to the home of Hahyonhwatha.

Then Dekanahwideh said: " It is right. I shall go with you."

They then returned and when they arrived back at the abode of Hahyonhwatha, the chief warrior spoke and said, " We have returned with Dekanahwideh, and he is now in your charge." Lord Hahyonhwatha then said: " I am now surely ready to fully accept the Good News of Peace and Power, and it now rests with you as your opinion in this matter."

---

[1] This event took place on the cliff overlooking the lower falls of the Mohawk. The tree was a bitter hickory, (gŭs'thik), which stood at the doorway of a woman named De'siio'. When Dekanawida climbed the tree he sang the air of " the six songs of the pacification hymn."

[2] The column of smoke from Dekanawida's fire is said always to have " pierced the sky." The term is, Wagayĕⁿgwa'i'dĕⁿwagaiyaestä', *It forms smoke, smoke pierces the sky.*

The chief warrior then said: " I was in great doubt, but have now truly concluded to accept the Good News of Peace and Power." Then Royaner (Lord) Hahyonhwatha said: " Now faithfully see these matters are settled and finished."

Then he further said: " Dekanahwideh, you may now listen to the answer we have concluded to give you. We have received the message which you brought us, and we have jointly concluded to accept the message of Good News of Peace and Power and we have now concluded all we have to say, and the matter shall now rest with you entirely."

Dekanahwideh then said: " This day is early and yet young, so is the new mind also tender and young, so also is the Good Tidings of Peace and Power, and as the new sun of Good Tidings of Peace and Power arose, so it will proceed on its course and prosper; so also will the young mind, and the Good Tidings of Peace and Power shall prevail and prosper. Therefore in the future your grandchildren forever shall live in peace."

Then Dekanahwideh answered again: " You, chief warrior, you have had power in warfare, but now this is all changed. I now proclaim that since you had doubts, you shall be hereafter known in the land by the name of Tha-ha-rih-ho-ken (De-ka-ri-ho-ken),[1] which means doubting or hesitating over two things as to which course to adopt."

And Dekanahwideh said: " You, the deputy chief warrior, I charge you that you shall be called and known hereafter in the land by the name of Sa-de-ga-rih-wa-den[2] (one-who-respects-all-matters-as-important-equally) because you truly have concurred in and justly confirmed all that you have heard."

Then Dekanahwideh also said: " I shall now pass on and go east, and we shall meet again tomorrow[3] to add to what we have already accomplished."

Then Dekanahwideh passed on in his journey.

Then in Lord Hahyonhwatha's family composed of three[4] daughters, the eldest was taken ill and in a little time she died.[5]

---

[1] In Onǫndaga, Degaihō'kĕⁿ'. His name appears first on the roll of " Rodiyaner."

[2] Tcă'dekaiiwāt'dĕ, sometimes translated, *Two stories diverging in conclusions.*

[3] " Tomorrow," or " on another day " frequently means the next year. Dekanawida in going east possibly went to the Abenaki or other New England Indians. See Prince, *op. cit.*

[4] Newhouse says seven.

[5] A Mohawk account. Cf. Newhouse, who says the daughters all perished through the witchcraft of Osïʼnoʼ. One account says that he took the form

The mind of Hahyonhwatha was troubled. His colleagues and the people assembled at his home and condoled with him and admonished him to forget his sorrow, and he acceded to their desire. Shortly afterwards the second daughter took sick and in a short time died. Then the sorrow and trouble of the Lord Hahyonhwatha was greatly increased, and again his colleagues and people assembled at his abode and again they tried to induce him to forget his sorrow and trouble, but he could not answer them. So Deharihoken said: " I will not tell you my mind (my purpose). I think that we should look for something which would console the mind of our lord in his trouble and bereavement." Then he also said: " I would lay before you warriors, for your consideration, that you cheer him by playing a game of lacrosse." [1]

Then Sadekarihwadeh said: " I will now tell you my mind, first let the people all assemble to console him. This shall be done as alas our lord has now only one daughter left alive."

Then Dekarihoken confirmed all that Sadekarihwadeh had said.

Then the people assembled at the home of the Lord Hahyonhwatha and they spoke unto him words of condolence that he might forget his grief and bereavement.

But the lord did not answer them. So then the warriors decided that they would play a game of lacrosse in order to cheer him and during the time that they were playing, the last daughter of Hahyonhwatha came out of the family abode to go after some water and when she had gone half way to the spring she saw flying high up in the air above a beautiful bird.[2] She paused in her journey and the bird flew downwards toward her. She cried out aloud, being frightened, and said, " O, see this bird! " after which she ran away.

Then the warriors saw it and as it was then flying low, the warriors followed it, and as they were looking at the bird they did not notice the daughter of Hahyonhwatha before them and in their haste they ran over and trampled her to death, and it transpired that the daughter of Hahyonhwatha was with child.

Then Sadekarihwadeh went and told Hahyonhwatha that a strange bird called Teh-yoh-ronh-yoh-ron (a high flying bird which

---

of a screech owl and conjured from a tree overlooking the daughters' lodge; another that he became a poison shadow at the bottom of a spring.

[1] Each game had a reputed medicinal effect.

[2] This was the magic Hä'goks, sometimes called " the wampum eagle." Another descriptive name is given later in the text.

pierces the skies) had come amongest them and that it was due to
the visit of the bird that his daughter was killed.

Then Hahyonhwatha answered sadly and said: " I have now
lost all my daughters and in the death of this, my last daughter,
you have accidently and unwittingly killed two beings." [1]

And Hahyonhwatha further said: " I must now go away to the
west," and he started immediately on his way. He met Dekanahwideh on the trail and Dekanahwideh warned him of the danger on
his way, especially with reference to a certain man who was watching, saying as follows:

" There is danger in front of you, there is a man watching your
way in front of you. It is necessary for you to approach him
without his becoming aware of your coming until you get to him.
If you can get up to him while he is unaware of your approach
then we shall surely prosper in our mission. You will then speak
to him and ask him what thing he is watching for. He will answer
you and say that he is watching to protect the fields of corn as the
people of other nations and also animals destroy the crops and he
is watching therefore that the crops might be preserved, so that the
children might live from the harvest."

Then Hahyonhwatha proceeded on his journey and when he
arrived where the man was sitting beside a fire near a big tree and
watching; he quickly spoke, asking, " What are you doing?" And
the man answered and said: " I am watching the fields of corn
to protect them from other nations and also from animals that our
children might live from the harvest."

Hahyonhwatha then said to the man: " Return home now and
tell your lord that the Good News of Peace and Power has come."
So he returned and told his Lord the message given to him by
Hahyonhwatha. Then the lord said: " Who is it who told you
this strange news?" Then the man who had been watching said:
"A man suddenly appeared to me when I was watching the fields
of corn and he told me the news."

Hahyonhwatha went to the other end of the corn field and there
met Dekanahwideh. Dekanahwideh said: " We have now announced the (Ka-ya-ne-reh) Good Tidings of Peace and Power,
therefore you shall abide in this hut near these corn fields, which
you will only leave when you receive an invitation from the people.

---

[1] Other versions say that this event took place before Hiawatha met
Dekanawida, his grief over his losses, driving him into a self-imposed exile,
during which he lamented all evil conditions. Later he met Dekanawida. A.
Cusick, and Baptist Thomas, New York Onondagas, both concurred in this.

You must not go unless the invitation is official. A woman shall first come to you early tomorrow morning who will be the first to see you, then you shall cut and prepare some elderberry twigs.[1] You shall cut them into pieces and remove the heart pulp and then you shall string them up." " Then the lord (Royaner) shall send a messenger to you to invite you, but you must not accept the invitation until he shall send to you a string of twigs similar to your own."

Then Hahyonhwatha went on his journey and found the hut beside the cornfield and built a fire, and in the morning a woman came to the cornfield and saw the smoke from the fire at the end of the cornfield and when she arrived there she saw a man sitting with his head hanging down. Then the woman hurried home and went straightway to where the lord (Royaner) lived and when she arrived she told him that she had seen a strange man sitting beside a fire in the cornfield.

Then the lord asked her: " What thing was this man doing there?" And the woman answered and said that the man was sitting there quietly looking on the ground.[2]

Then the lord said: " This must be the man who sent the message of the Good Tidings of Peace and Power. I shall therefore now send a messenger to bring him hither."

He then summoned the chief warrior and the deputy chief warrior to come to him and when the two had come, the lord said to them: " You shall go after the man who is at the fire in the cornfield and bring him to me. The lord then said to the deputy chief warrior: " I send you to go after him," and the deputy chief warrior went to bring this man, and when he arrived at the place where the man had built the fire, he saw a man sitting there and he was looking at a string of elderberry twigs which was hanging on a pole horizontally placed in front of him.

Then the deputy chief warrior said: " I am sent after you by the lord (Royaner)."

The man did not answer and so the deputy chief warrior repeated the message of the lord three times, but the man did not give any

---

[1] Wampum at first seems to have been any kind of cylindrical bead, large or small. The Mohawk name is o'tgo'rha; Seneca, o'tko'ä'. The quills of feathers and porcupines were used as wampum (o'tgo'rha). Indeed Baptist Thomas, an Onondaga informant, says porcupine quills were used and not elderberry twigs as stated in this version.

[2] Hiawatha kept repeating the phrase, äsanatcik, meaning, *they should give me a wampum token.*

reply. Then the deputy chief warrior turned and returned to the lord, and when he arrived, he said to the lord: "He did not reply."

The lord then asked: "What did you see?" Then the deputy chief warrior answered and said, "I saw a string of elderberry twigs hanging on a pole in front of him and he was looking at it." Then the lord answered and said: "I now understand; I shall therefore make a similar string out of quills which will cause him to come." The lord then made two strings of quills and put them on a thong.

The lord then said: "I have now completed the strings and you shall both go after him and bring him here. You shall therefore take these strings of quills with you to him and they shall become words and that will induce him to come. They then went on their errand and when they had arrived at the fire the chief warrior said: "The lord has again sent us after you, and this string of quills are his words which are to bring you to him."

Then Hahyonhwatha answered and said: "This is what should have been done." He then took the string of quills and said: "After I get through smoking[1] I shall go to the lord."

They then returned to the lord and when they had arrived they said that the man had now answered and that when he had finished smoking his pipe he would come.

The lord then told them to tell the people so that they would all assemble when the man should arrive.

The chief warrior and the deputy chief warrior then went to tell the people to assemble as soon as possible to the abode of the lord.

The people had therefore all assembled when Hahyonhwatha arrived. The lord said to him: "You have come amongst us and doubtless you have some important matter to convey to us. The people have already assembled and are prepared to listen to the matter which you may have to communicate to us."

Then Hahyonhwatha answered: "I have come here to deliver to you the message of Good Tidings of Peace and Power so that our children in the future may live in peace."

Then the lord said: "We shall defer answering you until the return of a certain man for whom we are waiting, but in the meantime we desire that you shall remain in our village with us."

Then Hahyonhwatha answered and said: "This can be safely

---

[1] To have gone in haste without a semblance of deliberation would have been considered insulting.

done as I came to you with the message of Good Tidings of Peace and Power."

Then the lord said: " I shall therefore entertain you myself. This will be done because the message which you have brought to us may be the same as the other man's for which we are waiting, and he has sent word that he is coming." Then Hahyonhwatha said: " I approve of all this."

The assembled people then dispersed and when night came the lord told Hahyonhwatha that he could sleep in the inner room. Then he (Hahyonhwatha) went in and retired. Shortly after he heard a voice outside which said: "Are you stopping here?" and Hahyonhwatha replied, " Yes." Now the voice from outside said that it was very urgent for him to come out.

So Hahyonwatha went out and he saw Dakanahwideh standing outside. Dekanahwideh then said: " It is now urgent that we proceed directly on our journey.[1] You have now accomplished all that is necessary to be done here at present; we can go to another settlement now and afterwards return. The man you are now waiting for will likely have returned by that time."

" There is one settlement left to be visited, although I have been there before and had conversation with the man. I have promised him that I will visit him again and for that reason when you left home you heard a loud toned voice in front of you saying, 'A-son-kek-ne-eh.' [2] We will now proceed on our journey."

They then went and while they were on their way Dekanahwideh said, " Let us stop here and wait a while, and you will look toward the southeast. So they stood still and Hahyonhwatha looked toward the southeast and saw the smoke arising and reaching to the sky.

Then Dekanahwideh asked: " What do you see? "

Hahyonhwatha said: " I see smoke piercing the sky."

Then Dekanahwideh answered: " That smoke which you saw is where the abode of Dyon-yon-ko is. The reason you see the smoke piercing the sky is because the Good Tidings of Peace and Power have come to the people of that settlement but unfortunately, owing to the selfishness and lack of energy of these people, the Good Tidings of Peace and Power have not prospered and have not extended to other settlements.[3]   It is thus good that these people

---

[1] Baptist Thomas says Hiawatha left this council because of a dispute on the part of the people, who forgot him in their effort to honor another man.
[2] " It has not yet occurred," asoñ'de'nëi'.
[3] It is said that the New England Indians (Adirhon'daks), the Cherokee (Oya'de), the Wyandott (Thästähetci), the Tionante (Tyonontate'ka'), the

have received the Good Tidings of Peace and Power. We shall therefore take power from them which will enable us to complete the work we have undertaken to accomplish."

They then heard the loud toned voice saying: "A-soh-kek-ne ————eh " (it is not yet; which means, impatiently waiting). Then Dekanahwideh said: " It is now very urgent for us to proceed on our journey to the place from whence this voice proceeds." They then went and they had not gone far when they came to a lake. Then Dekanahwideh said: " It is now left with you to decide what we shall do; you have seen the lake and it is beside this lake that the man lives whose loud voice you have heard saying: 'Asohkene————eh.' "

Dekanahwideh then also said: " There are two ways which we can pursue to get across the lake, and you can have your choice. We can take the boat which you see lying flat on the ground and paddle over or we can magically pass above the lake, and so get over it." Dekanahwideh also said: " That man whom you heard calling in a loud voice is able to cause the boat to upset if he sees it and the people within it to become drowned; he has ended the lives of many people in this way in the lake." [1]

Then Hahyonhwatha said: " My choice is that we pass over above the lake." Then Dekanahwideh said: " It is best to approach this man from behind; the reason we should do this is that he has been so long impatiently waiting that it would not be wise to approach him from the front and it might cause trouble." Then Dekanahwideh also said: " We shall now therefore proceed on our journey."

Then they went on their journey and arrived at the other side of the lake. They had not gone far when Hahyonhwatha saw the man sitting on a high knoll where it was his custom to sit. When silently they arrived where he was sitting, Dekanahwideh stood on the right side and Hahyonhwatha on the left. The man had not yet seen them when he called again: "A-soh-kek-ne————eh!"

Then Hahyonhwatha saw what this man was doing and as soon as the man called out in the loud voice the lake became very rough and troubled and great billows formed on its surface.

Then Dekanahwideh spoke and said: " I have now returned

Neuter Nation (Atirhagenrat), the Erie (Djikon'saseoano') and others, including the Delaware and some southern tribes, were invited into the confederacy.

[1] Onondaga lake at a point near the present village of Liverpool.

and according to my promise. I promised to bring some one with me and I have now fulfilled this promise."

Then the man who was sitting down turned around and saw Dekanahwideh and said: "Who is the man that has come with you?"

Dekanahwideh then said: "Look to your left and you will see." Then he looked to his left and saw the man standing there; then he said to the man (Hahyonhwatha): "What are you doing here?"

Hahyonhwatha answered and said: "I am standing here beside you because our minds are with you and are turned toward you, for the Good Tidings of Peace and Power have now arrived. You will therefore now see as you turn around in every direction the columns of smoke arising." [1]

Then the man raised his head and carefully looked around and he asked: "Who will accomplish this, that the Good Tidings of Peace and Power be propagated?"

Dekanahwideh said: "Tomorrow in the day time the delegates will come and approach you; then all things will be completed."

Then the man said: "I shall wait until all the delegates shall have arrived."

Then Dekanahwideh said: "We must now return but we must all meet again tomorrow."

So Dekanahwideh and Hahyonhwatha went away and returned again to the abode of the lord where Hahyonhwatha had been lodging when Dekanahwideh called him out and when they had arrived there the lord found out that Hahyonhwatha had returned. Then the lord called him in and told him that the man for whom they had been waiting had returned and said: "We are now ready to answer your message."

Then Hahyonhwatha said: "I am also now ready and I am accompanied by my coworker."

Then the lord answered and said: "You will now bring him in." Then Hahyonhwatha called Dekanahwideh and he came in.

Then the lord said: "The man for whom we have been waiting has now returned and he has delivered his message fully and according to our understanding it is the same as your message. We now understand and we therefore have now decided to accept your message."

---

[1] Smoke arises from settlements of people at peace with each other. The tall column of smoke symbolized the establishment of the Gayanĕsshä"gowa.

Then Dekanahwideh said: "We shall now conclude the object of this message." He then asked the question: "To whom among us did the message of the Good Tidings of Peace and Power first come?"

The lord answered and said: "It is to the man who was guarding the cornfield."

Then Dekanahwideh said: "Where is the man? You shall now bring him here." So the lord called him in and when he had come the lord said: "This is the man who guarded the fields of corn so that our children might live on the harvest."

Dekanahwideh said: "I now ask you if you are indeed the man who guards the cornfields and what your magical power is when you are so guarding the cornfields."

Then the man answered and said: "I rely entirely on my bow and arrows and when I go to the cornfields I take all my arrows with me."

Then Dekanahwideh asked the question: "How or in what manner do you carry your power?" (meaning his bows and arrows).

The man then answered and said: "I place them in a quiver and place the quiver on my back."

Then Dekanahwideh said: "You shall now therefore be called "Oh-dah-tshe-deh"[1] (meaning, the quiver bearer), as your duty as a guardian of the cornfields is now changed because the Good News of Peace and Power has now come. Your duty hereafter shall now be to see that your children (instead of fields) shall live in peace."

Then Dekanahwideh again asked the lord: "In the past (during the long time he had been guarding the cornfields), what did you do with reference to that part of the crops which were damaged?"

Then the lord answered and said: "I used to send the warriors to gather the damaged crops and they brought them to me and I would divide the corn in equal shares among the people."

Then Dekanahwideh said: "You shall now therefore hereafter be called Ka-non-kwe-yo-da.[2] It shall therefore now be your duty to propagate the Good Tidings of Peace and Power so that your children may live in peace."

Then Dekanahwideh said: "Where is the man for whom you have been waiting?" The lord then called this man and when

---

[1] Odatcë"te', quiver bearer, principal Oneida chief.
[2] Kanoⁿkweⁿyō'doⁿ', *A row of ears of corn standing upright.*

he had arrived, Dekanahwideh said: "Are you the man for whom this people have been waiting so long to return?" Then the man answered, "I am that man." Then Dekanahwideh said: "What was the cause of your long delay in coming?" The man answered and said, "I was waiting for that other man who passed here, and who promised to return but who did not return, and while I was vigilantly watching and waiting for him I could not see him and he failed to return as promised, and when I was on the point of returning I tore down my hut which I had built, then I looked back to my home for the path by which I had come. It had been plainly open before me but now on each side of the path was the forest. I then left and came home here and then I found that already the people had all heard of the Good News which I wished to bring them, so I simply corroborate what they have already heard (from Hahyonhwatha)."

Then Dekanahwideh said: "Everything is now completed, and as you have now torn down your hut, your duty is now changed. You looked back and saw plainly the path through the forest. You shall therefore be known in the land by the name of De-yo-ha'-kwe-de.[1] Your duty shall therefore be to propagate the Good Tidings of Peace and Power so that your children in the future may live in peace." Then Dekanahwideh also said: "I will now tell you that the people through whose settlements I have passed have all accepted the Good Tidings of Peace and Power. Hahyonhwatha shall therefore now go after his colleagues and I shall now visit the settlement at the big mountain [2] and see what is happening there. I have been there before but I have not yet received an answer and what I think now is that we ought to join together in this great work for it is now urgent that it would be done for our time is getting shortened and we have only until tomorrow [3] to complete the whole compact." Then he, Dekanahwideh, also said: "It would be best to appoint two delegates to go and find the smoke."

Then Hahyonhwatha said: "Where shall we meet again?"

Dekanahwideh answered and said: "We shall meet again by the lake shore where my boat lies." [4]

Then Ohdahtshedeh spoke and said: "I shall lie across the pathway like a log and when you come to me you will come in

---

[1] Teyoha'gwĕñtĕ', *Hollow voice in the throat.*
[2] Ganundawao, Bare Hill, the Seneca capitol.
[3] The term "tomorrow" means *a year hence.*
[4] At the mouth of the Oswego river; Oswĕ'gen', meaning, *the place of the outpouring.*

contact with a log and I shall then join with you" (meaning that he, Ohdahtshedeh, would be lying in wait for them and when they should come to the log, which means his settlement, he could accompany them). Then Ohdahtshedeh further said that he would agree to appoint two delegates to go and look for smoke (smoke means settlements).

Then Ohdahtshedeh said: "It is now left with you, the warriors, as to which of you will volunteer to go."

Then the chief warrior said: "I shall be one of those who volunteer to go." Then Ohdahtshedeh also said: "There is one more required to go; who will therefore volunteer?"

For a long time no one gave answer. Then Ohdahtshedeh asked the question anew and still again no one answered. Then Ohdahtshedeh said: "I shall ask the question once again, for the last time, and if any one desires to volunteer let him speak at once", and from the outside of the gathering a man spoke out and said that he would be one of the volunteers.

Then Dekanahwideh said, "Go and call that man who is speaking from the outside." The man was called in and he was asked to stand by the chief warrior in the meeting. Then Dekanahwideh said to the chief warrior: "You are the first to accede to the request of the lord to volunteer, therefore, your duty shall be to obey orders whenever the (lord) has any duties to give you." Then Dekanahwideh said to the warrior who was the second to volunteer: "As you came from the outside of the meeting, you shall therefore in the future be an assistant to the chief warrior in his duties, and whenever the chief warrior assigns his duties to you, you shall perform his duties and carry out his instructions." Then Dekanahwideh said: "It is now completed; you have all been assigned your duties. You will now go and search for the smoke and wherever you see smoke you shall go there and when you arrive there you shall see the lord of the settlement, then you shall tell him your message. You will say we were sent here by the lords (Ro-de-ya-ners-onh) who take you by the hand and invite you to the place of meeting. You will say to the lord you will send delegates and on their way to the conference to pass where the lord lives at the big mountain and you shall invite him to accompany you. Then if the lord asks you the place of meeting you shall say, 'by the lake where lives the Great Wizard who calls out in the loud-toned voice.'"

They then separated, the chief warrior and his assistant going on their mission, and Dekanahwideh and Hahyonhwatha going to their own home settlements, and when Hahyonhwatha had arrived home he said, "Everything is now completed and we shall (all colleagues) now all go to the conference. You shall therefore all make ready."

The people watched the two volunteer delegates start on their mission and saw them become transformed into high-flyers (a species of hawk)[1] and they arose high in the air and soared southward and when they descended and alighted near the settlement they were retransformed and proceeded to the village.[2] Here they inquired the abode of the lord, and they were conducted to him and when they had arrived they saw a man. Then the chief warrior asked: "Are you the lord?"

And he answered and said: "I am. Are you seeking for me?"

The chief warrior then said: "Yes, truly we are looking for you."

Then the lord said: "I will now ask you upon what mission have you come here."

Then the chief warrior said: "We are sent by the lords (Rodeyanersonh) who invite you to go to the meeting place of the conference, and you are to take your power with you" (meaning peaceful intent). "You shall therefore invite the lord who lives on the great mountain to accompany you."

Then the lord spoke and said, "Where shall we meet in conference," and the chief warrior answered and said, "By the lake."

Then the lord said: "I have known about this for a long time. I shall therefore now accept your message." Then he took his pipe and said: "When I finish smoking I shall attend the conference" and the chief warrior and his assistant saw the pipe which was an exceedingly large one and larger than any pipe which they had ever seen before. They then returned to their own settlement and when they had returned Ohdahtshedeh asked, "Did you discover the smoke?" Then the chief warrior answered and said: "Everything is right, all is well, and we have discovered the object which you desired; when we saw the smoke we went there and when we arrived we found the lord and we repeated to him fully all our message, and when he had heard all, he answered and said, 'I had known about this for a long time, and knew that I was required to attend the great conference and I now therefore accept and

---

[1] The two birds into which the messengers were transformed were Hă'goks' and Skadjiĕ'na.

[2] To the Cayuga capitol town. The Cayuga have the council name of Sononawendo'na, Great Pipe People.

approve the message.' He promised to pass on his way to the conference, the settlement at the great mountain,[1] and the people there are to accompany him to the conference."

Then Ohdahtshedeh said: "It is now time that Hahyonhwatha should return, and as soon as he returns we shall at once go to the conference."

Dekanahwideh himself had also gone to the settlement of the great mountain and when he had arrived at the abode of the lord of the settlement he said: "It is now very urgent that you should reply to the message which I have left here before."

The lord answered and said: "The chief warrior and his deputy have failed to unanimously agree with me to accept the message of Good Tidings of Peace and Power, and I am now bewildered and I am at loss to discover any course which might lead me to overcome this difficulty. The reason why we are thus placed is that the chief warrior and his deputy, who have the power and the control of the people, have disagreed with us to accept the message."

Then Dekanahwideh said: "That which has occurred with you will not make a difference. The reason why it will not make any difference is that you, being the lord, have accepted the message. You are not alone, for they are many who have now accepted the message and they will assist you to successfully consider the difficulty in which you are placed."

Then moreover Dekanahwideh said: "You will now notify the brother lord whose abode is on the *other side of the river* [2] that it is now urgent for him to come over the river, so that we might meet together here." Then the lord sent a messenger to notify the lord, whose abode was on the other side of the river, and shortly after the lord arrived at the appointed place.

Then Dekanahwideh said: "We have now all met together. I will therefore ask your mind."

Then the lord who had come from over the river spoke and said: "We lords on either side of the river have decided to accept your message which you left. The only difficulty which we have now to contend with is that our chief warrior and his deputy have failed to agree with us to accept the message, and they have the power to control the people, and we lords on either side of the

---

[1] The Seneca capitol. The Senecas were divided into two bands, one of which seems to have been allied with the Erie.

[2] Probably the Genesee river. "The other lord" means the chief of the trans-Genesee Seneca.

river are totally bewildered and fail to see a way out of the difficulty." [1]

Then Dekanahwideh said: "I now fully understand everything and I will encourage you with reference to this matter which has occurred to you. You are not alone for many have accepted the message of Good Tidings of Peace and Power. Therefore, owing to that which has occurred to you, you (the lord) whose abode is on this east side of the river and to whom the message first came shall be known in the land by the name of Ska-nya-dah-ri-yoh,[2] and you, the lord who came from over the river who has agreed in mind with your colleague on this side of the river, shall be called in the land by the name of Sa-denka-ronh-yes." [3]

Then Dekanahwideh also said: "This is now completed Now it is for you to make ready, for in a little while a man will come whom you will accompany to the conference." They then in the distance heard the man call, "A-soh-kek-ne——eh," meaning "It is not yet."

Then Hahyonhwatha distinctly heard where he was. Then Hahyonhwatha said to his colleague: "The time is now come when we should go to the conference." They then started to go to the place appointed for the conference and they arrived at the place where the log (the Lord Ohdahtshedeh) was lying across the path.

Ohdahtshedeh said: "We have been impatiently waiting for we have heard the man calling with a loud voice now for a long time. It is at the place appointed for the meeting of the conference."

Then Hahyonhwatha said: "Let us now proceed to the conference." They then went to the conference. Then Dekanahwideh said, "I shall now return to my abode and we shall all meet at the place appointed for the conference." Then the Lords Deh-ka-eh-yonh, Ji-non-dah-weh-hon [4] and Dyon-yonh-koh came from their settlement and when they arrived at the abode of Skanyadahriyoh, they said that the lords had decided and arranged that all should call here on their way to the conference and that they were to invite all to accompany them.

---

[1] The difficulties of the Senecas are related in all versions of this tradition. Two separate bodies of the Senecas are described in nearly all stories of the origin of the league.
[2] Ganiodai'io' (Seneca), Handsome Lake.
[3] Sadegai'yēs (Onondaga), or Dyădegaihyēs.
[4] Djinondawē'hon'.

Then Skanyadariyoh said: "We are ready now and we have been waiting for a long time."

They then journeyed on their way to the conference. Dekanahwideh had arrived at the place of meeting first, and after him arrived Hahyonhwatha, Ohdahtshedeh and their colleagues and shortly afterwards Skanyadariyoh, Dehkaehyonh and their colleagues arrived.

After they had all assembled in conference, Dekanahwideh stood up and said:

"This conference met here composed of four nations being now assembled, you will therefore now first consider what we shall do with reference to a certain woman, our mother, who has not yet arrived." They then considered the matter and they decided that they would proceed with the business on hand and the matter would be in progress when she arrived.

Then Dekanahwideh said: "The first thing we shall do will be to cross over the lake and it shall be Hahyonhwatha and Ohdahtshedeh and Dehkaehyonh and Skanyadariyoh and Sadehkaronhyes, who are the rulers with power who shall cross first. If these lords can safely get across the lake and make peace, then you, the whole delegation, can cross. Therefore you shall now watch and you shall see a display of power when they leave the shore in their boat. I shall therefore appoint Hahyonhwatha to guide the boat."

They then entered the boat and he (Dekanahwideh) stood in front of the boat and Hahyonhwatha sat in the stern and the rest of the lords then noticed that the boat was made of white marble. Then they embarked in this boat from the shore and they had not proceeded far on their journey when they heard a voice calling out, "A-soh-kek-ne———eh," and as soon as this voice had called out a strong wind arose and caused the lake to become very rough and troubled and great billows[1] formed upon its surface and more especially around the boat. Then those in the boat became frightened and said: "We are now going to die," but Dekanahwideh spoke and said: "There is no danger because Peace has prevailed."

Then Dekanahwideh further said to the wind and lake, " Be thou quiet, Gä-hä",[2] and rest." Then the wind and the roughness of the lake ceased. They had not gone much farther when the man across the lake called out "Asohkekne———eh," and then the wind and roughness of the lake became still more violent. Then again

---

[1] The lake was troubled because certain ceremonial words were spoken, making it become alive.
[2] The Wind God.

Dekanahwideh said: "You, the wind and the lake, be still, for we have not crossed the water yet." Then again the lake became calm. Then Hahyonhwatha began to paddle hard and the boat went so swiftly that when they reached the shore, the boat plowed deeply into the dry land on the shore bank.

Then Dekanahwideh said: "We will now get out of the boat for we have now arrived at the place where we desire to go." Then he got out and the other lords followed him and they continued on their journey and they had only gone a short distance when they beheld a man sitting on a high, round knoll and when they arrived where he was sitting they stood all around him and Dekanahwideh stood directly in front of him, then he spoke and said: "We have now arrived, we representing the four nations. You will therefore now answer the message which we have left here with you. These lords who now stand all around you have now accepted the Good Tidings of Peace and Power, which signifies that hereafter the shedding of human blood shall cease, for our Creator the Great Ruler never intended that man should engage in any such work as the destruction of human life. There are many who have perished in the direction you are now facing, and these lords have come to induce you to join them so that the shedding of human blood might cease and the Good Tidings of Peace and Power might prevail."

Then the man looked around and saw these men (the lords) standing all around him, but he did not answer but kept silent. Then these lords looked at his head while he was sitting on the ground and they saw his hair moving as if it were all alive and they saw that the movements of the hair greatly resembled that of serpents, and they looked at his hands and saw that his fingers were twisting and contorting continually in all directions and in all manner of shapes, and they became impatient because he would not answer the message.

Then Dekanahwideh said to Hahyonhwatha: "You shall now recross the lake and the chief warrior and De-ha-rih-ho-ken and Dyon-yonh-koh and our mother Ji-kon-sah-seh, shall accompany you back in the boat (when you return here)."

Then the man who was sitting on the ground smiled a little. Then Hahyonhwatha hurriedly went back and reembarked in the boat and recrossed the lake and when he had come to shore on the other side of the lake, they asked what had occurred.

Hahyonhwatha answered and said: "It is not yet complete, I have therefore come after the chief warrior, De-ha-rih-ho-ken and

Dyon-yonh-koh and our mother Ji-kon-sah-seh," [1] and they answered him and said: " She has now arrived."

Then all those whom he had named got into the boat. Then Hahyonhwatha said: " You will take as a sign that if we can get across the lake in safety and the lake remains calm all the way across then our message of peace will be accepted." They then embarked on the lake [2] and the boat was rapidly propelled and as they looked at the lake they saw that it was calm all the way across and they arrived on to the shore in safety, and when they had returned to where the man was sitting, Hahyonhwatha said, " Everything is completed, we are now all assembled here."

Then Dekanahwideh said: " We shall now first give thanks to the Great Ruler. We will do this because our power is now completed." He also said: " It shall be that each nation shall now have a voice in the thanksgiving and I shall therefore be the first to lead. He then exclaimed " Yo————hen ! "

Then Ohdahtshedeh also repeated " Yo————hen " and after him followed Dehkaehyonh who also repeated " Yo————hen." The next in order was Skanyadahriyoh who also repeated " Yo————hen " and after him Hahyonhwatha repeated " Yo————hen."

When Dekanahwideh started to address this man, the man became troubled and after all of the lords finished addressing the man his sympathy was affected and he shed tears. Then Dekanahwideh said: " We, the delegates of all the nations who have accepted the Good Tidings of Peace and Power, are now assembled here.

" The course, therefore, that we shall now pursue is that of the representatives of each nation giving utterance to their opinion upon this matter."

Ohdahtshedeh was the first to address the assembly and he said: " I shall be the first to give utterance to my opinion upon this matter. In my opinion this man may approve of our mission if we all lay our heads before him." (This means that the nations here represented would be submissive to this man Tha-do-dah-ho).

Then Dekanahwideh and Skanyadahriyoh spoke and said: " We acquiesce to all that Ohdahtshedeh has said."

Then Dekanahwideh said to Thadodahho: " Now you will answer and state if you are satisfied with the submission of these

---

[1] Djikon'sase is a character who should be better known in Iroquois mythology. There are several traditions about her, in the various events of Iroquois tradition. The name passed as a title from one generation to another.

[2] Mud Lake, or Diok'to, Otisco Lake.

lords who have laid their heads before you," but even then Thadodah-ho did not answer.

Then Dekanahwideh said: "You Dyon-yonh-koh will now give utterance and express your opinion on this matter, as you now have the authority."

Then Dyon-yonh-koh spoke and said to Thadodah-ho: "The Creator, the Great Ruler, created this day which is now shedding its light upon us; he also created man and he also created the earth and all things upon it. Now look up and see the delegates of the Four Nations sitting around you, also see the chief warrior and this great woman our mother (Jiknosahseh), standing before you, all of whom have approved of this message. The lords and all the chief warriors and this great woman, our mother, have all agreed to submit the Good Tidings of Peace and Power to you, and thus if you approve and confirm the message, you will have the power and be the Fire-Keeper of our Confederate Council, and the smoke from it will arise and pierce the sky, and all the nations shall be subject to you."

Then the twisting movements of the fingers and the snakelike movements of the hair of Thadodahho ceased.

Then he spoke and said: "It is well. I will now answer the mission which brought you here. I now truly confirm and accept your message, the object of which brought you here."

THE DEER'S HORNS THE EMBLEM OF POWER

Then Dakanahwideh said: "We have now accomplished our work and completed everything that was required with the exception of shaping and transforming him (by rubbing him down), removing the snake-like hair from him and circumcising him."

The lords therefore all took part in doing this and Ohdahtshedeh was the first to rub down Thadodaho and the others followed his example so that the appearance of Thaddodahho might be like that of other men.

When this had been done then Dekanahwideh again said: "You, the chief warrior, and you, our mother, you have the control of the power (the authority), and we will now put upon him a sign, by placing upon his head the horns of a buck deer. The reason why we do this is because all people live upon the flesh of the deer, and the reason that we take the emblem of the deer horns is that this institution, the Great Peace, shall be the means of protecting our children hereafter."

Then Dekanahwideh also said: "We shall now use these symbolic deer's horns by placing them upon the heads of each other. It shall be thus then that these horns shall be placed upon the head of a man who shall be called a lord by his people — he shall have the power to rule his people." Then Dekanahwideh further said: "And now you, the chief warrior and our mother, shall place these horns upon the head of him, Thadodahho."

Then they looked and saw antlers lying on the ground in the midst of them, and Dekanahwideh said: "Pick these horns up and put them upon him." Then the mother went forward and picked them up. Then the chief warrior and the woman each grasped the horns and placed them on his head. [a]

Then Dekanahwideh said to the man who was still sitting on the ground: "Now arise," and the man stood up.

Then Dekanahwideh said: "You, the nations who are assembled here, behold this man who stands up before us. We have now placed the deer's horns upon his head as an emblem of authority. The people shall now call him Lord Tha-do-dah-ho, in the land." Then Dekanahwideh said: "It shall now, in the future among us, the United Nations, thus be a custom that whenever a lord is to be created we shall all unite in a ceremony (such as this)."

POSITIONS OF THE CONFEDERATE LORDS

Then Dekanahwideh said: "Skanyadahriyoh and Sadehkarohyhes shall be the uncles of Dehkaehyonh. We have now formed the confederacy, and we shall now have two sets of lords, one on each side of the council fire.

"Then also Hahyonwhatha and Ohdahtshedeh, father and son, shall sit and face each other, one on each side of the council fire.

"Then Skanyadahriyoh and Sadehkaronhyes shall sit on one side of the council fire and their nephew Dehkaehyonh shall sit on the opposite side.

"On one side of the council fire shall then be seated Hayonhwatha, Skanyadahriyoh and Sadehkaronhyes and on the opposite side shall sit Ohdahtshedeh and Dehkaehyonh and it shall be that we shall place Thadodahho in the center between the two sets of lords in the council.

We shall establish this relationship as follows: You, Thadodahho, shall be the father of Ohdahtshedeh and Dehkaehyonh and Hahyonwhatha, Skanyadahriyoh and Sadehkaronhyes shall be your brothers and you shall be the principals of the confederation which we have just made and completed.

[a] see page 118.

"The first matter which I shall lay before you for your consideration is that as clans[1] are already established among the people, that the several clans form relations as brothers and cousins.

So the lords answered and said: "We have decided to adopt your suggestion."

Then he, Dekanahwideh said: "You, Hahyonhwatha, shall be the first to come and appoint your colleagues; you are of the Turtle Clan and shall therefore appoint your colleagues of the same clan."

Then when this was done Hahyonhwatha said: "This is now all ready, they have accepted and they are as follows: De-ha-rih-ho-ken, Sa-de-ka-rih-wa-deh."

Then Dekanahwideh said: "These shall therefore be your brother colleagues, you of the Turtle Clan. The brethern of the Wolf Clan shall be Sa-renh-ho-wa-neh,[2] De-yon-heh-kon[3] and On-renh-reh-ko-wah[4] and our cousins of the Bear Clan[5] shall be De-hen-nah-ke-re-neh,[6] Ah-stah-weh-seh-ron-ron-tha[7] and Soh-sko-ha-roh-wa-neh."[8]

Then Dekanahwideh said: "You, Hahyonhwatha, have now completed appointing your colleagues of your nation, as the Good Tidings of Peace and Power first originated at Kan-yen-geh, you shall be called Ka-nyen-geh-ha-kah[9] (Mohawk)."

Then Dekanahwideh said to Hahyonhwatha: "Now it shall fall upon your son Ohdahtshedeh who sits upon the opposite side of the council fire to appoint his brother colleagues." Then Ohdaht-shedeh appointed his brother colleagues of the Turtle Clan as follows: So-non-sehs[10] (Long House), Tho-nahonh-ken-ah[11] and A-tye-donj-eneh-tha.[12] And then he, Ta-na-o-ge-a, appointed his cousins of the Bear Clan as follows: Deh-ha-da-weh-de-yons,[13] Deh-ha-nyen-da-sah-deh[14] and Roh-wa-tsha-don-hon.[15] These being the

---

[1] In some traditions the origin of the clans is stated as coeval with the beginning of the Confederacy; the more accurate view is that clans had long existed.

[2] Saihowa'ne.

[3] Dionhekwi.

[4] Orhehe"gowa.

[5] Hodigwaho".

[6] Dehenagai'ne', Dragging horns.

[7] Hastamě'sěntä', Dropped rattle.

[8] Soskohai'ine'.

[9] Kanyěngěhä'kă, Flint people; cf. kanyeñgě', flinty place.

[10] Sono"s'es.

[11] Tonaogen"ä.

[12] Hadyä'donent'ha, Swallows his own body.

[13] Dehadahonděnyonk.

[14] Dehanye'däsäyeñ', Two legs together.

[15] Howashadononkho'.

second nation who accepted the message of Peace and Power and as their settlement (from whence they came) was where the great historic stone was situated, O-neh-yont, they were called O-neh-yo-deh-ha-ka.[1] (Oneidas).

Then Dekanahwideh said: " It shall now rest with you, the uncles, Skanyadahriyoh and Sadehkaronhyes, to appoint your colleagues." Then Skanyadahriyoh said: " I (myself) shall appoint two of my brothers and my cousin, Sa-deh-ka-ronh-yes, shall appoint two of his brethern." Then Skanyadahriyoh of the Turtle Clan also said : " I therefore now appoint Ka-no-kye [2] of the Turtle Clan and Sa-tye-na-wat [3] of the Bear Clan as my colleagues."

Then Sa-deh-ka-ronh-yes of the Snipe clan said : " I now appoint Sa-ken-jo-wah-neh [4] of the Pigeon Hawk Clan and Nis-ha-yeh-nehs [5] of the Snipe Clan as my colleagues."

Then Dekanahwideh said: " You have all appointed your colleagues and Kanokye [6] and Sakenhiwahneh [7] shall be cousins, and Nishayehnehs and Satyenawat [8] shall be cousins." He then said, " You, Skanyadahriyoh and Sadehkaronhyes of the Seneca Nation, have now completed appointing your colleagues. Your settlement is at the big mountain and you shall therefore be called O-neh-do-wah-ka [9] (people of the big mountain) Senecas."

Then Dekanahwideh also said: "And now your son Deh-ka-eh-yonh,[10] who sits on the opposite side of the council fire, shall name and appoint his colleagues."

Then Dehkaehyonh of the Big Bear Clan appointed his colleagues, saying as follows : " I shall now appoint my son Ji-non-dah-weh-honh [11] of the Ball Clan and my mother Ka-da-gwa-seh [12] of the Bear Clan and my brother Sho-yonh-wehs [13] of the Young Bear Clan and Hathatrohneh [14] of the Turtle Clan, Dyon-yonh-koh [15] of the Hand Clan, and Deh-yoh-doh-weh-kon [16] of the Wolf Clan, and

---

[1] Onäyont, or Hadiniyutgä".
[2] Ga'nongäï'.
[3] Sadyĕ'nawat.
[4] Sagendjo'nä.
[5] Nishayene"thä'.
[6] Ga'nongä-ï'.
[7] Gakĕniwanĕ'.
[8] Sadyĕ'nawat.
[9] Onundawäga. Nundawä'g'g, The hill people.
[10] De'hagä'enyok.
[11] Djinon'däwe'hon.
[12] Kadägwa'dji.
[13] Sho'yoñwēs, Long wind.
[14] Ha-tha"troh-ne'.
[15] Dion'yoñko'.
[16] Diotowĕ"kon, Two colds.

Dyon-weh-thoh [1] of the Snipe Clan. These are the brother colleagues.

Then Deh-ka-eh-yonh appointed the cousin of the chief so named as follows: Nah-don-dah-heh-ha [2] of the Plover Clan and Desda-heh [3] of the Young Bear Clan.

Then Dekanahwideh said: "You, Deh-ka-eh-yonh [4] of the Cayuga Nation, have now finished appointing your colleagues and you shall therefore be called Queh-you-gwe-hah-ka [5] (Cayuga) from your custom of portaging your canoe at a certain point in your settlement."

Then Dekanahwideh also said: "I shall now leave it to you, Tha-do-dah-ho, to appoint your colleagues."

Then Thadodahho of the Bear Clan said: "The first I shall appoint will be Onh-neh-sah-heh, [6] my cousin of the Beaver Clan, and Ska-nya-da-ge-wak [7] of the Snipe Clan and Ah-weh-ken-yath [8] of the Ball Clan and Deh-ha-yat-kwa-eh [9] of the Turtle Clan, and these are all brothers."

Then Thadodahho appointed their son, Ho-noh-we-yeh-deh [10] of the Wolf Clan, and then Thadodahho appointed his (Ho-nohwe-yeh-dehs) uncles as follows: Kon-weh-neh-senh-don of the Deer Clan and Ha-he-honk also of the Deer Clan and then their brothers as follows: Ho-yonh-nye-neh [11] of the Eel Clan and Sodeh-kwa-seh [12] also of the Eel Clan and Sa-ko-ken-o-heh [13] of the Pigeon Hawk Clan, and then he (Thadodahha) appointed the sons of the latter as follows: Ho-sah-ha-wa [14] of the Deer Clan and Ska-nah-o-wa-da [15] of the Small Turtle Clan.

Then Dekanahwideh spoke and said: "We have now come to appointing the lords of the Five Nations hereby represented. These lords have now all been crowned with deer's horns in conformity and in a similar manner to Thadodahho who was first crowned. Therefore we have now accomplished and completed the work of laying the foundation of the confederation."

---

[1] Dionwăthoⁿ".
[2] Nadondahē'hă'.
[3] Desgä'hĕ'.
[4] De'hagă'eⁿyok.
[5] Gwⁱio"gwehä'ka, drawn up from the water people.
[6] Oni'säähä'.
[7] Skanyă'dadji'wak, Bitter throat.
[8] Awekeⁿ"yat, Near the shore.
[9] Dehayatgwa'ĭĕⁿ. Red spots on wings.
[10] Honowiyĕ"ghī.
[11] Hoyoⁿnyĕⁿ"ni'.
[12] Sodĕ'gwäsĕⁿ', Bruised all over.
[13] Sägogĕⁿ"hĕ', I shall see them again.
[14] Hosähähwi.
[15] Skanawä'di.

PACIFICATION OF THE SENECA CHIEFS

Then Dekanahwideh spoke again and said: "I will now lay before your confederate council for your consideration one matter, and that is with reference to the conduct of the chief warriors of O-non-do-wa-ka (Senecas) who have refused to act in conjunction (or accord) with the lords in accepting the message of Good Tidings of Peace and Power."

Then the lords sent messengers for these two chief warriors of the Onondowaka (Senecas) to appear. And when they had come to the council, Lord Hahyonhwatha addressed these two chief warriors and said: "This Confederate Council now in session, together with their warriors, have unanimously accepted the message of Peace and Power and only you two chief warriors have not yet accepted and neither have expressed yourselves on this matter."

Then Hayonhwatha further said: "This Confederate Council and their chief warriors have unanimously decided to leave all the war power and military control of the people in your hands providing you accept the message so that in case of war with other nations you shall be the leaders of the people of the Confederate Nations in defense of their confederacy." Then one of these two warriors spoke and said: "We are agreed to accept the message."

Then Dekanahwideh continued his address and said: "Now our power is full and complete and the two chief warriors of the Onondowaka (Senecas) have agreed to accept the message of Good Tidings; therefore we shall now add to the number of the lords of the confederacy (Eh-ji-twa-nah-stah-soh-de-renh),[1] we shall call it Ka-na-stah-ge-ko-wah [2] and these two chief warriors shall represent the door of the long house. Ka-noh-hah-ge-ko-wah,[3] meaning *the great black door through which all good and evil messages must come to reach the confederate house of lords or council,* shall be the name of the door, and if any person or nation has any news, message or business matter to lay before the Confederate Council, he or they must come through this door."

Then Dekanahwideh again further said, "We shall now crown these two chief warriors with deer's horns [4] and make them lords also. We shall now first crown with deer's horns Deyohneohkaweh [5] of the Wolf Clan and then we shall also crown Kanonkedahwe [6]

---

[1] Nedjitwanastashoñdä'.
[2] Kana'stadjigo'wa, Black timbers.
[3] Kanohwa'gêgo'na.
[4] Skänondononä"gä, Deer horns.
[5] Deyoñeñhogä"wĕ', Open door.
[6] Kanon'gida'hwĭ', Hair burned off.

of the Snipe Clan and these two shall be cousins and they shall guard the door of the long house.[1] And we shall now floor the doorway with slippery elm bark, and it shall be that whenever we have visitors from other nations who will have any message or any business to lay before the Confederate Council, these two door-keepers shall escort and convey them before the council, but whenever the visitor or visitors have come for evil purposes, then Kanonkedahwe shall take them by the hand and lead them in and they shall slip on the slippery elm bark and fall down and they shall be reduced to a heap of bones (He-yoh-so-jo-de-hah [2] in Onondaga language; Ehyohdonyohdaneh in Mohawk), and the bones of the enemy shall fall into a heap before the lords of the confederacy." (A heap of bones here signifies a conquered nation to be dealt with by the lords of the confederacy who shall decide as to what manner they will be allowed to exist in the future.)

LAWS OF THE CONFEDERACY

Then Dekanahwideh again said: "We have completed the Confederation of the Five Nations, now therefore it shall be that hereafter the lords who shall be appointed in the future to fill vacancies caused by death or removals shall be appointed from the same families and clans from which the first lords were created, and from which families the hereditary title of lordships shall descend."

Then Dekanahwideh further said: "I now transfer and set over to the women who have the lordships' title vested in them, that they shall in the future have the power to appoint the successors from time to time to fill vacancies caused by death or removals from whatever cause."

Then Dekanahwideh continued and said: "We shall now build a confederate council fire [3] from which the smoke shall arise and pierce the skies and all nations and people shall see this smoke. And now to you, Thadodahho, your brother and cousin colleagues shall be left the care and protection of the confederate council fire, by the Confederate Nations."

---

[2] The term "long house" as applied to the confederacy is not generally used by the Canadian Iroquois in their manuscript copies of the confederate laws and legends. A mistaken notion that the long house idea originated with Handsome Lake accounts for it. Newhouse used the term "long house" in his earlier manuscripts but later erased it supplying the word "confederacy." He explained this by saying that he had heard an old man say that long house meant Handsome Lake's new religion, the thing that destroyed the knowledge of the old ways. Thus the term was tabooed in connection with the confederacy.

[2] En'yosodjodä"ha.

[3] Gadiista'iĕn'.

Then Dekanahwideh further said: " The lords have unanimously decided to spread before you on the ground this great white wampum belt Ska-no-dah-ken-rah-ko-wah [1] and Ka-yah-ne-renh-ko-wah,[2] which respectfully signify purity and great peace, and the lords have also laid before you this great wing, Ska-weh-yeh-seh-ko-wah,[3] and whenever any dust or stain of any description falls upon the great belt of white wampum, then you shall take this great wing and sweep it clean." (Dust or stain means evil of any description which might have a tendency to cause trouble in the Confederate Council.)

Then Dekanahwideh said: " The lords of this confederacy have unanimously decided to lay by you this rod (Ska-nah-ka-res)[4] and whenever you see any creeping thing which might have a tendency to harm our grandchildren or see a thing creeping toward the great white wampum belt (meaning the Great Peace), then you shall take this rod and pry it away with it, and if you and your colleagues fail to pry the creeping, evil thing out, you shall then call out loudly that all the Confederate Nations may hear and they will come immediately to your assistance."

Then Dekanahwideh said: " Now you, the lords of the several Confederate Nations, shall divide yourselves and sit on opposite sides of the council fire as follows: " You and your brother colleagues shall sit on one side of the council fire (this was said to the Mohawks and the Senecas), and your sons, the Oneidas and Cayugas, shall sit on the opposite side of the council fire. Thus you will begin to work and carry out the principles of the Great Peace (Ka-yah-ne-renh-ko-wah) and you will be guided in this by the great white wampum belt (Ska-no-dah-ke-rah-ko-wah) which signifies Great Peace."

Then Dekanahwideh said: " You, Thadodahho, shall be the fire keeper, and your duty shall be to open the Confederate Council with praise and thanksgiving to the Great Ruler and close the same."

Then Dekanahwideh also said: " When the council is opened, Hayonhwatha and his colleagues shall be the first to consider and give their opinion upon any subject which may come before the council for consideration, and when they have arrived at a decision, then shall they transfer the matter to their brethren, the Senecas, for their consideration, and when they, the Senecas, shall have

---

[1] Skanon'dä'kerhagona.
[2] Gayanässhägona (Onon.).
[3] Another belt known as the great wing, Dega'yadonwa'ne (Onon.).
[4] Ganagä'is.

arrived at a decision on the matter then they shall refer it back to Hahyonhwatha and his colleagues. Then Hahyonhwatha will announce the decision to the opposite side of the council fire.

"Then Ohdahtshedeh and his colleagues will consider the matter in question and when they have arrived at a decision they will refer the matter to their brethren, the Cayugas, for their consideration and after they have arrived at a decision, they will refer the matter back to Ohdahtshedeh and his colleagues. Then Ohdahtshedeh will announce their decision to the opposite side of the council fire. Then Hahyonhwatha will refer the matter to Thadodahho and his colleagues for their careful consideration and opinion of the matter in question and if Thadodahho and his colleagues find that the matter has not been well considered or decided, then they shall refer the matter back again to the two sides of the council fire, and they shall point out where, in their estimation, the decision was faulty and the question not fully considered, and then the two sides of the council will take up the question again and reconsider the matter, and after the two sides of the council have fully reconsidered the question, then Hahyonhwatha will again refer it to Thadohahho and his colleagues, then they will again consider the matter and if they see that the decision of the two sides of the council is correct, then Thadodahho and his colleagues will confirm the decision."

Then Dekanahwideh further said: "If the brethren of the Mohawks and the Senecas are divided in their opinion and can not agree on any matter which they may have for their consideration, then Hahyonhwatha shall announce the two decisions to the opposite of the council fire. Then Ohdahtshedeh and his brother colleagues, after they have considered the matter, and if they also are divided in their decision, shall so report, but if the divided factions each agree with the decision announced from the opposite side of the council, then Ohdahtshedeh shall also announce their two decisions to the other side of the council fire; then Hahyonhwatha shall refer the matter to Thadodahho and his colleagues who are the fire keepers. They will fully consider the matter and whichever decision they consider correct they will confirm."

Then Dekanahwideh said: "If it should so happen that the lords of the Mohawks and the lords of the Senecas disagree on any matter and also on the opposite side of the council fire, the lords of the Oneidas and the lords of the Cayugas disagree among themselves and do not agree with either of the two decisions of the

4

opposite side of the council fire but of themselves give two decisions which are diverse from each other, then Hahyonhwatha shall
refer the four decisions to Thadodahho and his colleagues who
shall consider the matter and give their decision and their decision
shall be final."

Then Dekanahwideh said: "We have now completed the system
for our Confederate Council."

Then Dekanahwideh further said: "We now, each nation, shall
adopt all the rules and regulations governing the Confederate
Council which we have here made and we shall apply them to all
our respective settlements and thereby we shall carry out the principles set forth in the message of Good Tidings of Peace and
Power, and in dealing with the affairs of our people of the various
dominions, thus we shall secure to them contentment and happiness."

Then he, Dekanahwideh, said: "You, Ka-nyen-ke-ha-ka (Mohawk), you, Dekarihoken, Hahyonhwatha and Sadekarihwadeh,
you shall sit in the middle between your brother lords of the Mohawks, and your cousin lords of the Mohawks, and all matters
under discussion shall be referred to you by your brother lords and
your cousin lords for your approval or disapproval.

"You, O-nen-do-wa-ka (Senecas), you, Skanyhadahriyoh and
Sadeh-ka-ronh-yes, you shall sit in the middle or between your
brother lords and your cousin lords of the Senecas and all matters
under discussion shall be referred to you by them for your approval
or disapproval.

"You, Ohnenyohdehaka (Oneidas), you, Ohdahtshedeh, Kanon-
kweyoudoh and Deyouhahkwedeh, you shall sit in the middle between your brother lords and your cousin lords of the Oneidas and
all matters under discussion shall be referred to you by them for
your approval or disapproval.

"You, the Que-yenh-kwe-ha-ka (Cayugas), you, Dekaehyonh
and Jinondahwehonh, you shall sit in the middle between your
lords and your cousin lords of the Cayugas and all matters under
discussion shall be referred to you by them for your approval or
disapproval."

Then Dekanahwideh said: "We have now completed arranging
the system of our local councils and we shall hold our annual Confederate Council at the settlement of Thadodahho, the capitol
or seat of government of the Five Nations' Confederacy."

Dekanahwideh said: "Now I and you lords of the Confederate
Nations shall plant a tree Ska-renj-heh-se-go-wah[1] (meaning a tall

---

[1] Skarhehĕ"gowa.

and mighty tree) and we shall call it Jo-ne-rak-deh-ke-wah [1] (the tree of the great long leaves).

"Now this tree which we have planted shall shoot forth four great, long, white roots (Jo-doh-ra-ken-rah-ko-wah).[2] These great, long, white roots shall shoot forth one to the north and one to the south and one to the east and one to the west, and we shall place on the top of it Oh-don-yonh [3] (an eagle) which has great power of long vision, and we shall transact all our business beneath the shade of this great tree. The meaning of planting this great tree, Skarehhehsegowah, is to symbolize Ka-yah-ne-renh-ko-wa, which means Great Peace, and Jo-deh-ra-ken-rah-ke-wah, meaning Good Tidings of Peace and Power. The nations of the earth shall see it and shall accept and follow the roots and shall follow them to the tree and when they arrive here you shall receive them and shall seat them in the midst of your confederacy. The object of placing an eagle, Skadji'enä', on the top of the great, tall tree is that it may watch the roots which extend to the north and to the south and to the east and to the west, and whose duty shall be to discover if any evil is approaching your confederacy, and he shall scream loudly and give the alarm and all the nations of the confederacy at once shall heed the alarm and come to the rescue."

Then Dekanahwideh again said: "We shall now combine our individual power into one great power which is this confederacy and we shall therefore symbolize the union of these powers by each nation contributing one arrow, which we shall tie up together in a bundle which, when it is made and completely tied together, no one can bend or break."

Then Dekanahwideh further said: "We have now completed this union by securing one arrow from each nation. It is not good that one should be lacking or taken from the bundle, for it would weaken our power and it would be still worse if two arrows were taken from the bundle. And if three arrows were taken any one could break the remaining arrows in the bundle."

Then Dekanahwideh continued his address and said: "We shall tie this bundle of arrows together with deer sinew which is strong, durable and lasting and then also this institution shall be strong and unchangeable. This bundle of arrows signifies that all the lords and all the warriors and all the women of the Confederacy have become united as one person."

---

[1] Onä"dedjisko'na skaskohäi'nä', Big long leaves, big limber tree.
[2] Djok'dehēsgo'na.
[3] The "upper world eagle" is called skadji'ēnä'.

Then Dekanahwideh again said: "We have now completed binding this bundle of arrows and we shall leave it beside the great tree (Skarehhehsegowah) and beside the Confederate Council fire of Thadodahho."

Then Dekanahwideh said: "We have now completed our power so that we the Five Nations' Confederacy shall in the future have one body, one head and one heart."

Then he (Dekanahwideh) further said: "If any evil should befall us in the future, we shall stand or fall united as one man."

Then Dekanahwideh said: "You lords shall be symbolized as trees of the Five Confederate Nations. We therefore bind ourselves together by taking hold of each other's hands firmly and forming a circle so strong that if a tree shall fall prostrate upon it, it could neither shake nor break it, and thus our people and our grandchildren shall remain in the circle in security, peace and happiness. And if any lord who is crowned with the emblem of deer's horns shall break through this circle of unity, his horns shall become fastened in the circle, and if he persists after warning from the chief matron, he shall go through it without his horns and the horns shall remain in the circle, and when he has passed through the circle, he shall no longer be lord, but shall be as an ordinary warrior and shall not be further qualified to fill any office."

Then Dekanahwideh further said: "We have now completed everything in connection with the matter of Peace and Power, and it remains only for us to consider and adopt some measure as to what we shall do with reference to the disposal of the weapons of war which we have taken from our people."

Then the lords considered the latter and decided that the best way which they could adopt with reference to the disposal of the weapons would be to uproot the great tall tree which they had planted and in uprooting the tree a chasm would form so deep that it would come or reach the swift current of the waters under it, into which the weapons of war would be thrown, and they would be borne and swept away forever by the current so that their grandchildren would never see them again. And they then uprooted the great tree and they cast into the chasm all manner of weapons of war which their people had been in the custom of using, and they then replaced the tree in its original position.

Then Dekanahwideh further continued and said: "We have completed clearing away all manner of weapons from the paths of our people."

Then Dekanahwideh continued and said: "We have still one matter left to be considered and that is with reference to the hunting grounds of our people from which they derive their living."

They, the lords, said with reference to this matter: "We shall now do this: We shall only have one dish (or bowl) in which will be placed one beaver's tail and we shall all have coequal right to it, and there shall be no knife in it, for if there be a knife in it, there would be danger that it might cut some one and blood would thereby be shed." (This one dish or bowl signifies that they will make their hunting grounds one common tract and all have a coequal right to hunt within it.[1] The knife being prohibited from being placed into the dish or bowl signifies that all danger would be removed from shedding blood by the people of these different nations of the confederacy caused by differences of the right of the hunting grounds.)

Then Dekanahwideh continued and said: "We have now accomplished and completed forming the great Confederacy of the Five Nations together with adopting rules and regulations in connection therewith."

Then he, Dekanahwideh, continued and said: "I will now leave all matters in the hands of your lords and you are to work and carry out the principles of all that I have just laid before you for the welfare of your people and others, and I now place the power in your hands and to add to the rules and regulations whenever necessary and I now charge each of you lords that you must never seriously disagree among yourselves. You are all of equal standing and of equal power, and if you seriously disagree the consequences will be most serious and this disagreement will cause you to disregard each other, and while you are quarreling with each other, the white panther [2] (the fire dragon of discord) [3] will come and take your rights and privileges away. Then your grandchildren will suffer and be reduced to poverty and disgrace."

Then he, Dekanahwideh, continued and said: "If this should ever occur, whoever can climb a great tree (Skarehhehsegowah) and ascend to the top, may look around over the landscape and will see if there is any way or place to escape to from the calamity of the threatening poverty and disgrace, so that our children may have a home where they may have peace and happiness in their day.

---

[1] Diondowĕs'tă', hunting ground.
[2] Usually translated *lion*.
[3] Oshondowĕk'gona.

And if it so occurs that he can not see any way or place to escape the calamity, he will then descend the tree. You will then look for a great swamp elm tree (Aka-rah-ji-ko-wah) [1] and when you have found one with great large roots extending outwards and bracing outwards from the trunk, there you will gather your heads together."

Then Dekanahwideh continued and said: "It will be hard and your grandchildren will suffer hardship. And if it may so occur that the heads of the people of the confederacy shall roll and wander away westward, if such thing should come to pass, other nations shall see your heads rolling and wandering away and they shall say to you, 'You belong to the confederacy, you were a proud and haughty people once,' and they shall kick the heads with scorn, and they shall go on their way, but before they shall have gone far they shall vomit up blood." (Meaning that the confederacy shall still have power enough to avenge their people.)

Then Dekanahwideh further said: "There may be another serious trouble. Other nations may cut or hack these four great roots which grow from the great tree which we have planted and one of the roots shoots to the north and one to the south and one to the east and one to the west. Whenever such thing happens, then shall great trouble come into the seat of your lords of the confederacy."

Then Dekanahwideh said: "I shall now therefore charge each of your lords, that your skin be of the thickness of seven spreads of the hands [2] (from end of thumb to the end of the great finger) so that no matter how sharp a cutting instrument may be used it will not penetrate the thickness of your skin. (The meaning of the great thickness of your skins is patience and forbearance, so that no matter what nature of question or business may come before you, no matter how sharp or aggravating it may be, it will not penetrate to your skins, but you will forbear with great patience and good will in all your deliberations and never disgrace yourselves by becoming angry.) You lords shall always be guided in all your councils and deliberations by the Good Tidings of Peace and Power."

Then Dekanahwideh said: "Now, you lords of the different nations of the confederacy, I charge you to cultivate the good feeling of friendship, love and honor amongst yourselves. I have now

---

[1] Gain'dadjikgo'na.
[2] Djadŭk'nioyionk'gage', seven fingers.

fulfilled my duty in assisting you in the establishment and organization of this great confederacy, and if this confederation is carefully guarded it shall continue and endure from generation to generation and as long as the sun shines. I shall now, therefore, go home, conceal and cover myself with bark and there shall none other be called by my name." (b)

Then Dekanahwideh further continued and said: "If at any time through the negligence and carelessness of the lords, they fail to carry out the principles of the Good Tidings of Peace and Power and the rules and regulations of the confederacy and the people are reduced to poverty and great suffering, I will return."

Then Dekanahwideh said: "And it shall so happen that when you hear my name mentioned disrespectfully without reason or just cause, but spoken in levity, you shall then know that you are on the verge of trouble and sorrow. And it shall be that the only time when it shall be proper for my name to be mentioned is when the condolence ceremonies are being performed or when the Good Tidings of Peace and Power which I have established and organized are being discussed or rehearsed."

Then the lords (Ro-de-ya-ner-shoh) said: "We shall begin to work and carry out the instructions which you, Dekanahwideh, have laid before us."

Then they said: "We shall therefore begin first with the Confederate Council of the Five Nations and other nations who shall accept and come under the Great Law of the confederacy will become as props, supports of the long house.

"The pure white wampum strings shall be the token or emblem of the council fire, and it shall be that when the fire keepers shall open the council, he shall pick up this string of wampum and hold it on his hand while he is offering thanksgiving to the Great Ruler and opening the council." And then they also said: "That while the council is in session the strings of the white wampum should be placed conspicuously in their midst and when they should adjourn then, the fire keepers should pick up these strings of wampum again, offer thanksgiving, close the council and all business in connection with the council should then be adjourned."

Then they said: "We shall now establish as a custom that when our annual Confederate Council shall meet we shall smoke the pipe of peace." [1]

---

[1] Swĕⁿno"ändwahē'n'. (b) see page 118.

And they, the lords, then said: "We shall now proceed to define the obligations and position of the lords of the Confederacy as follows:

"If a lord is found guilty of wilful murder, he shall be deposed without the warning (as shall be provided for later on) by the lords of the confederacy, and his horns (emblem of power) shall be handed back to the chief matron of his family and clan.

"If a lord is guilty of rape he shall be deposed without the usual warning by the lords of the confederacy, and his horns (the emblem of power) shall be handed back to the chief matron of his family and clan.

"If a lord is found guilty of theft, he shall be deposed without the usual warning by the lords of the confederacy and his horns (the emblem of power) shall be handed back to the chief matron of his family and clan.

"If a lord is guilty of unwarrantably opposing the object of decisions of the council and in that his own erroneous will in these matters be carried out, he shall be approached and admonished by the chief matron of his family and clan to desist from such evil practices and she shall urge him to come back and act in harmony with his brother lords.

"If the lord refuses to comply with the request of the chief matron of his family and clan and still persists in his evil practices of unwarrantably opposing his brother lords, then a warrior of his family and clan will also approach him and admonish him to desist from pursuing his evil course.

"If the lord still refuses to listen and obey, then the chief matron and warrior shall go together to the warrior and they shall inform him that they have admonished their lord and he refused to obey. Then the chief warrior will arise and go there to the lord and will say to him: 'Your nephew and niece have admonished you to desist from your evil course, and you have refused to obey.' Then the chief warrior will say: 'I will now admonish you for the last time and if you continue to resist, refuse to accede and disobey this request, then your duties as lord of our family and clan will cease, and I shall take the deer's horns from off your head, and with a broad edged stone axe I shall cut down the tree' (meaning that he shall be deposed from his position as lord or chief of the confederacy). Then, if the lord merits dismissal, the chief warrior shall hand back the deer's horns (the emblem of power) of the deposed lord to the chief matron of the family or clan."

Whenever it occurs that a lord is thus deposed, then the chief matron shall select and appoint another warrior of her family or clan and crown him with the deer's horns and thus a new lord shall be created in the place of the one deposed.

The lords of each of the confederate nations shall have one assistant and their duty, each of them, shall be to carry messages through the forests between our settlements and also in the absence of the lord through illness or any other impediment he shall be deputed by him (his lord) to act in his place in council.

The lords then said: "We have now completed defining the obligations and positions of a lord (Royaner) and therefore in accordance with the custom which we now have established, it shall be that when a lord is deposed and the deer's horns (emblem of power) are taken from him, he shall no longer be allowed to sit in council or even hold an office again."

Then the lords continued and said: "What shall we do in case some of us lords are removed by sudden death and in whom so much dependence is placed?"

"In such case (this shall be done), the chief matron and the warriors of the family and clan of the deceased lord, shall nominate another lord from the warriors of the family and clan of the dead lord to succeed him, then the matter will be submitted to the brother lords and if they (the brother lords) confirm the nomination, then the matter will be further submitted to their cousin lords and if they also confirm the nomination, then the candidate shall be qualified to be raised by the condolence ceremony (Honda nas)."

Then the lords continued and said: "In case the family and clan in which a lordship title[1] is vested shall become extinct, this shall be done: It shall then be transferred and vested in the hands of the confederate lords and they will consider the matter and nominate and appoint[2] a successor from any family of the brother lords of the deceased lord, and the lords may in their discretion vest the said lordship title in some family, and such title will remain in that family so long as the lords are satisfied.

"If ever it should occur that the chief matron in a family or clan in which a lordship title is vested should be removed by death and leave female infants who, owing to their infancy can not nominate a candidate to bear their lordship title, then the lords (of the same nation) at their pleasure may appoint an adult female of a sister family who shall make a temporary appointment, shall

---

[1] Nihosĕnnodĕ', *the title.*
[2] The term is Nahonyawădăgä yä'dĕn.

come before the lords and request that the lordship title be restored to them, then the lords must obtain the title and restore it accordingly."

Then the lords continued and said: "We now have completed laying the foundation of our rules and methods (Kayanehrenokowa) and we will now proceed to follow and carry out the working of these rules and methods of the confederacy, and the local affairs of our respective settlements, and whenever we discover a warrior who is wise and trustworthy and who will render his services for the benefit of the people and thus aid the lords of the confederacy, we will claim him into our midst and confer upon him the title of 'He has sprung up as a Pine Tree [1]' (Eh-ka-neh-do-deh) and his title shall only last during his lifetime[2] and shall not be hereditary and at his death it shall die with him."

Then the lords (Rodiyaner) again considered and said: "We have now completed the appointment of our lords. It may so occur that before we may be quietly reseated in our respective places, we may sustain another loss by death (of a lord) and in that case we shall do this: While yet the dying lord is suffering in the agonies of death, his brother lords will come and remove his deer's horns from his head and place them beside the wall and if by the will of the Great Ruler he recovers from his illness, he shall then reclaim his crown of deer's horns and resume the duties of a lord. They further considered this matter and said: "While the lord is ill we will place a string of black wampum at the head of his bed and if he dies anyone belonging to his clan may take this string of black wampum and announce his death to the whole circle of the confederacy as follows:

"If a Lord among the three brothers,[3] Mohawk, Seneca and Onondaga, dies, the chief warrior or a warrior will convey the string of black wampum to their son, Ohdahtshedeh or Dehkaeh-yonh, or their colleagues, and he will leave it there, and while on his way from the home of the dead lord he will repeat at regular intervals the mourning cry, three times thus —'Kwa – – – ah; Kwa – – – ah; Kwa – – – ah.'

"Then Ohdahtshedeh or Dehkaehyonh or their colleagues will convey the string of black wampum to their four brothers, and so

---

[1] Waganeda'nyŭk.
[2] E^{n}kanedode^n, *the pine tree shall grow.*
[3] A'sĕ'nihoñdadĕn''gĕn, three brothers.

on until the whole circle of the confederacy shall become aware of the death of the lord. And if a lord among the two (now four) brothers (the Oneida and Cayuga) dies, then the chief warrior or any warrior deputed will carry and convey the string of black wampum to Dekarihoken or Skanyadahriyoh or Thadodahho, or their brother colleagues, and the chief warrior or any warrior so deputed will, while on his way, repeat the mourning cry three times at regular intervals as follows: 'Kwa ─ ─ ─ah; Kwa ─ ─ ─ ah; Kwa ─ ─ ─ ah;' [1] and if a chief warrior on either side of the council dies (or now if a chief of Tuscarora, Delaware, Nanticoke or Tuteli member [2] of the council dies), then the mourning messenger will, while on his way to announce the death of either of these, repeat the mourning cry twice only as follows: 'Kwa ─ ─ ─ ah;· Kwa ─ ─ ─ ah.' In case of the sudden death of a lord, then his colleagues will remove his crown of deer's horns and will put it to one side where the chief matron of the family or clan to which he belonged will find and take it up again.

"If from whatever cause the crown of deer's horns are not removed from the head of the lord at the time of his death, then his colleagues will remove the same at the time of his burial and will place it beside the grave where the chief matron will find and pick it up again."

Then the lords said: "If a lord dies we will do this: we will put up a pole horizontally, and we will hang a pouch upon it, and we will put into the pouch a short string of wampum, and the side of the council fire which has sustained the loss by death shall do it and the side which has not sustained the loss will depute one of their lords to take the pouch off the pole, then he shall follow the path and go to the opposite side of the council fire where the loss has been sustained, and when he arrives at the house where the lord died he will stand at one end of the hearth and he will speak consoling words to the bereaved, and he will cheer them up, and this will be our mode of condolence, and these shall consist of eleven passages to be expressed in this condolence (Ka-ne-kon-kets-kwa-se-rah) [3] and eleven wampum strings shall be used in this ceremony.

---

[1] Kwa ă".
[2] Captive or adopted tribes having a seat and a voice in their own national affairs but no voice in the confederate council.
[3] Ganigohagetc'gwĕⁿ', Their spirits are lifted up.

THE CONDOLENCE CEREMONY

The beginning of the condolence ceremony used immediately after the death of a chief (or lord) and which is subsequently followed by the preliminary ceremony called, "At the wood's edge."

1 Now hear us our uncles, we have come to condole with you in your great bereavement.

We have now met in dark sorrow to lament together over the death of our brother lord. For such has been your loss. We will sit together in our grief and mingle our tears together, and we four brothers will wipe off the tear from your eyes, so that for a day period you might have peace of mind. This we say and do, we four brothers.

2 Now hear us again, for when a person is in great grief caused by death, his ears are closed up and he can not hear and such is your condition now.

We will therefore remove the obstruction (grief) from your ears, so that for a day period you may have perfect hearing again. This we say and do, we four brothers.

3 Continue to hear the expression of us four brothers, for when a person is in great sorrow his throat is stopped with grief and such is your case; now, we will therefore remove the obstruction (grief) so that for a day period you may enjoy perfect breathing and speech; this we say and do, we four brothers.

The foregoing part of the condolence ceremony is to be performed outside of the place of meeting.

Then the bereaved will appoint two of their chief warriors to conduct the four brothers into the place of meeting.

4 Continue to hear the expression of us four brothers, for when a person is in great grief caused by death, he appears to be deformed, so that our forefathers have made a form which their children may use in condoling with each other (Ja-wek-ka-ho-denh) which is that they will treat him a dose of soft drink (medicine) and which when it is taken and settled down in the stomach it will pervade the whole body and strengthen him and restore him to a perfect form of man. This we say and do, we four brothers.

5 Continue to hear the expression of us four brothers. Now

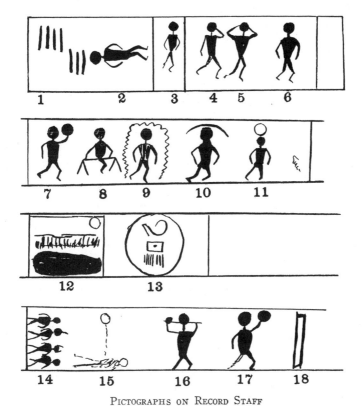

PICTOGRAPHS ON RECORD STAFF

(1) The seven parallel lines represent the four elder brothers and the three younger brothers of the eight clans who are mourning. (2) The prostrate figure is that of the dead chief of the eighth clan. (3) A chanter of condolence appears to comfort the sorrowing friends and relatives, (4) he lifts one hand to say, "we are mourning," (5) then both arms are raised to the heavens and he asks the people to look to the sun and be gladdened, and (6) then he points to the earth where sorrow shall be buried. (7) "Behold the sun in its brightness shining (8) for there sits the new chief (royaneh) on a bench with four legs, like the roots of the great tree." (9) Now the chief is in a bower of pine boughs where his enemies cannot discover him, there he sits and thinks of his duties. (10) Night covers him and he still meditates, (11) but the morning sun comes again like a circle of horns over his head and he approaches like the new sun. It shines over the new chief and (12) it shines over the grave of the chief who died. (13) Then shall the clans come in council and the new chief appears before them on a new mat, but the path is not yet clear or straight, until the (14) mourning clans arise and take their minds from (15) the dead chief whose spirit has gone after ten days from his body. Then (16) the new chief takes his staff and (17) goes forward with his sun before him, as a light to his mind and that people may see he is royaneh. Then (18) is his door open and his path made clear.

when a person is brought to grief by death, such person's seat or bed seems stained with human blood; such is now your case.

We therefore wipe off those stains with soft linen so that your seat and bed may be clean and so that you may enjoy peace for a day, for we may scarcely have taken our seats before we shall be surprised to hear of another death. This we say and do, we four brothers.

6 Continue to hear the expression of us four brothers. When a person is brought to grief through death, he is confined in the darkness of deep sorrow, and such is now the case of your three brothers. This we say, we four brothers.

7 When a person is brought to grief by death, he seems to lose sight of the sky (blinded with grief) and he is crushed with sorrow. We therefore remove the mist from your eyes, so that the sky may be clear to you. This we say and do, we four brothers.

8 When a person is brought to grief by death he seems to lose the sight of the sun; this is now your case. We therefore remove the mist so that you may see the sun rising over the trees or forest in the east, and watch its course and when it arrives in midsky, it will shed forth its rays around you, and you shall begin to see your duties and perform the same as usual. This we say and do, we four brothers.

9 Now when the remains are laid and cause the mound of clay (grave), we till the ground and place some nice grass over it and place a nice slab over it, so that his body (that of the dead lord) may quietly lay in his resting place, and be protected from the heavy wind and great rain storms. This we say and do, we four brothers.

10 Now continue to listen, for when a person is brought to grief, and such is your condition, the sticks of wood from your fire are scattered caused by death, so we the four brothers, will gather up the sticks of wood and rekindle the fire, and the smoke shall rise and pierce the sky, so that all the nations of the confederacy may see the smoke, and when a person is in great grief caused by the death of some of our rulers, the head is bowed down in deep sorrow. We therefore cause you to stand up again, our uncles and surround the council fire again and resume your duties. This we say and do, we four brothers.

11 Continue to listen for when the Great Spirit created us, he created a woman as the helpmate of man, and when she is called

Record staff containing the history of a condolence and raising ceremony of a royaneh or councellor.

away by death, it is grievously hard for had she been allowed to live she may have raised a family to inhabit the earth, and so we four brothers raise the woman again (to encourage and cheer up their downcast spirits) so that you may cheerfully enjoy peace and happiness for a day. This we say and do, we four brothers.

12 Now my uncle lords, you have two relations, a nephew and a niece. They are watching your course. Your niece may see that you are making a misstep and taking a course whereby your children may suffer ruin or a calamity, or it may be your nephew who will see your evil course and never bear to listen when the woman or warrior approach you and remind you of your duties, and ask you to come back and carry out your obligations as a Royaner or lord of the band. This we say and do, we four brothers.

13 They say it is hard for any one tc allow his mind to be troubled too greatly with sorrow. Never allow yourself to be led to think of destroying yourself by committing suicide for all things in this world is only vanity. Now we place in your midst a torch. We all have an equal share in the said light, and would now call all the Rodhanersonh (lords) to their places and each perform the duties conferred upon each of them. This we say and do, we four brothers.

Now we return to you the wampum which we received from you when you suffered the loss by death. We will therefore now conclude our discourse. Now point out to me the man whom I am to proclaim as chief in place of the deceased.

THE HIAWATHA TRADITION

Related by Baptist Thomas (Sa ha whi) an Onondaga (Turtle Clan) as he had it from Thomas Commissary (Ostowägō'nă* Big Feather).

When a man's heart is heavy with sorrow because of death he wanders aimlessly (wa-hē-des-yas-sha-dā'′-na').[1] That is why Ha-yĕnt-watha went away from the Mohawks. His only sister — he had only one sister — died. She was Da-si-yu' and she died. She was not a comely woman but her brother loved her and so Ha-yent-watha mourned and no one came to comfòrt him. Not one person came to him in his grief to comfort him, therefore his mind was clouded in darkness. His throat was dry and heavy and bitter. So he went away for he did not wish to stay among a people who had no hearts of sympathy for sorrow. The Mohawks had grown callous and so accustomed to troubled times that they did not care for the sorrows of others and even despised the tears of mourners. They were always fighting. Even they sent out war parties among their own relatives in other towns. Hayentwatha often said this was wrong but no one listened to him. So when his great sorrow came he went away. He took a canoe and went upstream. He paddled up the Mohawk river and when he landed to camp he talked to himself about his sorrow. " I would comfort others in sorrow," he said, " but no one comforts me."

After a long time he reached the portage and carried his canoe to Wood creek.[2] Here he camped three days. He took up his journey again and camped at one of two islands and went through Oneida lake. Then he went up the river and came to Three River point. Here he heard a broken branch creaking against a tree. It cried giis, giis, giis, so he named this spot Dyo-neda-tonk. So then he went up the river into Onondaga lake. He landed on the north side, (near the present site of Liverpool),[4] and built a hut. Here he made a camp fire and stayed for three days. Then he saw the monster. He was a long way off and he was looking at Hayĕnt-watha. So Hayĕntwatha moved his camp but the next morning the monster came nearer. This being was Thă-do-dā'-ho'. So the next evening Hayĕntwatha moved his camp again and in the

---

[1] Onondaga vocabulary.
[2] This portage is called De-hon-yugwha-tha.
[3] Odĭ-nĕs'-shi-yū, People of the sand and they shall be of the Snipe Clan.
[4] This spot he named Gă'skwasoĕtge'.

morning again he saw the monster before his camp fire. It seems that he had snakes in his hair and covering his shoulders and one great one came up from his thighs and went over his shoulders. Hayĕntwatha looked at Thădodaho and said " Shon-nis'?" (who are you?) The monstrous being did not reply but his face looked very angry. Again Hayĕntwatha changed his camp and built a shelter on one of the two islands in the lake. This spot he named Si-ye-ge. As before, the monster camped silently near him. He was nearer than ever before and seemed watching him from the corner of his eyes.

So then again Hayĕntwatha moved his camping place. He crossed the lake and camped at the point on the south shore. As he built his lodge he looked inland and saw seated on a knoll, the monster Thădodă'ho'. He then observed that what ever move he made the snake-bearing monster was ever before him. He seemed to anticipate his movements. This fact frightened Hayĕntwatha and he prepared to take up his journey again.

His sorrow was not diminished but hung like a black cloud over him. His heart was very heavy and there was no clear sky for him. He carried no war weapons and the monster frightened him. So Hayĕntwatha journeyed in his canoe up Onondaga creek. So in this manner he came to the Onondaga village. How long he stayed at the Onondaga town, my grandfather, Tom Commissary, did not say. Some say he stayed there and married. Some say he enjoined the Onondaga towns to be at peace and stop their quarreling. After a time when another great sorrow came, some say it was because his daughters died, he again continued his journey but Thădodă'ho' went before him and Hayĕntwatha saw him.

So Hayĕntwatha went south up Onondaga creek and he came to a certain spot where a brook enters the creek[1] and he saw there a pond and a grassy place. There it is said he saw a very large turtle and some women playing ball. Some say boys were playing ball but I say that women were playing ball because my grandfather said so. So Hayĕntwatha called this place Dwĕⁿ-the'-gă^s, and said from this spot comes the Ball Clan (Dwĕⁿ-the-gă^s Hadinya'-tĕⁿ') of the Great Turtle.

Hayĕntwatha continued his journey and went over Bear mountain.[2] First he camped at night at the foot of the high hill. Here

[1] A brook running through Cardiff, N. Y.
[2] Southwest of Cardiff, Lafayette township, Onondaga county.

he built a shelter. That night he heard a song and its words were what he believed and had spoken many times to the Onondaga chiefs and to the Mohawks.

In the morning he ascended the mountain and there he found five stalks of corn springing from four roots and there was only one large stalk at the root from which the five stalks grew. On each stalk were three large ears of ripe corn. Near the corn he saw a large turtle with a red and yellow belly and it was the turtle that danced. He danced the Ostowago'na, the great feather dance. So then Hayĕntwatha said "Did you sing last night? I heard singing." Then the turtle replied, " I sang. Now this is the great corn and you will make the nations like it. Three ears represent the three nations[1] and the five stalks from a single stalk represent the five nations and the four roots go to the north and west the south and the east."

Hayĕntwatha proceeded on his journey and after a time he came to a group of lakes. He called it Tgă-ni-yä-da-hä-nion (the lake group on hill) (the present Tully group of lakes). On one of these lakes were many ducks swimming very closely together. The ducks covered the lake. So Hayĕntwatha stopped to look at so strange a sight. " What are you doing there, so many of you?" he said all to himself. The ducks heard him and at the same moment, whoo! every one of them flew into the air and lifted up the water, so quickly did they fly up. The bottom of the lake was left dry and Hayĕntwatha walked across it. As he walked he saw many small shells and he gathered a deer skin full of shells so many were there. When he reached the opposite shore he saw a man limping toward him. He was dragging a large snapping turtle. " What troubles your walk?" asked Hayĕntwatha. " I have a blister on my crotch " answered the man.

Then said Hayĕntwatha to himself, " In the future this man and his brothers with all his female relations shall be known as Hodī-ho'ŏ'ĕn'h. They have blisters on their crotches and they shall be of the Small Turtle Clan."

Then again he proceeded on his journey and after a time he saw an old corn field and a field shelter house with a roof of stalks. So he went there for a camp.

The great sorrow had not left him so he sat by his campfire and talked to himself. Then he strung up the shells and placed three strings on a pole laid across two upright poles. He continued to talk.

---

[1] The original confederates were the Mohawk, Oneida and Onondaga.

A little girl saw the smoke of the campfire and went out into the field. She went close to the shelter house and listened to what Hayĕntwatha said. Then she returned and told her father what she had seen. He then sent two men to invite Hayĕntwatha to the village.

Hayĕntwatha did not reply to them but with his head bowed before his fire he said aloud to himself, " These people should know that every invitation should be confirmed by a string of shells such as hang before me; they should give me a strand (ä-sa-na-tcik′)." The men returned to their chief and told what they had heard. Then he ordered them to string up some beads of large porcupine quills and carry them to the stranger to become words of invitation. This they did and Hayĕntwatha said, " It is now right."

The warriors who came with the two messengers returned to the village and after smoking his pipe Hayĕntwatha went to the village with the two guides. At the settlement the council was in session and Hayĕntwatha was invited to sit on one side of the fire. The discussion was a spirited one and none of the head men could agree on any question. During the debate a great man came in. The room was crowded and the head man who had invited Hayĕntwatha arose and gave his place to the great man. The debate continued and Hayĕntwatha silently departed, angry at the slight he had received. In the council room the debate was as devoid of result as before when the head man arose and said, " I have staying with me a friend. He is a stranger and I do not know from whence he came. Perhaps he can settle our dispute."

Then everyone looked for the stranger but Hayĕntwatha was not there. The head man could not find him. So then the head man said, " I think I have made a great mistake. He must have been a great man and I have offended him. He has magically disappeared."

So the man who was able to settle the quarrel of the people was not there.

When Hayĕntwatha left the council he journeyed on to the outskirts of another settlement and made a camp. Here he commanded his two guardian birds to come to him. Their names were Hă'-goks′ and Skadjiē'na.[1] He said, " Go and see if smoke arises from any settlement."

Then the birds arose and when they returned they said, " Smoke arises from the Oneida villages."

---

[1] Said by some informants to have been two human messengers bearing these names and not actually birds.

So then Hayĕntwatha went eastward and in all the Oneida towns he heard the people talking about the Great Law and about the Great Peace. Dekanawida had told of it but the people failed to understand it. So then Hayĕntwatha said, " I must meet that man for my mind is not yet unburdened." So he continued on his journey down the river, toward the Mohawk country, for he greatly wished to see Dekanawida.

Editor's Footnotes

(a) In Parker all the Confederate Lords unite in rubbing (to reshape and transform) the newly redeemed Thadoda-ho; the horns of office are placed on his head jointly by Jikonsahseh and the Chief Warrior. However, Chief Thomas has it that the 49 chiefs united with Dekanawida to elevate this 50th Chief. Because no clan mother was involved in this instance the title belongs to no clan, although the holder as an individual will have a clan. Over the years the people (at Ohsweken) became confused about this title and it settled among the Deer clan and was treated as any other clan-held title. Of late, in a general scheme to rationalize title duplication, it has been accepted by the Chiefs at Ohsweken that henceforth there shall be only one Thadoda-ho and he will be installed by the Onondaga in New York State.

(b) According to the principal surviving oral custodian of this material at Ohsweken, Cayuga Chief Jacob E Thomas (June 19, 1991), when Dekanawida left he told people to use his name only when Condoling, and that it was not to be given to others since he was not dead (names should not be duplicated among the living, something which today is becoming increasingly difficult to observe). He said: "I am going to bury myself", meaning he was disappearing but not dead. This is somewhat akin to the concept expressed in the last sentence in this paragraph in Parker. He said he would return when all the people called out his name in their distress.

To accomodate the wish (paragraph 3) that his name not be "mentioned disrespectfully without reason or just cause" certain soubriquets have arisen. The most common of these is Honon^{h}shonne:don^h, "He Constructed the House" (ie: he created the symbolic political Longhouse of the League which stretched across Iroquoia). A second is Tandaho'ne^{h}s^{h}an', "He has no Father", sometimes rendered in English as "The Fatherless One", alluding to his miraculous parthenogenetic conception. In the last year of his life, 1912, Chief John Arthur Gibson dictated a 525-page manuscript of this great epic to the scholar Alexander Goldenweiser. During his translation of this material from Onondaga into English Chief Thomas found a third euphemism: Honek^{h}o:.wanen^h, "He has a Great Mind". Interestingly, Chief Thomas notes that there is no 'Iroquois' equivalent for the most often used English alias: "The Peacemaker".

WGS

APPENDIX A

THE PASSAMAQUODDY WAMPUM RECORDS

RECORDED BY J. D. PRINCE [1]

Many bloody fights had been fought, many men, women and children had been tortured by constant and cruel wars until some of the wise men among the Indians began to think that something must be done, and that whatever was to be done should be done quickly. They accordingly sent messengers to all parts of the country, some going to the south, others to the east, and others to the west and northwest. Some even went as far as the Wabanaki.[2] It was many months before the messengers reached the farthest tribes. When they arrived at each nation, they notified the people that the great Indian nations of the Iroquois, Mohawks and others had sent them to announce the tidings of a great Lagootwagon or general coun il for a treaty of peace. Every Indian who heard the news rejoiced, because they were all tired of the never-ending wars. Every tribe, therefore, sent two or more of their cleverest men as representatives to the great council.

When all the delegates were assembled they began to deliberate concerning what was best to do, as they all seemed tired of their evil lives. The leading chief then spoke as follows: "As we look back upon our blood-stained trail we see that many wrongs have been done by all of our people. Our gory tomahawks, clubs, bows and arrows must undoubtedly be buried for ever." It was decided, therefore, by all concerned to make a general Lagootwagon or treaty of peace, and a day was appointed when they should begin the rites.

For seven days, from morning till night, a strict silence was observed, during which each representative deliberated on the speech

---

[1] See "Klooskape, The Master." Funk & Wagnalls Co., 1899.

[2] According to Indian tradition, six Iroquoian tribes united in confederation in the interests of peace. This was the famous League of the Six Nations: Onondagas, Mohawks, Oneidas, Senecas, Cayugas and Tuscaroras. The first five of these completed their league as early as the middle of the fifteenth century under the Onondaga chief Hiawatha. The object of the federation was to abolish war altogether (see Brinton, The American Race, p.82,83). It is evident that the Passamaquoddy tradition embodied in this part of the Wampum Records refers to these proposals made by their Iroquois neighbors.

he should make and tried to discover the best means for checking the war. This was called the " Wigwam of silence."

After this, they held another wigwam called m'sittakw-wen tlewestoo, or " Wigwam of oratory."   The ceremonies then began. Each representative recited the history of his nation, telling all the cruelties, tortures and hardships they had suffered during their wars and stating that the time had now come to think of and take pity on their women and children, their lame and old, all of whom had suffered equally with the strongest and bravest warriors. When all the speeches had been delivered, it was decided to erect an extensive fence and within it to build a large wigwam.   In this wigwam they were to make a big fire and, having made a switch or whip, to place " their father " as a guard over the wigwam with the whip in his hand.   If any of his children did wrong he was to punish them with the whip.   Every child of his within the inclosure must therefore   obey his orders implicitly.   His duty also was to keep replenishing the fire in the wigwam so that it should not go out.   This is the origin of the Wampum laws.

The fence typified a treaty of peace for all the Indian nations who took part in the council, fourteen in number, of which there are many tribes.   All these were to go within the fence and dwell there, and if any should do wrong they would be liable to punishment with the whip at the hands of " their father."   The wigwam within the fence represented a universal house for all the tribes, in which they might live in peace, without disputes and quarrels, like members of one family.   The big fire (ktchi squt) in the wigwam denoted the warmth of the brotherly love engendered in the Indians by their treaty.   The father ruling the wigwam was the great chief who lived at Caughnawaga.   The whip in his hand was the type of the Wampum laws, disobedience to which was punishable by consent of all the tribes mentioned in the treaty.

After this, they proceeded to make lesser laws, all of which were to be recorded by means of wampum, in order that they could be read to the Indians from time to time.   Every feast, every ceremony, therefore, has its own ritual in the wampum; such as the burial and mourning rites after the death of a chief, the installation of a chief, marriage etc.   There were also salutation and visiting wampum.

CEREMONIES CUSTOMARY AT THE DEATH OF A CHIEF

When the chief of the tribe died, his flag pole was cut down and burnt, and his warlike appurtenances, bows and arrows, tomahawk and flag were buried with him. The Indians mourned for him one year, after which the Pwutwusimwuk or leading men were summoned by the tribe to elect a new chief. The members of one tribe alone could not elect their own chief; according to the common laws of the allied nations, he had to be chosen by a general wigwam. Accordingly, after the council of the leading men had assembled, four or six canoes were dispatched to the Micmac, Penobscot and Maliseet tribes if a Passamaquoddy chief had died.[1] These canoes bore each a little flag in the bow as a sign that the mission on which the messengers came was important. On the arrival of the messengers at their destination, the chief of the tribe to which they came called all his people, children, women and men, to meet the approaching boats. The herald springing to land first sang his salutation song (n'skawewintuagunul), walking back and forth before the ranks of the other tribe. When he had finished his chant the other Indians sang their welcoming song in reply.

As soon as the singing was over they marched to some imwewigwam or meeting house to pray together. The visiting Indians were then taken to a special wigwam allotted to their use over which a flag was set. Here they were greeted informally by the members of the tribe with hand-shaking etc. The evening of the first day was spent in entertaining the visitors.

On the next day the messengers sent to the chief desiring to see all the tribe assembled in a gwandowanek or dance hall. When the tribe had congregated there, the strangers were sent for, who, producing their strings of wampum to be read according to the law of the big wampum, announced the death of the chief of their tribe, " their eldest boy " (ktchi w'skinosismowal), and asked that the tribe should aid them to elect a new chief. The chief of the stranger tribe then arose and formally announced to his people the desire of the envoys, stating his willingness to go to aid them, his fatherless brothers, in choosing a new father. The messengers, arising once more, thanked the chief for his kindness and appointed a day to return to their own people.

The ceremony known as kelhoochun then took place. The chief notified his men that his brothers were ready to go, but that they

---

[1] From here on the recorder mentions only the neighboring Algonkin tribes as belonging to the federation which he has in mind. The northern Algonkin tribes were very probably in a loose federation with the Iroquois merely for purposes of intertribal arbitration. These Algonkin clans themselves, however, seem to have been politically interdependent, as one clan could not elect a chief without the consent of all the others.

should not be allowed to go so soon. The small wampum string called kellhoweyi or prolongation of the stay was produced at this point, which read that the whole tribe, men, women and children, were glad to see their brothers with them and begged them to remain a day or two longer; that "our mothers" (kigwusin), that is, all the tribal women, would keep their paddles yet a little while. This meant that the messengers were not to be allowed to depart so soon.

Here followed the ceremony called N'skahudin. A great hunt was ordered by the chief and the game brought to the meeting hall and cooked there. The noochila-kalwet or herald went about the village crying wikw-poosaltin, which was intelligible to all. Men, women and children immediately came to the hall with their birchbark dishes and sat about the game in a circle, while four or five men with long-handled dishes distributed the food, of which every person had a share. The feast was called kelhootwi-wikw-poosaltiu. When it was all over the Indians dispersed, but returned later to the hall when the messengers sang again their salutation songs in honor of their forefathers, in reply to which the chief of the tribe sang his song of greeting.

When the singing was over the chief seated himself in the midst of the hall with a small drum in one hand and a stick in the other. To the accompaniment of his drum he sang his k'tumasooi-n'tawagunul or dance songs, which was the signal for a general dance, followed by another feast.

The envoys again appointed a day to return, but were deterred in the same manner. As these feasts often lasted three weeks or a month, a dance being held every night, it was frequently a long time before they could go back to their own tribe, because the chief would detain them whenever they wished to return. Such was the custom.

THE CEREMONY OF INSTALLATION

When they reached home, however, and the embassies from the other Wabanaki tribes had also returned, the people of the bereaved tribe were summoned to assemble before the messengers, who informed them of the success of their mission. When the delegates from the other tribes, who had been appointed to elect the chief, had arrived and the salutation and welcome ceremonies had been performed, an assembly was called to elect the chief.

This took place about the second day after the arrival of the other Wabanaki representatives. A suitable person, a member of the bereaved tribe, was chosen by acclamation for the office of chief.

If there was no objection to him a new flag pole was made and prepared for raising, and a chief from one of the kindred tribes put a medal of wampum on the chief-elect who was always clothed in new garments. The installing chief then addressed the people, telling them that another " eldest boy " had been chosen, to whom they owed implicit obedience. Turning to the new chief, he informed him that he must act in accordance with the wishes of his people. The main duties of a chief were to act as arbiter in all matters of dispute, and to act as commander in chief in case of war, being ready to sacrifice himself for the people's good if necessary.

After this ceremony they marched to the hall, where another dance took place, the new chief singing and beating the drum. A wife of one of the other chiefs then placed a new deer skin or bear skin on the shoulders of the new chief as a symbol of his authority, after which the dance continued the whole night.

The officers of the new chief (geptins) were still to be chosen. These were seven in number and were appointed in the same manner and with the same ceremonies as the chief. Their duties, which were much more severe, were told them by the installing chief. The flag pole, which was the symbol of the chief, was first raised. The geptins stood around it, each with a brush in his hand, with which they were instructed to brush off any particle of dust that might come upon it. This signified that it was their duty to defend and guard their chief and that they should be obliged to spill their blood for him, in case of need and in defense of the tribe. All the women and children and disabled persons in the tribe were under the care of the geptins. The chief himself was not allowed to go into battle, but was expected to stay with his people and to give orders in time of danger.

After the tribal officers had been appointed, the greatest festivities were carried on; during the day they had canoe races, foot races and ball playing, and during the night, feasting and dancing. The Indians would bet on the various sports, hanging the prizes for each game on a pole. It was understood that the winner of the game was entitled to all the valuables hung on this pole. The festivities often lasted an entire month.

THE MARRIAGE CEREMONY: THE ANCIENT RITE

It was the duty of the young Indian man who wished to marry to inform his parents of his desire, stating the name of the maiden. The young man's father then notified all the relatives and friends of the family that his son wished to marry such and such a girl. If the friends and relations were willing, the son was permitted to offer his suit. The father of the youth prepared a clean skin of the bear, beaver or deer, which he presented to his son. Provided with this, the suitor went to the wigwam of his prospective bride's father and placed the hide at the back of the wigwam or nowteh. The girl's father then notified his relations and friends, and if there was no objection, he ordered his daughter to seat herself on the skin, as a sign that the young man's suit was acceptable. The usual wedding ceremonies were then held, namely, a public feast, followed by dancing and singing, which always lasted at least a week.

THE MARRIAGE CEREMONY IN LATER DAYS

After the adoption of the Wampum laws the marriage ceremony was much more complicated.[1]

When the young man had informed his parents of his desire to marry and the father had secured the consent of the relations and friends, an Indian was appointed to be the Keloolwett or marriage herald, who, taking the string of wampum called the Kelolwawei, went to the wigwam of the girl's father, generally accompanied by as many witnesses as cared to attend. The herald read the marriage wampum in the presence of the girl and her father, formally stating that such and such a suitor sought his daughter's hand in marriage. The herald, accompanied by his party, then returned to the young man's wigwam to await the reply. After the girl's father had notified his relatives and friends and they had given their consent, the wedding was permitted to go on.

The usual ceremonies then followed. The young man first presented the bride-elect with a new dress. She, after putting it on, went to her suitor's wigwam with her female friends, where she and her company formally saluted him by shaking hands. This was called wulisakowdowagon or salutation. She then returned to her father's house, where she seated herself with her following of old women and girls. The groom then assembled a company of his friends, old and young men, and went with them to the bride's wigwam to salute her in the same manner. When these salutations were over a great feast was prepared by the bride, enough for all the people, men, women and children. The bridegroom also prepared a similar feast. Both of these dinners were cooked in the

---

[1] Mitchell interpolated this remark.

open air and when the food was ready they cried out k'waltewall " your dishes." Every one understood this, which was the signal for the merry-makers to approach and fall to.

The marriage ceremonies, however, were not over yet. The wedding party arrayed themselves in their best attire and formed two processions, that of the bride entering the assembly wigwam first. In later times it was customary to fire a gun at this point as a signal that the bride was in the hall, whereupon the groom's procession entered the hall in the same manner, when a second gun was fired. The geptins of the tribe and one of the friends of the bride then conducted the girl to the bridegroom to dance with him. At midnight after the dancing a supper was served, to which the bride and groom went together and where she ate with him for the first time. The couple were then addressed by an aged man (noiimikokemit) on the duties of marriage.

Finally, a number of old women accompanied the newly made wife to her husband's wigwam, carrying with them her bed clothes. This final ceremony was called natboonan, taking or carrying the bed.

APPENDIX B

SKETCHES OF AN INDIAN COUNCIL, 1846

(From Schoolcraft's Census of 1845)

A grand council of the confederate Iroquois was held last week, at the Indian council house on the Tonawanda Reservation, in the county of Genesee. Its proceedings occupied three days, closing on the third instant. It embraced representatives from all the Six Nations — the Mohawk, the Onondaga, the Seneca; and the Oneida, the Cayuga and the Tuscarora. It is the only one of the kind which has been held for a number of years, and is the last which will ever be assembled with a full representation of all the confederate nations.

With the expectation that the council would commence on Tuesday, two or three of us had left Rochester so as to arrive at the council house Monday evening; but owing to some unsettled preliminaries, it had been postponed till Wednesday. The Indians from abroad, however, arrived at the council grounds, or in their immediate vicinity, on Monday; and one of the most interesting spectacles of the occasion, was the entry of the different nations upon the domain and hospitality of the Senecas, on whose ground the council was to be held. The representation of Mohawks, coming as they did from Canada, was necessarily small. The Onondagas, with the acting Tod-o-dah-hoh of the confederacy, and his two counsellors, made an exceedingly creditable appearance. Nor was the array of Tuscaroras, in point of numbers at least, deficient in attractive and imposing features.

Monday evening we called upon, and were presented to, Blacksmith, the most influential and authoritative of the Seneca sachems. He is about 60 years old, is somewhat portly, is easy enough in his manners, and is well disposed and even kindly towards all who convince him that they have no sinister designs in coming among his people.

Jemmy Johnson is the great high priest of the confederacy. Though now 69 years old, he is yet an erect, fine looking, and energetic Indian, and is both hospitable and intelligent. He is in possession of the medal presented by Washington to Red Jacket in 1792 which among other things of interest, he showed us.

It would be incompatible with the present purpose to describe all the interesting men who there assembled, among whom were Captain Frost, Messrs Le Fort, Hill, John Jacket, Doctor Wilson and others. We spent most of Tuesday, and indeed much of the time during the other days of the week in conversation with the chiefs and most intelligent Indians of the different nations, and gleaned from them much information of the highest interest in relation to the organization, government and laws, religion, customs of the people, and characteristics of the great men, of the old and once powerful confederacy. It is a singular fact, that the peculiar government and national characteristics of the Iroquois is a most interesting field for research and inquiry, which has never been very thoroughly, if at all, investigated, although the historic events which marked the proud career of the confederacy, have been perseveringly sought and treasured up in the writings of Stone, Schoolcraft, Hosmer, Yates and others.

Many of the Indians speak English readily; but with the aid and interpretations of Mr Ely S. Parker, a young Seneca of no ordinary degree of attainment, in both scholarship and general intelligence, and who with Le Fort, the Onondaga, is well versed in old Iroquois matters, we had no difficulty in conversing with any and all we chose to.

About midday on Wednesday, the council commenced. The ceremonies with which it was opened and conducted were certainly unique, almost indescribable; and as its proceedings were in the Seneca tongue, they were in a great measure unintelligible, and in fact profoundly mysterious to the pale faces. One of the chief objects for which the council had been convoked, as has been heretofore editorially stated in the *American,* was to fill two vacant sachemships of the Senecas, which had been made by the death of the former incumbents; and preceding the installation of the candidates for the succession, there was a general and dolorous lament for the deceased sachems, the utterance of which, together with the repetition of the laws of the confederacy — the installation of the new sachems — the impeachment and deposition of three unfaithful sachems — the elevation of others in their stead, and the performance of the various ceremonies attended upon these proceedings, consumed the principal part of the afternoon.

At the setting of the sun, a beautiful repast, consisting of an innumerable number of rather formidable looking chunks of boiled fresh beef, and an abundance of bread and succotash, was brought into the council house. The manner of saying grace on this occasion was indeed peculiar. A kettle being brought, hot and smoking from the fire, and placed in the center of the council house, there proceeded from a single person, in a high shrill key, a prolonged and monotonous sound, resembling that of the syllable *wah* or *yah*. This was immediately followed by a response from the whole multitude, uttering in a low and profoundly guttural but protracted tone, the syllable *whe* or *swe*, and this concluded grace. It was impossible not to be somewhat mirthfully effected at the first hearing of grace said in this novel manner. It is, however, pleasurable to reflect that the Indians recognize the duty of rendering thanks to the Divine Being in some formal way, for the bounties and enjoyments which he bestows; and were an Indian to attend a public feast among his pale faced brethern he would be effected, perhaps to a greater degree of marvel, at witnessing a total neglect of this ceremony, than we were at his singular way of performing it.

After supper commenced the dances. All day Tuesday, and on Wednesday, up to the time that the places of the deceased sachems had been filled, everything like undue joyfulness had been restrained. This was required by the respect customarily due to the distinguished dead. But now, the bereaved sachemships being again filled, all were to give utterance to gladness and joy. A short speech from Captain Frost, introductory to the employments of the evening, was received with acclamatory approbation; and soon eighty or ninety of these sons and daughters of the forest — the old men and the young, the maidens and matrons — were engaged in the dance. It was indeed a rare sight.

Only two varieties of dancing were introduced the first evening — the trotting dance and the fish dance. The figures of either are exceedingly simple, and but slightly different from each other. In the first named, the dancers all move round a circle, in a single file, and keeping time in a sort of trotting step to an Indian song of Yo-ho-ha, or yo-ho-ha-ha-ho, as sung by the leaders, or occasionally by all conjoined. In the other, there is the same movement file round a circle, but every two persons, a man and a woman, or two men, face each other, the one moving forward and the other backward, and all keeping step to the music of the singers, who are now, however, aided by a couple of tortoise or turtle shell rattles or an aboriginal drum. At regular intervals there is a sort of cadence in the music, during which a change of position by all the couples take place, the one who had been moving backward taking the place of the one moving forward, when all again move onward, one-half of the whole, of course, being obliged to follow on by advancing backward.

One peculiarity in Indian dancing would probably strongly commend itself to that class among pale-faced beaux and belles denominated the bashful; though perhaps it would not suit others as well. The men, or a number of them, usually begin the dance and the women, or each of them, selecting the one with whom she would like to dance, presents herself at his side as he approaches, and is immediately received into the circle. Consequently, the young Indian beau knows nothing of the tact required to handsomely invite and gallantly lead a lady to the dance; and the young Indian maiden presents her personage to the one she designs to favor, and thus quietly engage herself in the dance. And, moreover, while an Indian beau is not necessarily obliged to exhibit any gallantry as toward a belle, till she has herself manifested her own pleasure in the matter, so therefore the belle can not indulge herself in vacillant flirtations with any considerable number of beaux, without being at once detected.

On Tuesday the religious ceremonies commenced, and the council from the time it assembled, which was about 11 o'clock a. m., till 3 or 4 o'clock p. m., gave the most serious attention to the preaching of Jemmy Johnson, the great high priest, and the second in the succession under the new revelation. Though there are some evangelical believers among the Indians, the greater portion of them cherish the religion of their fathers. This, as they say, has been somewhat changed by the new revelation, which the Great Spirit made to one of their prophets about 47 years ago, and which, as they also believe, was approved by Washington. The profound regard and veneration which the Indian has ever retained toward the name and memory of Washington is most interesting evidence of his universally appreciated worth; and the fact that the red men regard him not merely as one of the best, but as the very best man that ever has existed, or that will ever exist, is beautifully illustrated in a single credence which they maintain even to this day, namely, that Washington is the only white man that has ever entered heaven, and is the only one who will enter there, till the end of the world.

Among the Senecas, public religious exercises take place but once a year. At these times Jemmy Johnson preaches hour after hour, for three days; and then rests from any public discharge of ecclesiastical offices the remaining 362 days of the year. On this, an unusual occasion, he restricted himself to a few hours in each of the last two days of the council. We were told by young Parker, who took notes of his preaching, that his subject matter on Tuesday abounded with good teachings, enforced by appropriate and happy illustrations and striking imagery. After he had finished, the council took a short respite. Soon, however, a company of warriors ready and eager to engage in the celebrated " corn dance," made their appearance. They were differently attired; while some were completely enveloped in a closely fitting and gaudy colored garb, others, though perhaps without intending it, had made wonderfully close approaches to an imitation of the costume said to have been so fashionable in many parts of the state of Georgia during the last hot summer, and which is also said to have consisted simply of a shirt collar and a pair of spurs. But in truth, these warriors, with shoulders and limbs in a state of ñudity, with faces bestreaked with paints, with jingling trinkets dangling at their knees, and with feather war-caps waving above them, presented a truly picturesque and romantic appearance. When the center of the council house had been cleared, and the musicians with the shell rattles had taken their places, the dance commenced; and for an hour and a half, perhaps two hours, it proceeded with surprising spirit and energy. Almost every posture of which the human frame is susceptible, without absolutely making the feet to be uppermost, and the head for once to assume the place of the understanding, was exhibited. Some of the attitudes of the dancers were really imposing, and the dance as a whole could be got up and conducted only by Indians. The women in the performance of the corn dance, are quite by themselves, keeping time to the beat of the shells, and gliding along sideways, scarcely lifting their feet from the floor.

It would probably be well if the Indians everywhere could be inclined to refrain at least from the more grotesque and boisterous peculiarities of this dance. The influence of these can not be productive of any good; and it is questionable whether it would be possible, so long as they are retained, to assimilate them to any greater degree of civilization or to more refined methods of living and enjoyment, than they now possess. The same may be said of certain characteristics of the still more vandalic war dance. This, however, was not introduced at the council.

A part of the proceedings of Friday, the last day of the council, bore resemblance to those of the preceding day. Jemmy Johnson resumed his preaching, at the close of which the corn dance was again performed, though with far more spirit and enthusiasm than at the first. Double the number that then appeared — all hardy and sinewy men, attired in original and fantastic style, among whom was one of the chiefs of the confederacy, together with forty or fifty women of the different nations — now engaged and for two hours persevered in the performance of the various complicated and fatiguing movements of this dance. The appearance of the dusky throng, with its increased numbers and, of course, apportionably increased resources for the production of shrill whoops and noisy stamping, and for the exhibition of striking attitudes and rampant motions, was altogether strange, wonderful and seemingly superhuman.

After the dance had ceased another kind of " sport," a well-contested foot race, claimed attention. In the evening after another supper in the council house, the more social dances — the trotting, the fish, and one in which the women alone participated — were resumed. The fish dance seemed to be the favorite; and being invited to join it by one of the chiefs, we at once accepted the invitation, and followed in mirthful chase of pleasure, with a hundred forest children. Occasionally the dances are characterized by ebullitions of merriment and flashes of real fun; but generally a singular sobriety and decorum are observed. Frequently, when gazing at a throng of sixty or perhaps a hundred dancers, we have been scarcely able to decide which was the most remarkable, the staid and imperturbable gravity of the old men and women, or the complete absence of levity and frolicsomeness in the young.

The social dances of the evening, with occasional speeches from the sachems and chiefs, were the final and concluding ceremonies of this singular but interesting affair. Saturday morning witnesses the separation of the various nations, and the departure of each to their respective homes.

The writer would like to have said a word or two in relation to the present condition and prospects of the Indians, but the original design in regard to both the topics and brevity of this writing having been already greatly transcended, it must be deferred. The once powerful confederacy of the Six Nations, occupying in its palmy days the greater portion of New York State, now number only a little over 3000. Even this remnant will soon be gone. In view of this, as well as of the known fact that the Indian race is everywhere gradually diminishing in number, the writer can not close without invoking for this unfortunate people, renewed kindliness and sympathy and benevolent attention. It is true that, with some few

5

exceptions, they possess habits and characteristics which render them difficult to approach; but still they are only what the Creator of us all has made them. And let it be remembered, it must be a large measure of kindliness and benevolence, that will repay the injustice and wrong that have been inflicted upon them.

R. S. G.

Rochester, October 7, 1845

APPENDIX C

MINUTES OF THE SIX NATIONS COUNCIL OF 1839[1]

LIST OF CHIEFS

Selected and inaugurated at the Six Nations' Council at
the Six Nations Onondaga Council House, July 17, 1839
Sen (eca)

Of the Chicken Hawk Tribe

1 Shagĕhjowa, Joseph Silverheels of
Cattaraugus Reservation a Sachem of the
Long House of the Six nations
(Capt. Jones of Allegany, Gan'nage).

2 Sgăndiuhgwadi, Owen Blacksnake
James Robinson (Shaweegĕt) of Allegany
abdicated in favor of Blacksnake
A War Chief.

Of the Snipe tribe

1 Hah-jih-nya-wăs, Jacob Johnson
Walter Thomson (Honondahes) of Cattaraugus
Sachem of the Senecas

2 Degas swĕn'gaent, Davis Isaac
(English name not known) (Othowă) of Cattaraugus
War Chief.

Of the Swan tribe —

1 Deyúgăhăshă, John Mitten
(Old Greenblanket, Don dae hañ) of Buffalo reservation.
Sachem or as we might say sub-sachem for the Senecas, but
not entitled to a seat in the Six Nations' Council

2 Ga'năyuehse. James Pierce
English name not known (Toʔwihdoh)
War Chief.

Of the Deer Tribe

1 Swaowaeh, Jonah
White Chief Deganohsogă of Buffalo reservation
War Chief

2 Dóhsihdásgowa, John Baldwin
(George White Sa'gonondano of Buffalo.)
War Chief

[1] From the original manuscript.

3 Hăondyeyah, Lewis Kennedy
  (Capt. M'Gee Thoiwae) of Tonawanda
  Sachem of the Senecas.

  These four clans are brethren
  Of the Wolf tribe
1 Deonihhogă'hwă, Blacksmith
  Little Johnson of Buffalo (Jă-oyah-geăh) deposed
  of Tonawanda —
     Sachem of the Six Nations
2 Ganiyăs, John Dickie
  (No English name) (Dijihhnak) of Cattaraugus
     War chief and runner under the preceding.
3 Degaăont, John Kennedy jr
  (No English name) (Gagóh) of Buffalo
     War Chief
4 Gásgaodoh, John Joshua Bluesky
  (Two Guns) Gihdoondoh of Buffalo
  Killed in battle of Chippeway
     Sachem of the Senecas
5 Hayahsajih, Peter Johnson
  (Old Two Guns, brother
  of the preceding.)   (Degeyáhgoh)
     War Chief
6 Gayáhsodoh   George Green Blanket
  (No English name)   (Gonyus,)
                                   Buffalo
     War Chief
7 Dagéhsahĕh   Isaac Shanks
  (Reuben James)   (Jiyakhoh)
                                 Tonawandi
     Sachem of the Senecas
  Of *the Turtle tribe.*
1 Hadogut   Jacob Shongo
  (No English name)   Waonohsihdeh
                               of Allegany
     Sachem of Seneca
2 Gahnase   Abram John
  (No English name)   (Ganăyáhseh)
                               Of Cattaraugus
     Sachem of Senecas

3 Ganĭhdadeháoh
  (No English name) Danl Spring
            of Tonawandi
                War Chief.   James, Spring
4 Gahnăodoh   Ganănwĕhdŏoh
  (Thomson S. Harris)
  (deposed)   Buffalo
      War Chief
      Speaker for the women.
  Of the Beaver tribe
1 Aånishădekhah
      Abram Johny John
  Tall Chief   Howanyaondyo
  of Genesee   Buffalo
      Sachem for the Senecas
2 Ohgahdont   Isaac Johny John
  Guardian of the preceding during his minority
3 Doăhsah   Hemlock
  (Jack Berry)   (Jinohsowă)
                         Buffalo
      Sachem for the Senecas
4 Dayagodăhseh   George Turkey
  (Jack Snow)   (Dyneah)
                              Cattaraugus
      War Chief
5 Hayă'ndagă'nyahháh
  Joe Hemlock   Peter White
            Thayah'dah'ah
      War Chief   Cattaraugus
  Of the Bear Clan
1 Găhgwasah   Saul Logan
                         Shoiwagayăt
                         Buffalo
      War Chief
2 Aodogwĕh   Jack Doxtator
                         Hajă'anoh
                         Buffalo
      War Chief
  These five Clans are brothers like the preceding four.
      Of the Cayuga Nation
      Of the Swan Tribe

1 Wăowawănaok,   Peter Wilson
   No English name   (Dyawegaathet)
                    Buffalo
       Sachem of the Cayugas
2 Ganyáh'geodoh   Jacob Seneca
                    Hahsegwih
                    Buffalo
   War Chief and runner for the preceding.
        Of the Snipe Clan.
1 Gendăohoh'   Joseph Peter
  James Young   Darhsas
    War Chief

The preceding minutes were taken at the time of the transaction recorded and are the original thereof.

ASHER WRIGHT

RECORD OF A CONDOLENCE COUNCIL
The Mourning Council for the raising of chiefs

See writing on letter & consult other interpreters for the full meaning of the rest of the song.

Very mournful and solemn " There lays a number of with their horns on!! (Emblems of power like Hebrews)

Rehearsing the ancient custom that when they come we will give them a part of the five, (as he did in the beginning of the ceremony) Here ends the first song.

This was sung by Hyah'dajiwak after Col. Silversmith had presented the five as above. Then Elijah Williams answered by alluding to the loss they had & gave a string of wampum recounted the meanings of the several strings. Thanks them for wiping away their tears & this day thank the Great Spirit that they can thus cleanse away their grief and smoke the pipe of peace together, & then replies in a simular manner. We have come and found you also mourning and we also wipe away your tears, etc. Then Hayahdijiwak informed them that Gov. Blacksnake would take the lead of the Oneida party.

Then the Seneca side started —

(Dan'a says that if any portion of the Six Nations should go off he will be .... the confederacy)

Soon after the other side led by Blacksnake and young Jones repaired to the Council House and were received there by others who were seated there. Then came waiting & for many minutes one of the Oneidas second in the march walked the floor carrying the bag of old things & sang a wailing song, being frequently answered by the other side with a long wail & once by Elijah Williams. (What must be the feeling of these men.) Again Williams wails in a high tone & then others in a suppressed note an octave below. Wms. wails again & the low note is repeated & the bag bearer goes on singing. Now the wail and low tone are responded from the other side of the house. (I believe in his song he is repeating the names of the hadiyanne & then offices) of all the Six Nations. Now he is upon the Onondagas, and now they wail again as before. Now again. Now again. Is it repeated when he is coming to the names of the dead? Or is it at the finishing of those who belong to the same tribe? The latter I think or both.

Hai! Hai gayahaagweniohgwe!

Now he is upon the Cayugas. The exclamation hai! hai! seems a mourning interjection at the beginning of every sentence, between all the simple sentences & at the close of every paragraph. (Once Wms. made a little mistake & began to wail a word or two too soon & I noticed a little smiling) Now he is upon the Senecas. And now done & he has sat down by the side of Elijah Williams & now he has risen & began to speak instead of singing & desired them all to hear & said I have spoken the old way, continue it for one benefit, let it be followed forever.

Then silence and something which seemed like a consultation for several minutes followed. At length blankets were brought and a cord stretched across the Council House so as to separate the two parties from each other and cut off communication. Then another long interval of waiting. Then a bench was brought in to the Cayuga side and the wampum laid out before the masters of ceremonies, preparatory to the songs etc. These songs are the several articles of the ancient confederacy. Art I *Hai hai! Hai hi hi haih ne* etc. closing with a semitone downward slide of the voice etc.

It was so made everything was right when altogether they did it. There a relationship was made between them. (Song and response regular always interspersed with hai etc.) A chief warrior i. e. This wampum is so called, I suppose a chief or great woman. It was by their transaction that this operation goes forward.

After singing thus far he rose and made a wonderful speech to the dead man who invented the ceremonies, stating that, we have heard from our forefathers that these Nations will become extinct but we have now come to raise up chiefs and let the people hear the laws of our forefathers. Then he sung over the same speech.

Then Elijah Williams rose & recounted what was done in ancient times something like a declaration of independence repeating the names of the nations, or the others, united in one house & of the Sachems addressing the speech to "Ak sut" i. e. the other side, I suppose regarding them as the mother as it were of the Confederacy. (Here needs more inquiry)

Speaking of Ganinduiyes who used to live at Tonawanta, called him a Long Hickory Tree. After he had finished he received four papers of tobacco from the other side of the house & (shouted as it were.)

Then the other Oneida, Peter Williams, rose and took a string of wampum & explained the duties of a chief warrior as agreed by our forefathers that he must look to all the people and take care of them all old, young, women, children, creepers & the breast etc. So it was unanimously agreed (This was the black wampum)

---

2 A short wampum signifying that when a chief is buried his grave must be leveled as soon as possible (i. e. a new chief must be chosen)

3 As soon as done always gives over to the other side & Wm. had another Comforting all who have been called to mourning by the death of Chiefs so as not to feel their loss always.

4 Now another sun breaks through the clouds and enlightened the faces which were sad before.

5 When the council five bands have been all scattered they must be gathered together again, i. e. when death has scattered the chiefs they must be collected again around the council fire and fill their places.

6 This is to comfort and pacify & satisfy the minds of the Chiefs, so that they can come together cheerfully to transact business.

7 If any of the chiefs go contrary to the law, the chiefs & chief warriors must consult the mother and follow her advice, thus, say we three of the children who are charging you.

8 We have poured water into the thirsty throats that they may be able to feel comfortable and speak freely.

9 He must carry his bag always whenever he goes anywhere he must go and stand by the corner of the fire and draw out his speech from the bag and if need be draw out his arrows also and declare war.

———

10 Requesting them to appoint men to fill the places of the dead and tell us that we may know who they are — (And then he joked a little and said we three brothers have got through, it is time to adjourn & we can get to the tavern.)

Then Hayahdajiwak rose and requested the three brothers to have patience.

The curtain was put up in the other side of the house and preparations made to send back another set of wampums to be kept by this party.

(Meanwhile the four papers of tobacco had been divided among the three brothers.)

———

Now the other side commence with a kind of a shout to call attention & a repetition of the Songs nearly as before with a wampum before them on the little bench.

(It is said the words are the same as used by the Oneidas, although sung by an Onondaga. Probably a form either compounded to suit the occasion or perhaps one of the ancient languages as it was hundreds of years ago.)

———

In the song on the other side they mentioned the death of the fathers. Now these sing that the children are alive yet (of course we are not in mourning as before). Oyehgwohdoh was the name of the founder of the confederacy.

———

Sing again we must always hear what our ancestors have said and hear the Chief Woman who can call a council of the women and tell their voice in council among the chiefs & they are obliged to listen, as to a chief (or perhaps more seriously).

———

Now the wampums are sent back beginning with the black one.

It is true as you have said we have experienced a great loss etc. & we will do as well as we can etc.

(Note certain of the wampums not brought or delayed.)

Note the peculiar manner of recitation accent on the first syllable spoken & then again on the last. I think these replies accompanying the several strings of wampum were (or mean) " Now

the word shall go forth in relation to what you have spoken."
"Our children (or younger. brothers) all which you have said is
wise. It is a good matter. You are wise. Now hear, all which
you have spoken relative to this string of wampum is wise &
we will do accordingly "—

But there is some variation in the words used according to the
particular charge given by the party.

There are two sets of wampum & every time new chiefs are
elected these are exchanged and kept till the next election by the
two parties. (Did the two parties originate in the conjunction of
the two confederacies in ancient times?)

Then he proceeded to bring forward the newly elected chiefs.

1 Shagehjowa- Joseph Silverheels a sachem. Degahnoge

You have requested us to tell us who we appoint to a co-worker
with the chiefs in accordance with the example of our forefathers
and now we have brought him forward, now know him, & know
that he is called such an one.

---

2 In the place of Robinson i. e. next to the chief warrior,
Dyăńdiṇhgwadih, Owen Black Snake, Shaweegah'.

3 Twenty Summers, John Mitten.

(It is said that they have a string of wampum for every *name*
and that these are kept so that the names may not be lost.)

4 A man not here, living at Alleghany in place of Ganāynihse,
dead James Pierce.

---

5 In the place of Gaswăhgaah, lives at Cattaraugus, Chief
Warrior.

---

6 Daandieyah, a young man at Tonawandi.

---

7 Sgaowai, Jonah — White Chief, Gahnyagoh.

---

8 Daáshihdasgowa, John Baldwin.

---

9 Hahjihnyawăy Dea. Jacob Johnson
   Walter Thompson.

10 In place of Little Johnson, (deposed) Dasnihogăhweh, Blacksmith of Tonawandi, Găoyah'gea.

11 Janiyăhs, not present. John Dicker.

12 Degaăout, John Kennedy.

13 Gasgaa-doh' John Joshua Sachem Gih'oh, in place of Two Guns, father of Henry Two Guns and Daniel, killed in battle of Chippeway—

14 Hayasajih, War Chief Gih'-oh.

Peter Johnson (Degiyah'goh) in place of old Two Guns, brother of preceding.

15 Gayáhsodoh', George Green Blanket in place of his grandfather some time since dead.

16 Waádogut, Jacob Shongo, Dep. Sachem.

17 Dagehsadĕh young man from Tonawandi.

18 Gah'nase, Abram John sub Sachem.

19 Gah'neodoh' James Spring in place of T. S. Harris deposed.

20 Ganĕhdadíhdăoh. A young man from Tonawandi.

Then Hayahdajiwak said that is all and Peter Williams begun to speak when Col. Silversmith beckoned him down and Hayahdajiwak proceeded.

21 To put in Saul Logan Gaăhgwas-Chief or head of the warriors.

22 Othaoh'dogwĕh. Jack Doxtader, a chief of the warriors.

23 In place of Jack Berry Doăsah (Sub Sachem) lives at the falls.

24 Ohăneshadekhah'. Johnny Johnny John's son Sub-Sachem.

25 Isaac Johnny John. Guardian of preceding till he grew up.

26 Peter White of Cattaraugus Hayăndagănyathah.

27 George Turkey, Do Da-yagodăhseh War chiefs.

Now he says we have finished for the Senecas, Doorkeepers.

Then Peter Williams ansd. and charged the chiefs to take care of the people and not do anything contrary to the will of the people and not to trust in their own wisdom because they are elevated not to try to get above them but to promote their benefit and conform to the laws of the Six Nations.

If it had not been for the wampums which have been preserved it would have been difficult to have filled all these offices, of those which are dead, etc. etc.

Congratulates them highly and says there is only one thing lacking i. e. we begin to feel hungry — Then sat down but soon after rose. Held a wampum in his hand and made a speech & proceeded to put Peter Wilson 1 Waowawăvaok, a Cayuga chief in place of some old man and also Wm King resigned to him his office.

2 Jacob G. Seneca was put in his second Ganyahgeodoh.

3 Joseph Satourette in place of James Young, Gĕhdăodoh. — and made a speech afterward and presented a wampum but I had no interpreter at hand & could not understand whether another chief was put in or not.

About this time the provisions were brought in.

Peter Williams sat down & soon a shout was raised or wail. I do not know what to call it. (Elevated note drawn out & then the low octave followed) & was soon after repeated. After some moments repeated again and drawn out longer than before —

Then a long interval, while there were more provisions brought in, in which the assembled seemed to get in promiscuous conversation in a low tone and many were going out and coming in as if to relieve themselves after so long a confinement.

When Hayahdajiwak began to speak and as I supposed returned thanks and compliments & gave some notices etc. and then invited them according to the rule of our forefathers to take the food before they go out that they may be strengthened & then took a wampum and presented it to this side with an exhortation never to flinch from duty nor fail to come when called to a council of this kind. We exhort you and exhort ourselves.

Then Peter Williams took the same wampum and gave an answer that we were bound together again in fellowship according to the rules of our forefathers. We three brothers on this side of as you on that side and all together and keep the council houses in order. Thus we will all do according to the wishes of our forefathers.

Then Col. Silversmith sometime and exhorted them to keep the rules and create the new tunes and alluded to the dancing of the night and told them of strangers coming from abroad wish to have anything to do with our young women we shall not withhold them but shall act according to the rule and those who do not wish to have anything to do with these things can have an opportunity to· stay away etc.

(According to the old custom of the Northern & perhaps of all other Indians)

(And let them take warning, Dea. White says in a whisper to them not to act so bad.)

Ayokhiyatgah agwus weetgat agwus weetgäh agwus.

APPENDIX D

MINUTES OF THE
COUNCIL OF THE SIX NATIONS,
UPON THE CATTARAUGUS RESERVATION[1]

Dec. 1st, 1862

Andrew Snow made a few remarks that all the chiefs take places.

Dewathaaseh made a few congratulatory remarks of thanks. According to Indian customs thanked the Great Spirit for having preserved of those as were, now represented in council. He further stated that it devolved upon the Canada Indians to proceed with the exposition of the law.

Nowineehdoh' & Ganohgaihdawih' then opened the bag of wampum.

Nowineehdoh' arose & spake saying that we are now got together. When our forefathers finished the law they in the first place would return thanks — that was passed.

As far as was proceeded they would go on with the exposition of the law — In the first place think this, we are poor it will therefore depend our brother on the other side of the fire. That was the arrangement.

Seneca Johnson then arose & spoke exhorting the people to listen.

There is a goodly number — We therefore give thanks to the whole — It was the conclusion of my brother on the other side of the fire to devolve upon me.

In the first place you were told the other day of how the law came into existance, lastly the Tuscaroras came into the confederacy. Our forefathers foretold of the destiny of the Indians at the commencement of All. council. We have now come to that.

Long House used to sing when we were in power they went on in harmony. Hense they foretold what would happen.

They have now gone to their grave.

Their footsteps are a great way off that made the law.

What I say I am responsible for

---

[1] From the original manuscript by N. H. Parker.

I will commence here. my told the truth in saying that the fire was here — Jonodagăantyewa. He was to have a stick when he could not do it he was to whoop and in less than no time the chiefs that is all true we could not go further than what was said by Hohsănehdeh'. The Long House says Six Nations — Tuscarora came in last —

5 nations made the law so & so — they were to be united by this law. If any one go through, his horns would fall off from his head. Or if any should fall another should be raised.

But if any should refuse to come back by three time — they should take them off — Thus they arranged it, as it was to last forever (the law)

It is true in what he said by saying that they should pull the tree &c.

A Brand was taken from the real fire & laid into Canada after the expedition against the Indians. The chief went across the river. They had a great council at Găndayĕh by name. They said we should put up a tha — so no one could not get one (or over (?))

They went to work — the law — here it is. We do not know all Deaigă — & sa — know it all they have it written.

Concerning the tree —

Dasdaegih to watch the west root — south root Cherochees to charge of done by Six Nations East root 7 nations St Regis took charge of the ocean — North root. Ojigweh nation took charge of.

Long House did this large wampum there at Canada.

When peace was declared Long House put fire there into Canada to watch the north region — This is why they said the great white root should grow, & we should put our heads there should anyone strike the root &c.

This is the sum and substance of what the Canadians have.

Presented a belt with 12 black crosses. the words of Otawatgaenoot the name where a great council was held all summer.

Gosiweh was the name of the chief dwah'gahah'

They was to kill the chief of the Six Nations Sawanoonoh took the law

I said just now — Canada nations presented the wampum with a dark spot in the middle represent a bowl or dish with beaver tail in it — they also made a road — also presented a wampum — I say nothing about this wampum presenting it being the british —

This belt represents the encircling of the Six Nations similar to the one at Onondaga —

Israel Jimeson wished the speaker to turn it to the females. You see they the chiefs cannot get through.

Now this belt show the 12 nations said &c.

All the nations of the Six Nations were represented.

Dish represented with beaver meat in it They should eat together — use no knife for fear they should cut and draw blood.

This belt is with hearts to represent one heart. This the to other nations.

This belt Brant & Niăondahgowa throwed into the fire representing their repentence. So all must do

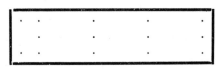

Again

I am merely what the proceedings were here and Canada 8 year council was held or called of all the nations & 4 years ago another was held of all the nations.

They were all united in the force of the law in Canada.

Now at this council many were present who were educated at that council.

As we now see here many are educated writing down the proceedings for future generations as it was the plan of our forefathers —-

At this council a vote was taken whether they should adher to the law all rose.

This is all I can do as I fear I might injure feelings as there those present who made the law

But the main fire is not here Still it was your minds here to have the exposition of law again that was right. You now can see whether you have erred from the path of this law —

The white man has found his gun — now fighting. Let it not be so with us.

— Speech ended —

Additional remarks — It was the intention of the Long House wherever a council was held to bring the fires together. We heard that you was to take from us the fire that is the reason &c.

———

I will explain concerning this belt encircling the reason
6 arrows in a bundle
— We are weak —

———

The fathers & son's repentence   this belt.

The Tuscarora said I am now at ease & therefore I shall not come to the fire.

I had a conversation with the British he asked me where I was going. I told him he said it was not right   I protect you here — I said wonderful — your law & interest are connected by iron &c. I said that those who erred were to be seen to &c.

S. S. D. Spoke   It turned upon the Tuscaroras no ·chiefs here & it may true that he mind in peace as he is now able to take of chel,—

Sigwaih'seh is here installed at Onondaga he wishes to be in the confederacy —

Now and then you know they are divided still he will always be present & hopes that the other party will come to repentance —

Thomas Jimeson

Spoke & said he was happy to my friends — I wish to explain — before the sale of lands I used to talk with my friends old Canada. I thought I would try to live a different life — I bought lands — pay taxes — White man collected taxes first it was small 2d year I went & paid taxes again pd a little more than $20 — Path Master came next increased a little every year — came up to $40 — & 50 days roads Taxes. finally they petitioned for a cor- poration about 2 year it went through —City tax came in collector posted bills to pay on 1st of Oct. quite high about $110. Taxes must be pd or land sold — on the next Aug I pd again a little & on 1st of Dec since 5 year for 2 years I paid $50.— then officers changed time came. Tax fell off also on county Tax.

George Buck spoke in brief

The principal business of the day has gone by — it was con- cluded that the exposition of the law be made —

The council was called some time since   Now you this day. You all Six Na have heard what was said by the keepers of the fire.

Both parties were here from Canada & here. you have heard all — ädwadegonih onäh

Detwathaahseh' spoke and said I will tell what happened where we came from — It was done in council. Sanctioned by Sardoha- hoh' Now I will tell about the chief. All claim him & for a reason — how we are to live encircling belt. I would say this is the same Six Nations joined in hands in the middle the house.

It is therefore important should he go through or over or go in ground to come out & some to do for the distruction of chil —

Again when he was chief he attended to interest of the land
not to sell — also the interest of women chil — not to make chil.—
or people cry — therefore his horns must fall on other nations west
did not look to us — heads will roll

Chiefs skin must be thick & have patience.

Warriors beyond the circle & women (?) next therefore 3
times &c. chiefs must consider their (?) warriors then women

Then all shall come together to consider.

Again how a chief shall speak chiefs shall have control of Deaths
of chiefs to sympathize with such family.

Chief shall hold office for life or good behavior.

Again we see our Canada friend. We see here the fire — the
minds seems the same concerning the law. So you ought to do.
I shall adher to it — Speech closed.

Wish to Amend

How the council should never speak of dividing land by dis-
banding the Na —

Again

When white man became brothers they traded land. Chiefs
said All lands sold should be in common.

Nowineedoh' to speak for or in behalf of the chiefs from abroad.

listen brothers

You see us here Onondagas —All is exposed the law in full this
day & all we can do —

You see us chiefs here this all they can do —

Their minds is, we have all construed the law should a council
be called at some other place Then you may have the whole.

Again this thing is come to pass according to your mind —

It now devolve upon you to consider We all see our troubles —
some day — it is therefore you should consider carefully.

How shall we do that our chil shall & have many days —
Therefore you consider carefully in regard to this matter.

This much we say in brief — I would say again you are wise
& you can see what to do.

Speech ended

Little Joe spoke

We have heard all the law exposed regard to what has been
said. We have no time now tomorrow we will tell you.

Dec. 2d 1862

Council of the Six Nations resumed its deliberation by opening
remarks of John Cook according to the custom of such councils —

Thanking the Great Spirit in preserving the lives of all now present & those who have come from abroad —

The council therefore was ready to proceed to *business.*

John Cook again spoke

saying his friends had now come from Canada as they were to do by and by.

It is this, that each tribe in N. Y. speak for themselves — to commune in order. When after all have spoken a certain one will be appointed to speak for the whole —

Tonawandas to council first, then Alle. then Catt — They were then ordered to take their accustomed seats

Tonawandas

Jubez Ground spoke as follows:

That it was the duty in all such gatherings to exchange words of thanks before proceeding to business.

It was announced that we were the first to explain our troubles in council — We have divided. Some of us thought we were not going right — Blksmith and Jemmy Johnson were strait till their death Had they been living it would not have been so —

The other side tells us that we have erred because we would not comply with the law. So we said to them

Hence the party thought it best to have a council called to hear the exposition of the law — Our party is strong in the faith of the law.

You understand how we stand We are divided. We stand on the Six Na law & will stand by it — This is the feeling of our party. So you understand.

They have firm reliance on the law —

Now we tell how large our party is who *will* adher to the law 282.

We were told that belt was left for repentance — We have none to leave as they not believe they have erred.

The above is the actual number who voluntarily wished to on our side joined us without threats. Thus much we explain to you and our position *in brief*

Seneca Johnson said

The No of your party as I understand is 282. Now I ask the whole No at Ton

Isaac Doctor said that we do not know exactly but the other side has the majority — our party was once over 300 but fell off to the other side by threats, such as you will have no more goods & money if you keep the other side & you go to Kansas.

Alle —

Isaac Halftown —

I am appointed to speak for Alle & I will be brief as respects the condition of our people — we have what the Ton have said

They say that the other side has the majority how they (?) will do in that case I do not know.

The Alle would be glad to get back

They expect to take their band and explain to those left at home

Daniel Two Guns said that he speaks for the old folks — they have not let go the law

They will in the first place have to talk with the Pres.   The Pres. have erred from the contract

In respect to our party we have a party but cannot say how many

So much in brief.   Daniel 2 guns added

I said we do not know but we will go to work and see & let you know how many wish to adher to the Six Nations Law.

Isaac Halftown spoke again saying (the Alle) we will take hold of it.

I now ask concerning the wampum belt of repentance.   You said &c

We Catt & Alle have erred we got white man law.

Shall we put the belt there too?

This is what I wish to know.

Little Joe said the thing today was going on what was to happen. The Cayugas also would have the privilege to speak he has erred it therefore may be of some help to those who have erred to hear them speak.

Joseph Isaac explained that they were ready to speak as soon

Seneca Johnson:

In reference to the question, let my brothers have patience until we answer to all that may be said.

Dr Wilson:

We will inform you how we feel we are much enlightened greatly in the exposition of the law — we therefore thank you — Now in reference to another matter, the white man long ago turned the Indians mind —

Concerning the arrows.   This is to be of one mind — we come from the west through the white man's advice we now have small pieces of land.   It now depends on you old folks to determine what to do —

Concerning the fires &c the white man has mixed his laws in criminal cases &c   Then went on to relate the condition of Catt & Alle Reservations from the commencement up to this time, but still the idea is (our idea) that the old fellows are still chiefs in Six Nations Council —

. Our idea is that there is lack in the exposition of the law. Still we hope that at some future time the whole will come together & still their faith remained the same relying on the law of the Six Nations

Adjourned to eat —

John Cook spoke for women

Jisgoh'goh gave notice who was to make answer —

Silverman spoke

Ganyodioyoh

Dewathaah'sech' said that our destruction is being brought about by the white man

In regard to murder and theft the laws of the white man has jurisdiction also in case of liquor Laws by U. S. made

Our condition is this Our old chiefs beg laws for the protection of timber.

_____

CERTAIN IROQUOIS TREE MYTHS AND SYMBOLS[1]

A student of Iroquoian folklore, ceremony, or history will note the many striking instances in which sacred or symbolic trees are mentioned. One finds allusions to such trees not only in the myths and traditions that have long been known to literature, and in the speeches of Iroquois chiefs in council with the French and English colonists, but also in the more recently discovered wampum codes and in the rituals of the folk-cults.

There are many references to the " tree of peace " in the colonial documents on Indian relations. Cadwallader Colden, for example, quotes the reply of the Mohawk chief to Lord Effingham in July 1684. The Mohawk agreed to the proposals for peace and their spokesman said: " We now plant a Tree who's tops will reach the sun, and its Branches spread far abroad, so that it shall be seen afar off; and we shall shelter ourselves under it, and live in Peace, without molestation." (Gives two beavers.)[2]

In a footnote Colden says that the Five Nations always express peace under the metaphor of a tree. Indeed, in the speech, a part of which is quoted above, the peace tree is mentioned several times.

In Garangula's reply to De la Barre, as recorded by Lahontan, are other references to the " tree." In his " harangue " Garangula said:

" We fell upon the Illinese and the Oumamis, because they cut down the Trees of Peace. . ." " The Tsonontouans, Gayogouans, Onnotagues, Onnoyoutes and Agnies declare that they interred the Axe at Cataracuoy in the Presence of your Predecessor the very Center of the Fort; and planted the Tree of Peace in the same place; 'twas then stipulated that the Fort should be used as a Place of Retreat for Merchants, and not as a Refuge for Soldiers. You ought to take care that so great a number of Militial Men as we now see . . . do not stifle and choke the Tree of Peace . . . it must needs be of pernicious Consequences to stop its Growth and hinder it to shade both your Country and ours with its Leaves." [3]

The examples cited above are only a few of many that might be quoted to show how commonly the Iroquois mentioned the peace

_____

[1] A. C. Parker; an extract from Amer. Anthropologist, v. 14, No. 4, 1912.
[2] Colden, History of the Five Nations, reprint, p. 58, New York, 1866.
[3] Lahontan, Voyages, v. 1, p. 42. London, 1735.

tree. There are also references to the tree that was uprooted " to afford a cavity in which to bury all weapons of war," the tree being replanted as a memorial.

In the Iroquoian myth, whether Cherokee, Huron, Wyandot, Seneca or Mohawk, the " tree of the upper world " is mentioned, though the character of the tree differs according to the tribe and sometimes according to the myth-teller.

Before the formation of the lower or earth world the Wyandot tell of the upper or sky world and of the " big chief " whose daughter became strangely ill.[1] The chief instructs his daughter to " dig up the wild apple tree; what will cure her she can pluck from among its roots." David Boyle[2] wondered why the apple tree was called " wild " but that the narrator meant wild-apple and not wild apple is shown by the fact that in some versions the Seneca call the tree the crab-apple. The native apple tree with its small fruit was intended by the Indian myth-teller, who knew also of the cultivated apple and took the simplest way to differentiate the two.

With the Seneca this tree is described more fully. In manuscript left by Mrs Asher Wright, the aged missionary to the Seneca, I find the cosmologic myth as related to her by Esquire Johnson, a Seneca, in 1870. Mrs Wright and her husband understood the Seneca language perfectly and published a mission magazine in that tongue as early as 1838. Her translation of Johnson's myth should therefore be considered authentic. She wrote :

" There was a vast expanse of water. . . . Above it was the great blue arch of air but no signs of anything solid. . . . In the clear sky was an unseen floating island sufficiently firm to allow trees to grow upon it, and there were men-beings there. There was one great chief who gave the law to all the Ongweh or beings on the island. In the center of the island there grew a tree so tall that no one of the beings who lived there could see the top. On its branches flowers and fruit hung all the year round. The beings who lived on the island used to come to the tree and eat the fruit and smell the sweet perfume of the flowers. On one occasion the chief desired that the tree be pulled up. The great chief was called to look at the great pit which was to be seen where the tree had stood."

The story continues with the usual description of how the sky-mother was pushed into the hole in the sky and fell upon the wings of the waterfowl who placed her on the turtle's back. After this mention of the celestial tree in the same manuscript is the story of

[2] Connelley, W. E., Wyandot Folk Lore. Topeka, 1889.
[2] Boyle, The Iroquois, in Archeological Report of Ontario for 1905, p. 147.

the central world-tree. After the birth of the twins, Light One and Toadlike (or dark) One, the Light One, also known as Good-minded, noticing that there was no light, created the "tree of light." This was a great tree having at its topmost branch a great ball of light. At this time the sun had not been created. It is significant, as will appear later, that the Good-minded made his tree of light one that brought forth flowers from every branch. After he had continued experimenting and improving the earth, " he made a new light and hung it on the neck of a being, and he called the new light Gaagwaa (ga gwa) and instructed its bearer to run his course daily in the heavens." Shortly after he is said to have " dug up the tree of light, and looking into the pool of water in which the stump (trunk) had grown, he saw the reflection of his own face and thereupon conceived the idea of creating Ongwe and made them both a man and a woman."

The central world-tree is found also in Delaware mythology, though so far as I can discover it is not called the tree of light. The Journal of Dankers and Slyter[1] records the story of creation as heard from the Lenape of New Jersey in 1679. All things came from a tortoise, the Indians told them. " It had brought forth the world, and in the middle of its back had sprung a tree upon whose branches men had grown."[2] This relation between men and the tree is interesting in comparison with the Iroquois myth, as it is also conceived to be the central world-tree. Both the Lenape and the Iroquois ideas are symbolic and those who delight in flights of imagination might draw much from both.

The Seneca world-tree is described elsewhere in my notes as a tree whose branches pierce the sky and whose roots extend to the waters of the underworld. This tree is mentioned in various cere-monial rites of the Iroquois. With the False Face Company, Hadigo sa sho o, for example, the Great Face, chief of all the False Faces, is said to be the invisible giant that guards the world tree (gain-dowa ne). He rubs his turtle-shell rattle upon it to obtain its power, and this he imparts to all the visible false faces worn by the com-pany. In visible token of this belief the members of the company rub their turtle rattles on pine-tree trunks, believing that thereby they become imbued with both the earth power and the sky power. In this use of the turtle-shell rattle there is perhaps a recognition of

---

[1] Journal of Voyage to New York in 1679–80, by Jasper Dankers and Peter Slyter. translated in Trans. L. I. Hist. Soc., v. I, 1867.
[2] With the New England Indians the idea was held that men were found by Glooskap in a hole by an arrow which he had shot into an ash tree.

the connection between the turtle and the world-tree that grows upon the primal turtle's back.

In the prologue of the Wampum Code of the Five Nations Confederacy we again find references to a symbolic "great tree." In the code of Dekanawide, the Iroquois culture hero exclaims:

"I am Dekanawide, and with the Five Nations' confederate lords (rodiyaner) I plant the Tree of the Great Peace. I plant it in your territory, Adodarho and the Onondaga nation, in the territory of you who are Fire Keepers.

"I name the tree the Tree of the Great Long Leaves. Under the shade of this Tree of Peace we spread the soft, feathery down of the globe thistle, there beneath the spreading branches of the Tree of Peace."

In the second "law" of the code, the four roots of the "tree" are described, and the law-giver says:

"If any individual or any nation outside of the Five Nations shall obey the laws of the Great Peace and make known their disposition to the lords of the confederacy, they may trace the roots of the tree, and if their minds are clean and obedient . . . they shall be welcome to take shelter beneath the Tree of the Long Leaves.

"We place in the top of the Tree of the Long Leaves an Eagle who is able to see afar; . . . he will warn the people."

In another place is the following:

"I, Dekanawide, and the union lords now uproot the tallest pine tree and into the cavity thereby made we cast all weapons of war. Into the depths of the earth, down into the deep underearth currents of water flowing to unknown regions we cast all the weapons of strife. We bury them from sight and we plant again the tree. Thus shall the Great Peace, Kaye narhe ko wa, be established."

These laws and figures of speech are evidently those which the Iroquois speakers had in mind when addressing "peace councils" with the whites.

Symbolic trees appear not only in Iroquois history, mythology, and folk beliefs, but also in their decorative art. The numerous decorative forms of trees embroidered in moose hair and porcupine quills by the eastern Algonquians, by the Hurons, and by the Iroquois appear to be attempts to represent the world-tree and the celestial tree, in some cases, with "all manner of fruits and flowers." Many, if not most, of the modern descendants of the old-time Indians, who copy these old designs, have forgotten their meanings, and some have even invented new explanations. A few of the more conservative, however, still remember the true meanings of their designs and from these much of interest has been learned.

Plate 2

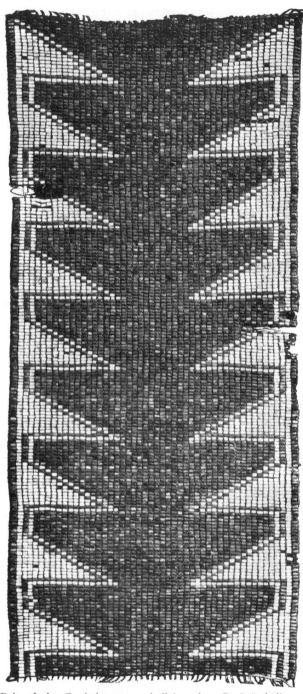

Great Belt of the Confederacy symbolizing the Gayänĕsshä''gowä as an
ever growing tree

Plate 3

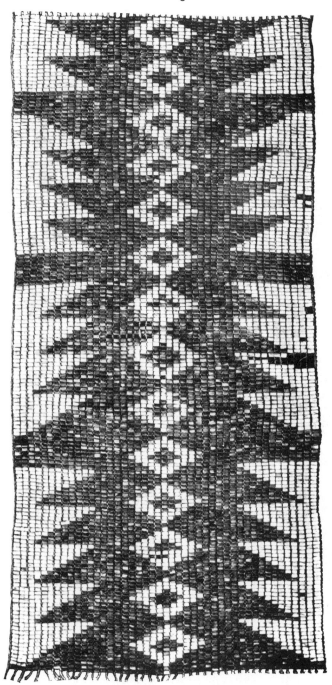

Belt of the covenant. Displayed by the speaker of the confederate council.

Plate 4

1   2

1 Nomination belt used to confirm the nomination of the civil chiefs
2 Welcome belt used in welcoming delegates

Plate 5

Reciting the Laws of the Confederacy

From an engraving in Lafitau's, Moeurs des Sauvages Ameriquains, published in 1724

Plate 6

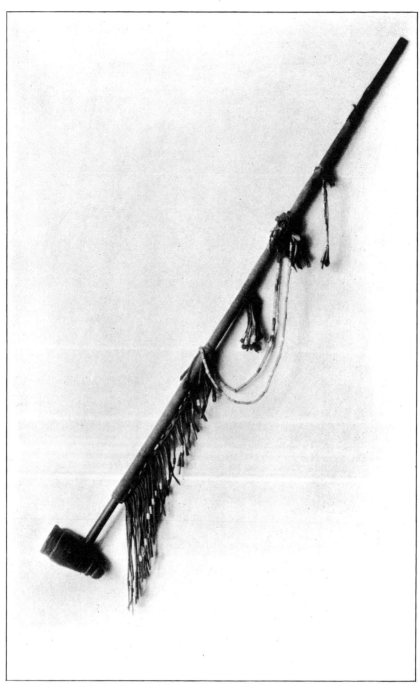

Council pipe used in the ceremonies of raising a civil chief. This pipe was last owned by Albert Cusick, who presented it to the State Museum in 1911.

Plate 7

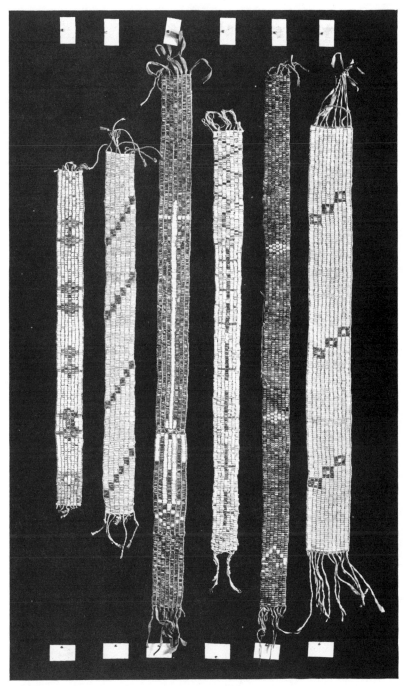

Commemoration belts of the Five Nations recording events and alliances

Plate 8

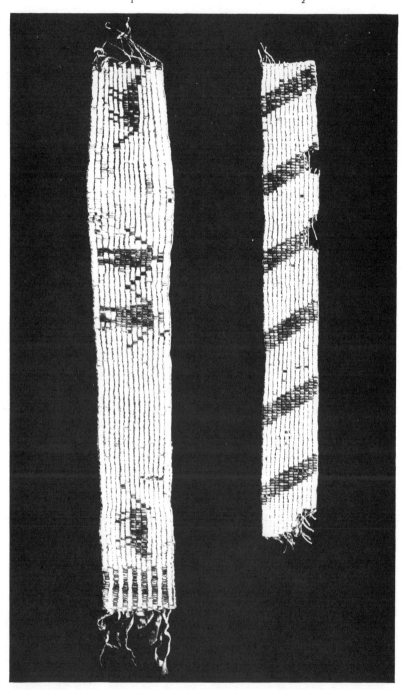

1 Wolf clan belt said to represent a pact of the Mohawk with the French
2 Tuscarora entrance belt

INDEX

"It is fortunate that Parker's reputation as an ethnologist does not rest on the two reviews which greeted the Constitution in succeeding years in the *American Anthropologist*." Thus writes Iroquoianist W N Fenton[1] of the two reviews of "the Constitution of the Five Nations" presented here for the first time since their publications in 1916, 1917. Following these is Parker's 1918 reply. Recently, the Grand Council of the Confederacy has expressed its concern over the various "Constitutions" within Iroquoia and is now working towards the preparation of an authorized oral and written text.

WGS

(431) *BOOK REVIEWS*

The Constitution of the Five Nations. ARTHUR C. PARKER. Albany: The University of the State of New York, 1916 (New York State Museum Bulletin, No. 184). 158 pp. and map.

Mr. Parker's latest contribution to Iroquoian ethnology comprises two principal documents and a number of minor sketches. Of these a brief version of the Hiawatha tradition (pp. 114-119) and the Appendix A: The Passamaquoddy Wampum Records (pp. 119-126) are of some interest. The Appendices B, C and D, on the other hand, contain material, in part previously published, of so superficial and fragmentary a character that the printing or reprinting of it could hardly be regarded as justifiable. The subjects are: Sketches of an Indian Council, 1846 (pp. 126-133); Minutes of the Six Nations Council of 1839 (pp. 133-144); and Minutes of the Council of the Six Nations, upon the Cattaraugus Reservation (pp. 144-152). There is finally an Appendix E, an extract from Mr. Parker's valuable article in the *American Anthropologist* (Vol. 14, No. 4, 1912) on "Certain Iroquois Tree Myths and Symbols."

The two principal sections of the work are of very considerable interest. They constitute what Mr. Parker calls "The Constitution of the Five Nations" or "The Iroquois Book of the Great Law," and are based on two manuscripts found by Mr. Parker in the Six Nations Reservation, Ontario, Canada, in 1910. The first manuscript was prepared by Seth Newhouse, a Mohawk (to be referred to as MS. 1), the second was compiled by some of the representative chiefs of the Six Nations Council, in 1900 (to be referred to as MS. 2). MS. 1 comprises an enumeration of the "Conferedate Iroquois Laws" somewhat incoherently intertwined with a version of the Deganawída legend. MS. 2 gives the fullest version of the legend recorded to date.

One notes with surprise the absence of reference to previous appearance in print of MS. 2. On May 16, 1911, Mr. Duncan C. Scott presented the identical account to the Royal Society of Canada. The legend, entitled "Traditional History of the Confederacy of the Six Nations," appeared in the *Transactions of the Society*, Third Series (1911), Vol. 5, Section 2, pp. 195-246. The two publications, Mr. Scott's and Mr. Parker's, seem to be identical

---

[1] Fenton, W.N., introduction to *Parker on the Iroquois*, pp 44-46, Syracuse University Press, 1968.

in all respects except that in Mr. Scott's publication an account of the ceremony called "At the Wood's (432) Edge" is given, which is taken from Hale's *Iroquois Book of Rites*. As Mr. Scott's publication could not have escaped the notice of Mr. Parker, the absence of any reference must be due to a regrettable oversight.

A comparison of MS. 1 and MS. 2 brings out some interesting points. With reference to the election of a new chief MS. 2 reads:—

> Then Deganawideh further said: "I now transfer and set over *to the women*[1] who have the lordships' title vested in them, that they shall in the future have the power to appoint the successors from time to time to fill vacancies caused by death or removals from whatever cause" (p. 97).

The statement in MS. 1 is much more explicit. We read:—

> When a Lordship title becomes vacant through death or other cause, the Royaneh women of the clan in which the title is hereditary shall hold a council and shall choose one from among their sons to fill the office made vacant. Such a candidate shall not be the father of any Confederate Lord. If the choice is unanimous the name is referred to *the men relatives of the clan. If they should disapprove* it shall be their duty to *select a candidate from among their own number.* If then *the men and women are unable to decide* which of the two candidates shall be named, then the matter shall be referred to the Confederate Lords in the clan. They shall decide which candidate shall be named. If *the men and the women* agree to a candidate his name shall be referred to the sister clans for confirmation. If the sister clans confirm the choice, they shall refer their action to their Confederate Lords who shall ratify the choice and present it to their cousin Lords, and if the cousin Lords confirm the name then the candidate shall be installed by the proper ceremony for the conferring of Lordship titles (p. 44).

We note then that whereas in MS. 2 the matter of electing a new chief is simply referred to the women of the proper clan and maternal family[2], in MS. 1 the men of the clan are introduced; they must ratify in any case, and they may have to select the candidate from among themselves. Provision is also made in MS. 1 for various possibilities of disagreement.

There is a difference also between the two MSS. with reference to the deposition of a chief. MS. 2 reads:—

> If a Lord is guilty of unwarrantably opposing the object of decisions of the Council and in that his own erroneous will in these matters be carried out, he shall be approached and admonished *by the chief matron of his family and clan* to desist from such evil practices and she shall urge him to come back and act in harmony with his brother lords.
>
> (433) If the lord refuses to comply with the request of the chief matron of his family and clan and still persists in his evil practices of unwarrantably opposing his brother lords, then *a warrior of his family and clan* will also approach him and admonish him to desist from pursuing his evil course.
>
> If the lord still refuses to listen and obey, then *the chief matron and warrior* shall go together to the [chief?] warrior and they shall inform him that they have admonished their lord and he refused to obey. Then *the chief warrior* will arise and go there to the lord and will say to him: "Your nephew and niece have admonished you to desist from your evil course, and you have refused to

---

[1] This and subsequent italics are mine.

[2] While the old version of the Deganawida legend does not say any more than that, it has of course been a matter of well-known practice to refer the women's candidate for ratification first to the chiefs of the sister clans of the tribe, then to those of the cousin clans, and finally to the chiefs of the confederacy in general session.

obey." Then the chief warrior will say: "I will now admonish you for the last time and if you continue to resist, refuse to accede and disobey this request, then your duties as lord of our family and clan will cease, and I shall take the deer's horns from off your head, and with a broad-edged stone axe I shall cut down the tree" (meaning that he shall be deposed from his position as lord or chief of the confederacy). Then, if the lord merits dismissal, *the chief warrior shall hand back the deer's horns* (the emblem of power) of the deposed lord *to the chief matron* of the family or clan.

Whenever it occurs that a lord is thus deposed, then *the chief matron shall select and appoint another warrior* of her family or clan and crown him with the deer's horns and *thus a new lord shall be created in the place of the one deposed* (pp. 106-7).

The corresponding section in MS. 1 differs appreciably:—

If at any time it shall be manifest that a Confederate Lord has not in mind the welfare of the people or disobeys the rules of this Great Law, *the men or the women of the Confederacy, or both jointly,* shall come to the Council and upbraid the erring Lord through his War Chief. If the complaint of the people through the War Chief is not heeded the first time it shall be uttered again and then if no attention is given a third complaint and warning shall be given. If the Lord is still contumacious the matter shall go to the *council of War Chiefs. The War Chiefs* shall then divest the erring Lord of his title by order of *the women* in whom the titleship is vested. When the Lord is deposed *the women* shall notify the Confederate Lords through their War Chief, and the Confederate Lords shall sanction the act. *The women* will then select another of their sons as a candidate and the Lords shall elect him. Then shall the chosen one be installed *by the Installation Ceremony* (p. 34).

Thus whereas in MS. 2 the matron, a warrior, and the warrior chief, are the only actors; in MS. 1 there is no reference to the matron as such, instead we find the men and women of the Confederacy, the women of the clan, and a council of war chiefs. Moreover, whereas in MS. 1 the new appointee, having been duly ratified by the chiefs, is installed in the regular ceremonial fashion; the matron of MS. 2 is the sole agent in this connection: the man she selects in place of the deposed chief, becomes chief without the usual ceremonials.

In addition to this, MS. 1 contains an important provision to which there is no parallel in MS. 2:—

(434) In case *a part or all the Lords pursue a course not vouched for by the people* and heed not the third warning of their women relatives, then the matron shall be taken to *the General Council of the women of the Five Nations.* If the Lords notified and warned three times fail to heed, then the case falls into the hands of *the men of the Five Nations.* The War Chiefs shall then, by right of such power and authority, enter the open council to warn the Lord or Lords to return from their wrong course. If the Lords heed the warning they shall say, "we will reply to-morrow." If then an answer is returned in favor of justice and in accord with this Great Law, then the Lords shall individually pledge themselves again by again furnishing the necessary shells for the pledge. Then shall the War Chief or Chiefs exhort the Lords urging them to be just and true.

Should it happen that the Lords refuse to heed the third warning, then two courses are open: *either the men may decide in their council to depose the Lord or Lords or to club them to death with war clubs.* Should they in their council decide to take the first course the War Chief shall address the Lord or Lords, saying: "Since you the Lords of the Five Nations have refused to return to the procedure of the Constitution, we now declare your seats vacant, we take off your horns, the token of your Lordship, and others shall be chosen and installed in your seats therefore vacate your seats."

Should the men in their council adopt the second course, the War Chief shall order his men to enter the council, to take positions beside the Lords, sitting between them wherever possible. When this is accomplished the War Chief holding in his outstretched hands a bunch of black wampum strings shall say to the erring Lords: "So now, Lords of the Five United Nations, harken to these last words from your men. You have not heeded the warnings of the women relatives, you have not heeded the warnings of the General Council of women and you have not heeded the warnings of the men of the nations, all urging you to return to the right course of action. Since you are determined to resist and to withhold justice from your people there is only one course for us to adopt." At this point the War Chief shall let drop the bunch of black wampum and the men shall spring to their feet and club the erring Lords to death. Any erring Lord may submit before the War Chief lets fall the black wampum. Then his execution is withheld (pp. 46-7).

In this passage the startling assumption is made that part or even all of the chiefs may prove unfaithful to the principles of the League; a new body, the General Council of women of the Five Nations, is introduced; the men again figure prominently; while the war chief is invested with powers, derived from the authority of the men, which seem to run counter both to the letter and the spirit of the Iroquois League as portrayed in MS. 2.

If a lord is found guilty of wilful murder, [according to MS. 2] he shall be deposed without the warning (as shall be provided for later on) by the lords of (435) the confederacy, and his horns (emblem of power) shall be handed back to the chief matron of his family and clan (p. 106).

MS. 1, on the other hand, decrees that:—

If a Lord of the Confederacy of the Five Nations should commit murder the other Lords of the Nation shall assemble at the place where the corpse lies and prepare to depose the criminal Lord. If it is impossible to meet at the scene of the crime the Lords shall discuss the matter at the next Council of their nation and request their War Chief to depose the Lord guilty of crime, to "bury" his women relatives and to transfer the Lordship title to a sister family (p. 35).

Thus the punishment of the chief is in MS. 2 a confederate function, in MS. 1 a tribal or national one; moreover, whereas in MS. 2 the guilty chief alone suffers, according to MS. 1 the entire maternal family is involved, and the chieftainship is transferred to another family.

There is, finally, still another provision in MS. 1 to which no parallel can be found in MS. 2:—

If any of the Royaneh women, heirs of the titleship, shall wilfully withhold a Lordship or other title and refuse to bestow it, or if such heirs abandon, forsake or despise their heritage, then shall such women be deemed buried and their family extinct. The titleship shall then revert to a sister family or clan upon application and complaint. The Lords of the Confederacy shall elect the family or clan which shall in future hold the title (p. 43).

Here MS. 1 provides for a contingency which has not been foreseen by the framers of MS. 2.

The main features, then, which differentiate MS. 1 from MS. 2 are these: (1) The family matron does not appear as a leading figure; (2) the men of the clan and League participate directly in the election and deposition of chiefs; and (3) in certain instances the supreme authority rests with the men; (4) the authority of the War Chiefs is great and their functions all important; (5) there is less hesitancy about depriving a maternal family of its hereditary chieftainship; (6) various instances of disagreement, faithlessness to the League and neglect of duty are guarded against; (7) certain statements reflect confused social conditions, such, for instance, as the vague reference to "the men and the women of the Confederacy"; (8) murder, finally, is treated with greater severity.

An analysis of the above features can leave no doubt that MS. 1 reflects Iroquois society at a much later stage in its development than is the case in MS. 2. The impression, in fact, derived from a study of MS. 1 is one of ancient Iroquois society distorted by abnormal social conditions and the intrusion of modern traits. This, of course, does not in any way detract from the value of the document, which, in fact, becomes of (436) peculiar interest as material for a study of the breakdown of a highly complex and coherent socio-political system, under the stress of modern conditions. It must be kept in mind, however, that whereas MS. 2 represents an exceedingly old traditional record, but weakly rationalized by the intrusion of later interpretations and additions; MS. 1, as an integral code, cannot justly be regarded as a genuine native product. It is, without doubt, based on a wide acquaintance, on the part of the compiler, with the beliefs, attitudes, and practices of the confederated Iroquois, but this native material has been welded into a highly formal and rationalized document, the product of a sophisticated mind, and, as such, conspicuously un-Indian in character. In a sense, then, "The Constitution of the Five Nations" is a figment. It does not exist. For, apart from the Legend of Deganawida, the Indians of the Iroquois League had no constitution, either written or unwritten.

A.A. Goldenweiser
American Anthropologist, (New Series)
Vol. 18, No. 3, 1916, pp. 431-436

(429)

The Constitution of the Five Nations. ARTHUR C. PARKER. (New York State Museum Bulletin, No. 184, Albany, N.Y.: April 1, 1916).

Traditional History of The Confederacy of The Six Nations. DUNCAN CAMPBELL SCOTT, F.R.S.C. (Royal Society of Canada, Proceedings and Transactions, 3rd Series, vol. V., Ottawa, Canada, 1912, Section 11, 195-246 pp.).

Civil, Religious and Mourning Councils and Ceremonies of Adoption of the New York Indians. REV. WILLIAM M. BEAUCHAMP. (New York State Museum Bulletin, No. 113, Albany, N.Y., June, 1907).

These three publications are considered here together because they deal with a common topic — the League of the Iroquois. They severally repeat old errors and so diffuse them broadcast under the patronage of learned institutions, and so the following strictures are made on the untrustworthy character of much of their contents, lest the unwary student be led into accepting misinformation for truth.

It must be noted that the second publication also forms a part of the contents of the first, in which the fact of its separate publication by Mr. Duncan Campbell Scott is not mentioned by the editor.

(430) The third publication is interesting chiefly as compilation of texts, notes, comments and quotations rather than as a serious study and analysis of the complex institutions mentioned in the title of the work. Thus, for example, a long list of etymologies is quoted from Morgan, although a large majority of them are worthless; the texts and translations cited from Hale are not revised and corrected, although in very many instances they are misleading or erroneous. The want of accurate knowledge of the languages of the peoples to which the work refers made Dr. Beauchamp the victim of the palpable blunders in translation which his chief informant, the Rev. Albert Cusick, was prone to make.

Mr. Parker tells us that two main manuscripts form the basis of his publication. He fails, however, to point out the value of either manuscript, or to explain the significance of the serious conflict of statements of essential facts or events between the two; we should have been told the essential fact that the document prepared by the Committee of Chiefs of the Six Nations was prepared as a substitute for the Newhouse document, which the chiefs in council had thrice rejected as faulty in arrangement and erroneous or spurious in many of its statements. We are told that these two manuscripts were "discovered" in 1910 on the Six Nations reserve, Ontario, Canada; it is however a fact that the Newhouse "Constitution," although in much briefer form, had been known since 1880, for in that year a copy of it had been left by its compiler on the Cattaraugus reservation for safe-keeping; the document of the chiefs of the Six Nations was prepared in the early spring of 1900 while the present writer was a guest of the late chief John Arthur Gibson, one of the Committee of Chiefs.

Again, Mr. Parker should have explained also that this document of the Committee of Chiefs, supplemented, however, by a portion of the native matter appearing in Hale's *The Iroquois Book of Rites*, 1883, had been published as early as 1912, by Duncan C. Scott, F.R.S.C., in the *Proceedings and Transactions of the Royal Society of Canada* as noted above.

The following comments deal chiefly with the contents of Bulletin 184, by Mr. Parker. The statement that Rev. Albert Cusick was

> employed for more than a month in correcting the Newhouse manuscript until he believed the form in which it is now presented fairly correct and at least as accurate as a free translation could be made

is contrary to the facts. The Newhouse manuscript has appeared in a number of varying versions, which were one and all originally recorded in the English language. But in 1897-8 the present writer induced Mr. Newhouse to undertake with him the translation of the best of these, (431) after recasting and rewriting certain portions of the various sections. This work was undertaken in order to preserve in Mohawk terms of juridical, governmental, and of ritualistic import, but not for publication in the material as found. So the matter of this document is in no accepted sense a "free translation" of a native text. It is indeed unfortunate that the translated matter quoted by Dr. Beauchamp and Mr. Duncan from Hale's *Iroquois Book of Rites* should have been used without radical and essential corrections in the forms and translations of vital portions of the Ritual, for the renderings of entire sections are faulty and misleading, and often quite contrary to the intent of the originals.

These editors were apparently quite unaware of the serious blunders in translation and statement they were unconsciously diffusing as sources of further error. A specimen of the untrustworthy character of much of the material in question may be cited here. The provision for a private visit of condolence and sympathy to the death-lodge three days after the burial the body of a dead chief (Duncan, *op. cit.*, Parker, *op. cit.*, 109) is to the point; this visit is to be made by a delegation from the "cousin" sisterhood of tribes, for the purpose of comforting the bereaved family and kindred with the substance of *eleven* (not *thirteen*) of the Fourteen Themes (Ne' Adondakshah) of the Requickening Address; what follows is intended to be the caption of this hearthside address and is in the words following:

> The beginning of the Condolence Ceremony used immediately after the death of a chief (or Lord) and which is subsequently followed by the thirteen ceremony called 'At the Wood's Edge.'

It is clear that the thirteen sections of the address cited here are for the formal public function and so are not at all in the form suitable for use at the private lodge hearthside. Besides there is no such thing as a thirteen Ceremony called "At the Wood's Edge." Mr. Parker quotes eleven strings of wampum, although he cites thirteen sections just as does Mr. Duncan; but the interpolated remarks in section 3, to wit:

> The foregoing part of the Condoling Ceremony is to be performed outside of the place of meeting. Then the bereaved will appoint two of their chief warriors to conduct the four brothers into the place of meeting,

should have been a loud hint to the editors that they were quoting wrong matter. This is a confusion of a private visit with a public function. Careless proofreading permitted an undue number of inexcusable misprints to appear. Skanawatih's (9 and 13) or Skanawita's (30) is evidently (432) printed for Dekanawida's. Abbreviations share in these errors of proofreading; *SPW* (pp. 52, 53, 54 and elsewhere) evidently should be *LPW*. Too much credence is placed in the authenticity of the so-called Passamaquoddy wampum traditions, which are of course concerned with the activities of the "Iroquois" settled at Caughnawaga and elsewhere on the St. Lawrence, Canada, and so have little or no bearing on the early history of the "Five Nations" of New York.

The number of federal chiefs was not fixed at fifty. This is an unhistorical number which is known only within the last century; it arose from a misinterpreted tradition concerning the episode in which one Bearfoot was a chief figure. The first traditionally authentic number is 47, to which in later times were added two Seneca chiefs, making 49 as the highest authentic roll of offical titles of federal chiefs. Authentic tradition is silent as to the original number. It is usually found by adding together the several tribal lists.

It is not traditional nor historical to say that for "many generations" the knowledge of "each law or regulation" of the League had been "preserved" by means of "a collection of wampum belts and strings," as the traditions published along with this statement clearly show, for these inform us that the founders of the League knew apparently little, if anything symbolic, about wampum, but rather something definite about "elderberry twigs" and "quills." Hence, the further statement (p. 8) that "Several of the wampum belts in the New York State Museum are Constitutional belts or memorials" seems indefensible, if it is desired to suggest that they were used by the founders of the League. Dr. Beauchamp (*New York State Museum Bulletin*, No. 41, vol. 8) has reached conclusions in accord with this remark.

The statements on page 13 concerning the use of the word "Longhouse" are based on misinformation and superficial observation. In no Iroquois tongue does the native name of the League signify "Longhouse." There is, therefore, never any confusion between the native names for the "Long House," the usual place of assembly, and that for the institution, called the League or Confederation. Trustworthy and discriminating interpreters and informants would so translate these native terms as to emphasize this important difference. The native name of the League is *Gano^{n}syoñ́ni'* (with initial K in some dialects) and signifies "The Extended Lodge," i.e., the Lodge that is Extensive; that is, spread out far, especially lengthwise. But the native name for the ordinary public assembly lodge is *Gano^n'ses* (in some dialects the last *e* becomes an *i*) and means "The Long Lodge," commonly shortened (433) to "Long-house"; and so there is no reason for confusion here. So it is a gratuitous remark to say that Handsome Lake destroyed "the old religious system," for there is nothing to show its truth; the great religious festivals, all antedating the time of Handsome Lake, are today still in vogue on the Grand River reservation and elsewhere.

The references (p. 14 and elsewhere) to the "Crooked Tongues" are due to hazy ideas about the facts in the matter. There is no historical or traditional evidence, known to the present writer, showing that the Neuter Nation, so-called, ever had lands lying northeast of Lake Ontario, or that a Huron village called Kahanayen was situated on them. The land in question was probably Huron territory for Dekanawida's date. Evidently, the name "Crooked Tongues" is used as a substitute translation of the Huron and Neuter name Attiwendaronk (Hatiwendaronk) which signifies "Their speech is awry," i.e., "They speak a language slightly different (*from the norm of ours*)." The source of the utter confusion of names and places probably arose from misunderstanding certain information which the present writer many years ago gave to Mr. Newhouse concerning the early inhabitants of what is now Ontario, Canada. This information contained the suggestion that Dekanawida was very probably a naturalized Huron captive among the Iroquois. Singularly, the Huron tribes do not figure in the traditions relating the events leading to the formation of the League. So the comments on page 15 concerning Dekanawida's troubles with his own people are probably fiction, and especially so is the alleged conversation carried on with Mohawk people; the Mohawk did not know the Wyandot (Huron) as the "Crooked Tongues," as the statement on page 14 implies. After crossing the Lake, Dekanawida was not in Mohawk hunting ground, but in that of the Oneida or Onondaga, being a long distance from the Mohawk villages.

There is also confusion between an alleged "immutability" in contradistinction from the asserted "continuity" of the institutions of the League. Amendments to already existing laws are monotonously frequent in the traditions. Again, it is not true that the term *oñgwe 'hoñ́we'* implies any notion of peculiar "originality" of descent or of "superiority" of race. This compound term signifies "native man," and is a limitation of the general term *oñ́gwe'*, "man-being," i.e., any living being having human attributes, the man of myth, to the "native" strictly *human* man. The Indian knew no race other than his own, for this term is also applicable to the Eskimo. Any other view is untenable.

There is no justification for the substitution of the words, "the soft, (434) white, feathery down of the globe thistle," for the original false translation, "The Great Belt of White Wampum," of the native term, Jonodaken-rahkowa, of the Newhouse manuscript of 1898, for these terms in no sense correct the incorrect rendering and they wholly miss the expressive symbolism of the native expression. The unhistorical character of the list of fifteen "original" clans, appearing in section 42 on page 42, in which seven are spurious, is clear to any careful student of the early clans of the Five Nations, for even one of the most important — the Wolf — has been suppressed without comment. The last three probably owe their existence to *otosis* — originating in the mishearing of names. The so-called "Ball" clan is a Hawk clan; the Opposite-Side-of-the-Hand is a Wolf clan; and the "Wild Potatoe" is a "Tuber Duck" clan; or is possibly due to the mishearing of a dialectic pronunciation of the name for Plover.

The Mohawk text first published by Hale in his *Iroquois Book of Rites*, then by Rev. Dr. Beauchamp, and finally by Dr. Scott (*op.cit.*, p. 238) gives no warrant for the astonishing statements (*Bulletin*, No. 184, pp. 27-28) concerning the clan towns, namely, "Now the party passed through these places" and "All these places are in the Mohawk country." The native text already mentioned states that some of these town belong to the Wolf clan, some to the two Turtle clans, and some to the Bear clan. It would have been thus unnecessary for the 'party' to march through these towns, for they were evidently not all in "the Mohawk country" but dispersed among all the tribes these represented; and the clans-people present are severally addressed as coming from these several towns, and it is further stated, and this is important, that these *four* clans made up the number of clans "in ancient times." The last statement bears on what has been said about the clan list in section 42.

In article 63 the words "two sons," which occur several times, represent a wrong translation of a native term of relationship which signifies, in this place, "parent and offspring," usually translated, "Father and Son," or "Mother and Daughter." Section 19 is scarcely more than an expansion of section 18, and its provision for an independent "Council of War Chiefs" is unhistorical; too many councils of coördinate jurisdiction would result from it. Sections 55, 56 and 57 are confused and so in their present form unhistorical. The alleged provision for the dissolution of the League is indefensible; the provisions of Section 56 and 57 are inconsistent one with another, and these in turn are traversed by the ordinances set forth in the second paragraph on page 103 (which is a part of the Committee's document).

(435) The song set forth in Section 105 is certainly not what its caption, "The Installation Song," represents it to be; there is, indeed, no such song. This song was personal to the first Wathatotarho (Adodarho), and so it is not an installation song of to-day. The first line should have been translated, "I possess a fine thing," instead of "It is good, indeed."

On page 91 the statement is made that circumcision was practised on one of the founders of the League. This statement of course is inaccurate, as the Iroquois performed no such rite. The native words have quite a different and symbolic meaning.

The expressions, "white lion," "fire dragon of discord," and "white panther," on page 103, are attempts at translating native words which together are the name of one of the primal man-beings of Iroquoian myths of creation who was therein the personification of Discord. The literal meaning of his name is "the white-bodied meteor or flying-dragon." He brought about discord in heaven (the sky-world) which resulted in the complete metamorphosis of beings. So to translate his native name by the words "white lion" is erroneous, for it does not express the ideas intended in the text. The original manuscript in 1900 contained the words "white lion" at this point. So the present writer pointed out that such a rendering was inaccurate because the early Iroquois did not know the lion but did know the meteor. And he suggested further that as the "Master or God of Discord" was here intended, the better expression in English would be "the white-bodied meteor, the white-bodied fire-dragon or panther, of discord"; the suggested correction was approved by Chief Abram Charles and the late Chief John Arthur Gibson of the Canadian Six Nations, to whom it was made. The native term in note 3 on page 103 signifies "Death, or the Destroyer," a very different idea from the one sought to be expressed in the text.

In regard to the ownership of land, the latter part of Section 42 contradicts Section 44. The two main documents (compare pp. 11 and 12 with 98 and 47, respectively) disagree flatly as to usage in color symbolism. And both are in error in regard to the meaning of the native term "Ska-no-dah-ken-rah-ko-wah," which signifies "the very great white mat (foundation)," for both erroneously translate "belt" where they should render "mat." They differ entirely as to its color: the Committee's statement being the correct one. The statement of the Committee's document (p. 103, 2nd paragraph) in regard to the community of hunting-grounds is correct; but the Newhouse assertion (p. 45, Sec. 57) is of course inaccurate, because it limits the right to the "one bowl" containing (436) "a beaver's tail" (i.e., the common game preserve) to the "Lords of the Confederacy." His use of the term "cooked" beaver's tail, shows clearly that he has still to learn the meaning of this wise and benevolent provision of the founders of the League.

Sections 99 to 104 do not belong in a work of this kind. And Sections 105 and 106 are wrongly labeled and are not a part of the Constitution of the League. Section 107 does not belong here; many things naturally were taken for granted as well-known common law. Sections 108 to 117, private "Funeral Addresses," do not form any part of the Constitution of the League, and so are out of place here; their crudity and naïveté should have excluded them from consideration.

Section 64 is certainly not a law or ordinance; Section 72 is merely an expansion of 71; Section 73 is contradicted by 57; Sections 19, 59 and 98 deal with the same matters and so in their present form are unhistorical, and so is the last part of Section 79. Sections 74 and 77 are unauthentic; 87 is largely a duplicate of 83; and Sections 82 and 89 are not parts of the "Constitution," so-called. And Sections 85 and 88 are entirely contrary to the basic principles of the League as founded by Dekanawida. Sections 93 to 96, having been translated from Lafitau's Moeurs, etc., by the present writer for Mr. Newhouse, are not traditionally part of the "Constitution."

Of the footnotes on the pages from 65 to 107, thirty-three are erroneous and misleading.

It is noteworthy that the Secretaries of the Committee of Chiefs of the Six Nations Council admit that the traditions which they recorded have been "much modified" by several causes. But these annalists failed to detect in some notable instances the elements which have been assimilated by the

League traditions from their mythic and other tales. Such, for example, are the following: the notion of "the white stone canoe" or the "marble canoe," and the "Ohsinoh" incidents. Now, the "stone" or "flint" canoe belongs to the cycle of stories which relate to the Winter God whose means of travel on water is a block of ice, which is poetically transformed into a "canoe." So this episode does not belong to the Dekanawida legend. Mr. J.V.H. Clarke (*Onondaga*, 1, 1849) records the Dekanawida story, but he writes "*white* canoe" only; the original Dekanawida canoe was probably a birchbark canoe. But tradition has expanded "white" into "white stone" as suggested above. Moreover, Clarke mentions one *Ho-see-noke* as "A kind hearted, merry chief" who in behalf of the Council comforted the vexed mind of Hiawatha; but it is found that the Newhouse story makes this man whose (437) name is in slightly different spelling, thus Ohsinoh (Osinoh) page 18, "a famous shaman" who destroys Hiawatha's daughters by "evil magic arts." Here we find a complete transformation of a man and his deeds.

It is to be noted that an extra verse has been unwarrantably added to the well-known "Six Songs" (Duncan, 239 p.), which derive their common name from the fact that just "six" verses constitute this chant; it is also quite erroneous to say, following Hale, "the Hymn called 'Hail'," for this designation rests on a mistranslation of the native name and on a worse misapprehension of the real import of the chant.

Other misprints are Jiknosahseh (p. 91), Djikonsase (p. 90), and Djikonsá'se' (p. 71), for Djigo^{n}sǎ'sě^n. It may be said here that there is no evidence that this person, the so-called Peace Woman, was in any sense a character "in Iroquois mythology." An examination of the provisions of Section 91 shows that they are in serious conflict with those of Section 59.

The inept and wholly whimsical comments on the pictographs published on page 111 indicate that here the editor was the dupe of cocksure but ignorant informants. The utterly fanciful character of these comments is indeed emphasized by the remarkable fact that this page of pictographs and comments appears as an inset in a misnamed and badly garbled summary of the "Re-Quickening Address of the League Ritual of Condolence and Installation." These pictographs from number 4 refer serially to the paragraphs of the summary beginning with number 1 on page 110, although the editor seems unaware of this interesting fact. It is to be noted that this *Address* deals with the *tribes* of the League but not with the *clans* of the League; the printed comments are incorrect in this respect.

The two pictographic groups of parallel lines respectively refer to the 'Father' and 'Mother' side of the League structure — the four representing the 'Mother' side and the three, the 'Father' side; the four lines represent the Oneida, the Cayuga, the Tuscarora, and the Delaware, the so-called 'Four Brothers'; and the three lines, to the Mohawk, the Seneca, and the Onondaga, the so-called 'Three-Brothers.' The prostrate figure indicates that 'Three Brothers' are the mourning side, and the first erect figure shows that the 'Four Brothers' are the celebrant side according to the Ritual and so are not mourning in the ritualistic sense, — a needful distinction.

Then the pictographs marked 4, 5, and 6 represent the three Acts or Words spoken "At the Wood's Edge," the key words being respectively "wipe away the tears," "clear out the ears," and "remove the (438) choking from the throat"; these acts are mentioned in paragraphs marked 1, 2, and 2, on page 110. Figure 7 (4 on p. 110) does not hold a "sun" as here stated, but "a cup," containing "the waters of pity"; figure 8 (5 on p. 110) does not denote "a bench with four legs," but rather the "seat" or "the reed mat," said to be stained with blood; figure 9 (6 on p. 112) denotes "the darkness" of grief; figure 10 (7 on p. 112) denotes "the loss of the sky" from grief; figure 11 (8 on p. 112) denotes "the loss of the sun" from grief; figure 12 (9 on p. 112) denotes "the grave," i.e., "the upturned earth"; figure 13 (idea not on p. 112) denotes "20 strings" as the price exacted for a homicide, which is the circle of protection for the two groups of parallel lines; figure 14 (11 on p. 112) denotes "the reverence due the person of the woman"; figure 15 (wanting on p. 112) denotes "the malific powers of the earth"; figure 16 (wanting on p. 113) denotes "the obligation of mutual respect and service"; figure 17 (wanting on p. 113) denotes "the torch of announcement, or of notification"; and figure 18 (wanting on p. 113) denotes "the doorway," i.e., the "end of the address." These brief strictures show how much real harm is done by the rush to published unstudied material, no matter by whom.

But to enumerate the redundancies, the contradictions, and the misconceptions in Mr. Parker's *Bulletin* would require a volume larger than the publication in question. It is most unfortunate for the cause of historical truth that great institutions insist on publication at the expense of study and accuracy. It may be mentioned that this publication of Mr. Parker has been most unfavorably reviewed by Dr. Goldenweiser in volume 18, no. 3, pp. 431-436, of *The American Anthropologist*. I have purposely not given out this unfavorable estimate of Mr. Parker's recent work until it had been reviewed by one whose motive Mr. Parker might not question.

J.N.B. Hewitt
American Anthropologist (New Series)
Vol. 19, No. 3, 1917, pp. 429-438.

(120) *THE CONSTITUTION OF THE FIVE NATIONS: A REPLY*

STUDENTS of Iroquoian social and political organization and folklore are fortunate in having so able a source of data as Mr. J.N.B. Hewitt. In the *Anthropologist*, vol. 19, no. 3, Mr. Hewitt criticized one of my recent publications, *The Constitution of the Five Nations*, and most ably pointed out both the faults of the native authorities who supplied my information and the errors in editing. In an earlier issue of the *Anthropologist* Dr. A.A. Goldenweiser published a criticism. In justice to the subject it would have been well and saved a possible misunderstanding if both critics had read page 12 and 13 of the introduction. There I said:

The two principal manuscripts that form the basis of this work were found on the Six Nations Reservation, Ontario, Canada, in 1910.

The first manuscript was a lengthy account of the Dekanawida legend and an account of the Confederate Iroquois laws. This material has been brought together by Seth Newhouse, a Mohawk who has expended a large amount of time and given the subject a lengthy study. His account written in Indian English was submitted to Albert Cusick, a New York Tuscarora-Onondaga, for review and criticism. Mr. Cusick had long been an authority on Iroquois law (121) and civic rites, and had been a chief informant for Horatio Hale, William Beauchamp, and in several instances for the present writer. Mr. Cusick was employed for more than a month in correcting the Newhouse manuscript until he believed the form in which it is now presented fairly correct and at least as accurate as a free translation could be made. The second manuscript was compiled by the chiefs of the Six Nations Council and in the form here

published has been reviewed and corrected by several of their own number including Chiefs John Gibson, Jacob Johnson and John William Elliott. The official copy was made by Hilton Hill, a Seneca, then employed by the Dominion Superintendent for the Six Nations. It has been reviewed and changes were suggested by Albert Cusick....
In presenting these documents the original orthography has been retained. The only attempt to record Iroquois names and words phonetically is in the notes. This will account for some variations in spelling....

In the light of the conditions under which the Bulletin under discussion was presented, a compilation of native documents, criticism seems gratuitous. Especially siginficant is Mr. Hewitt's attempt to controvert my statement of Mr. Cusick's help. One would almost suspect this to be designed to impute a falsehood, but in the light of Mr. Cusick's assistance, this imputation would seem to fall little short of maliciousness though probably not so intended.

The reference to "a free translation" should be apparent to anyone who has read the work under discussion. Suffice to say, no translation or presentation in English can gracefully and fluently express the Iroquoian idiom. Witness Mr. Hewitt's own literal translation of the "Iroquois Cosmology." It appears in clumsy, stilted English, involved and lacking in force of expression. Literal translation robs the native thought of much of its meaning and emphasis.

Our critic's reference to wampum would seem to imply that only one sort of wampum was recognized by us, though the manuscripts clearly name elderberry twigs, scouring rushes and porcupine quills. The wampum belts described as "constitution belts" may be regarded as such even though not made during the days of Dekanawida, in this sense being as truly memorials to the founding of the League as Lincoln's Gettysburg speech is Lincoln's still even though printed in today's newspaper. The belts are old and probably native made and they have been invested with the symbolism ascribed to them — memorials of the days when Dekanawida spoke.

The lack of accuracy, consistency and forethought on the part of the authors of the manuscripts is to be deplored but even though these Indian annalists wrote clumsily it did not occur to me that of my own (122) initiative I should alter their writings, even for the sake of presenting them as I personally desired to see them. Mr. Hewitt must learn that if ethnologists should habitually change the myths and native manuscripts that came into their hands, in order to bring about consistency, the finished production would shrink in value. The scientist takes what comes to him from the quarry, and though it is covered by corrosion and foreign matter, he presents it as found. It is his specimen upon which he does not chisel an inscription. That is written on a separate label.

An example of native inaccuracy is quoted by Mr. Hewitt in the following: "After a journey across the lake (Ontario) he came into the hunting territory of the Flint Nation." Mr. Hewitt correctly stated that the immediate landing place of Dekanawida would be in Oneida territory. Our Indian writer simply described things rapidly and without detailed chronological sequence, yet if some other writer had penned a line such as "After a journey across the ocean Olaf Jensen came into the forests of Minnesota," we think few critics would have deliberately gone out of their way to say that the assertion implied that Minnesota was on the Atlantic coast, especially if the statement had been made to those familiar with geography. We accept in a proper spirit the catalogue of our own blunders but we must insist that we do not believe in presenting the Indian manuscripts, we should eliminate their "crudity and naïveté from consideration," even to satisfy those who possess other versions of these Iroquois codes and legends. Indians who were life-long residents of their respective reservations produced the documents and stood for them. The writings represent in English, so far as they were able to make them, what they thought, believed, and lived in Iroquois. They do not necessarily represent what the present writer thinks accurate in detail or satisfactory.

Mr. Hewitt has had a large influence in directing the minds of his informants and no doubt, as he himself suggests, has contributed largely to their store of ancient lore, though we must confess it seems to us that "facts" so collected seem like re-importations; in other words, like telling one's informants what to say and how to say it. For example, Mr. Hewitt tells in his criticism how he instructed Mr. Newhouse in a certain translation of Lafitau, and says that Newhouse accepted the data and incorporated it in his code, Section 93-96. Mr. Hewitt also tells how he instructed the chiefs in the translation of certain names. It is thus evident that my distinguished critic has had an enormous advantage in previously instructing for a period of years his native informants. (123) They have accepted his statements as correct and incorporated them in their writings as original with them. The extent of this may be realized when it is said that some of the chiefs admitted that Mr. Hewitt wrote the introduction to the chief's version.

In our translation of the "record" staff, a cut of which was published, we simply followed the translation made by Abram Charles, a chief of the Cayugas, for Mrs. H.M. Converse, at least twenty years ago. Mr. Cusick apparently was satisfied with the translation. However, we suspected that it might be an attempt to call to mind the so-called condolence ceremony and thus we placed the picture to face that text, and with considerable difficulty, but Mr. Hewitt evidently thinks it is a coincidence.

We are grateful to Mr. Hewitt's criticism, for he has pointed out a store of facts that should have been made available years ago. Modestly he refrains from more extensive criticism, but we hope to have all the necessary data when he publishes his own version of "The Constitution of the League" for which he has prepared native texts in Mohawk and Onondaga. An English parallel in Mr. Hewitt's own fluent English will then be available and, of course, be above criticism, though there will be some who will suspect that the content and the "original text" have been rigidly supervised.

Apparently Mr. Hewitt agrees with Dr. Goldenweiser's earlier criticism, and yet Dr. Goldenweiser specifically states that "The Constitution of the Five Nations is a figment ... It does not exist ... either written or unwritten." Strangely, however, it appears as a coincident that Mr. Hewitt's texts and translations parallel those we have published, for the *Twenty-eighth Report of the Bureau of Ethnology* mentions his collection of "texts" in the Onondaga and Mohawk dialects,

> embodying the basic principles of the civil and political structures and organization of the League of the Iroquois and data relating thereto. The following captions will indicate sufficiently the subject matter of these texts: The Constitution of the League, the Powers of Thadodaho, Amendments, Powers and Rights of Chiefs, Powers and Rights of Women, Powers of the Women Chiefs, etc.

We confess that we do not quite understanding Mr. Hewitt's concluding statement,

> I have purposely not given out this unfavorable estimate of Mr. Parker's recent work until it had been reviewed by one whose motives Mr. Parker might not question.

The pure love of accuracy is sufficient motive, and should have prevented (124) any feeling of restraint in giving out "this unfavorable estimate," until some other ethnologist has taken the initiative. We trust that this inertia of Mr. Hewitt will now be overcome and that we may be prevented from getting into further sloughs of error by his speedy publication of his own version of the "Constitution of the Five Nations." We feel sure that the faults of our own attempt will but add to the luster of the greater work that is to come.

Like Kipling's hero in *The Neolithic Age*, I feel, as I survey the bulky criticism of my bulletin, as if "... a rival of Solutré told the tribe my style was *outré*...." But I am consoled, as every ethnologist must be who finds dozens of versions of myths and "constitutions," in the last verse of the poem, and for a pleasant thought, I present it to my critics.

> Here is wisdom for your use, as I learned it when the moose
> And reindeer roared where Paris roars tonight
> There are nine and sixty ways of constructing tribal lays,
> And—every—single—one—of—them—is—right.

NEW YORK STATE MUSEUM,
ALBANY, NEW YORK

Arthur C. Parker

American Anthropologist (New Series)
Vol. 20, No. 1, 1918

APPENDIX G
A MOHAWK CONDOLENCE AT OKA, P.Q., APRIL 1964
W.G. Spittal

The following notes have been inserted into the third IROQRAFTS reprinting of the *CONSTITUTION* to record a Condolence a century after the three in Parker's appendices. Neither scholarly nor analytical, but highly personalized and anecdotal, they are offered in the hope of their having some value in memorializing the establishment and brief existence of a new Iroquois Longhouse (seemingly not yet noted in the published Iroquoian literature), and in giving some of the flavour of one individual's experiences and observations during an important Iroquois ritual in the mid-twentieth century. Because no writing is permitted in Longhouses, the notes were jotted down as they tumbled from memory immediately upon returning to Ohsweken. The casual, colloquial "style" was adequate at the time for a young man's private journal, and has been left more or less intact here. Editing has been confined primarily to minor adjustments to clarify meanings and to rectify the writer's tendancy to creative spelling; the footnotes are recent.

* * * * * * * * * * * * * * *

Friday, April 24, 1964

Left Rachel in charge of the children at 07:20 and set out with Bunny, John and Mae for Oka. Vernie[1] had stayed behind as she was involved in cooking medicine for C.M.'s wife, suffering badly from cancer[2]. We had an interesting drive and arrived at the Oka ferry dock at 16:10. Encountered considerable difficulty in locating the settlement we were interested in. I exercised my high school French with barely satisfactory results and at 17:00 we arrived before the new Longhouse.

A small man in his 30's approached us (Samson Gabriel), and after a few words we were invited into the Longhouse. In the minds of Oka people for 25 years by their own statement, it was today only hurriedly roughed out in time for the Hai Hai[3]. The framework was of rough-sawn basswood, the rafters of similarly prepared birch on which some bark yet showed. Very heavy sheets of wall-weight sheet-metal — which had been used before and through which sunlight streamed from old nail holes – had earlier in the day been tacked into place. That morning water had been on the floor from a rain the night before. Windows, which don't open, had also been placed into the wall today, and like-wise, a rough-hewn door. A second door-hole to the West was covered by a sheet of plywood, time having been too short to prepare a door for it. The walls were covered by fibre building-board (an underlay material). The floor was plywood; counting its sheets I determined the size to be 26' by 28'. Rough plank benches were supported by struts from the wall. At this time only one stove was set up, at the east end. The grounds are below road level and inclined to collect water after a rain. The house rests on cement posts and is about 100 feet[4] or more from the road. An undeveloped government-drilled well (250'+) is in the yard, but at present is capped. There is no cook house or dining hall yet. A wire runs from the home of Solomon (brother of Samson) Gabriel to the Longhouse to illuminate three bulbs running down a plank nailed to the bare ceiling joists[5].

Solomon joined us and shortly invited us into his home for a meal. Our host was short and very stocky, a real bull of a man. His wife is about 32, rather lightly complexioned. They have four girls: 8, 10, 13 and 14. The entire family uses Mohawk almost all the time, Solomon getting mad if his daughters use English or French. They are beautifully mannered children, and very cute; their quiet use of Mohawk and their good manners were very impressive. After dinner we sat talking and about 21:00 Solomon, John and myself went into the Longhouse to chat. Albert Greene was there now with

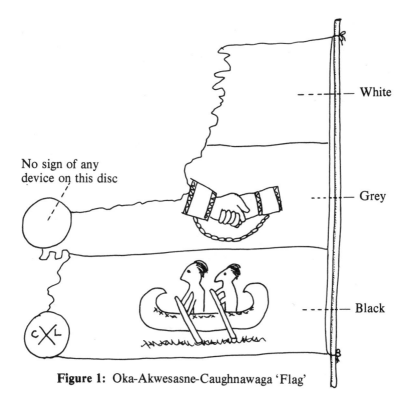

No sign of any device on this disc

— White

— Grey

— Black

Figure 1: Oka-Akwesasne-Caughnawaga 'Flag'

his passengers: Bill Fish, Nawa''hās, and a man from Middleport[6]. Albert had passed us in Kingston when we stopped to eat. It appears he must have come across the Lac du Deux Montagnes just minutes before we did. But it was 20:30 before they were able to locate the Longhouse. In half an hour Howard Skye appeared with his gang: Patterson Davey, Eugene Skye, and Deskahe[7]. Samson brought a five-foot pole into the Longhouse with cloth wrapped around it. Carefully unrolling it on the floor, he showed us a kind of Indian flag (Figure 1). As near as I could learn, the three bands of colour stood for the triangle of Mohawk Reserves (Oka, St. Regis, Caughnawaga) and that the "flag" had been brought to Oka when the Reserve had been settled[8]. I didn't ask more about it as it slipped my memory. There was a lot of individual conversation. About 23:30 Deskahe gave a brief Thanksgiving Address[9]. Someone else spoke briefly, then we had a 15-minute Gada'trõt sung by Nawa'hās and Howard, about ten of us joined in. About midnight we dispersed, going to the various homes which were to put us up. We stayed with Solomon, where our women had gone to sleep earlier.

Saturday, April 25, 1964

Our hosts were up and about shortly after 06:00. We had breakfast around 06:30[10]. During breakfast, Calvin Miller's station wagon appeared and unloaded into Solomon's house. In it were: Calvin, Josie, Ma'' mits, Oliver Jacobs, Peter Skye, Harry Henhawk, and Roy Buck[11]. They ate after us and then quite late our hosts were able to eat. John and I joined in their conversation for awhile, then I went into the Longhouse where most of our Younger Brothers were. More private conversations. Then Josie brought his group out to discuss arrangements with the Younger Brothers. John and I met outside for conversation. He drew my attention to a beautiful pine woods growing to the south, saying he'd been told that it was on Indian land, but was tied up by the Roman Catholic church, and the Indians couldn't cut it. The Reserve was set up as three and a half leagues along the river and three leagues deep. On this land was the Village of Oka (a very charming little place), plus homesteads of French scattered among the Indian households and a beautiful golf course in the afore-mentioned pine woods. The choice lands along the river were settled mainly by non-Indians (see Map).

The idea came to both of us and we set out for Oka to buy groceries to help out our hosts. At this time many women were busy making sandwiches in the kitchen and packing them away in boxes. We bought $10.19[12] worth of varied foodstuffs. On the street, a car loaded with Syracuse and Caughnawaga people stopped us for conversation. A second car with them was following on the next ferry.

We were approached by a man in his 60's in a variety store. He looked like any Frenchman, but proved to be a Mohawk named Charlie Gabriel. He wanted to converse and also get a ride out to the Longhouse. At the second corner up from the ferry, he stopped to relate an anecdote about the property which stood there – a new store building which was vacant and for rent. According to Charlie, years ago the priests in the church "kitty-corner" from

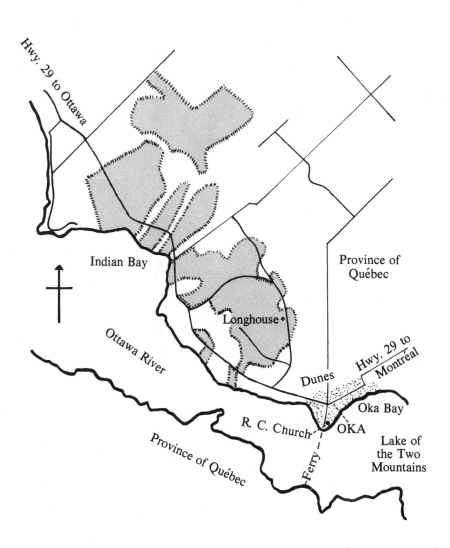

OKA RESERVE

us had given the Indians blankets infected with Yellow Typhoid germs, which deed killed off many of them. They were buried in various places about the area. Recently, when the foundations were being excavated for this new store, a considerable number of Indian bones were uncovered. The builder was advised to box the bones and return them to the Indians, but he wasn't interested and disposed of the bones "back in the country". Once the building was completed the owner moved in and set up his business. However, he could not make a success of it and was forced to sell out. Succeeding store-keepers likewise were unsuccessful in their efforts, and so the store was vacant and looking for a tenant. Meanwhile, the original owner continued to flounder, "going down all the time", and he has been obliged to sell other of his properties but still is unsuccessful. A second story concerned a Québec Provincial Police Officer who arrived, newly posted to the area, and proceeded to police the Indians very strictly. Soon he was involved in a car crash from which he will have a limp for the rest of his life. Charlie saw a relationship between the two.

Figure 2: Peg Shapes on Johnson Cook's Condolence Cane

We got back to our hosts about 10:40. A great many more people had arrived from other reserves and reservations[13]. I talked with a young fellow named Bill Lazore[14] from Syracuse, with whom I'd danced at Seneca Longhouse a couple of years ago. About 11:00 the Younger Brothers began walking from a house down the road. It was 11:15 when I saw them almost to Solomon's gateway where a fire was burning, and on the west side of which were the Elder Brothers. Here "At the Edge of the Woods" was performed. Josie read his portion from mimeographed pages[15]; I observed Howard following the version and running his finger along the lines in his new copy of Hale's *BOOK OF RITES*[16]. I got two or three photos here; saw "Goldie"[17] from Syracuse doing likewise and also John. Roy Buck began preaching for the Elder Brothers[18]. Then Peter handed him a 5" or 6" wampum string to preach on. Harry Henhawk carried it across the fire to Deskahe. There were three of these strings. Nawa'ʳ hãs spoke for their return and Eugene carried them back to Peter. It wasn't much longer before the Elder Brothers moved out and filed down and into the Longhouse. Once they had gone, we ten were led in double file by Ma'ʸ mits and Harry[19] while Deskahe sang the Hai Hai. In the Longhouse there was a little shuffling about to get seats, then "Chief"[20] began the Hai Hai. He carried a Condolence Cane which I'd seen Johnson Cook of Syracuse carrying and may have been his. It had the Spragg pictographs on it[21]. All the pegs were of deer antler, the Seneca pegs were the only odd-shaped ones, being but the points of antlers (see Figure 2). A beautiful antler handle, with a finely carved dog (wolf?) head and paws, finished it off. Howard had his Condolence Cane and Harry Henhawk carried a third. There were several other plain canes in evidence.

Elder Brothers from various communities filled the benches from the door, to the right, all the way about to their Chiefs, and later, when the house filled, even along the bench near me.

Unless there were Oneida or Cayuga in there whom I did not know, our little group was all that was present. "Chief's" Hai Hai lasted one hour and 32 minutes. While he preached, Howard placed a fancy carved cane showing the ten Cayuga Clans and other symbols across our two benches, then Deskahe laid Condoling Strings across it[22]. He took these from a new buckskin pouch dated "1964"[23]. A pitcher of water was set out at the west end of the house and "Chief" took occasional drinks to relieve his throat[24]. The rest of the ceremony was a typical Condolence and I saw nothing unusual in it. The house held around 100 persons during the day, but as the ceremony stretched on people took off, leaving about 50 or so inside. House filled up again at night when we danced.

Albert Greene created a bit of a stir when he appeared in his impressive full Indian regalia. No one else among the visitors was dressed in anything more than a rosette necktie to suggest "Indian". Later in the afternoon a Syracuse chief went out and changed into a fringed, but otherwise undecorated, leather outfit and a two-feather Onondaga gustō' we'[25].

There was some confusion when it came time to name the new chiefs. Solomon's brother, Moses, and their mother were brought onto the floor(see Figure 3) and also six others. Moses was the first to be given a title(I believe the Bear Clan – earlier in the day "Chief" had removed the seventh peg from the Mohawk roster on the cane[26] while we stood "at the edge of the woods"). Now came about ten minutes of discussion among the various persons on the floor as they explained what was coming up. It developed that they had not discovered who held titles to other Chiefships. Until next Fall, when another Condolence is planned, they have installed three temporary Chiefs and as many Clan Mothers; in the Fall they will either confirm the present holders or substitute those who actually should be in the positions[27]. Samson Gabriel and his wife, Frank Moses and a young woman(perhaps 20 years old), and Frank Gabriel (a nephew of Samson, Solomon, and Moses) and his sister were named.

As I indicated it was 11:00 when Younger Brothers began walking, thereby starting the rite. I suppose they had had Hai Hai in a house before starting, just as is done inside Lower Cayuga Longhouse before starting down the roads to Onondaga Longhouse. It was 18:30 when the last words of the Condolence were said. Now kettles of pork and beef were brought in, boxes of baker's bread and corn bread, and pots of rather greasy corn soup cooked with a few sliced carrots in it[28]. These were set on the long bench in front of the Chiefs; as soon as they had dug into them, the rest of us attacked the food with great zeal.

Dancing was now engaged in: Gada'trōt, Gīō'wa', Shaking-a-Bush and Rabbit. When that had concluded Deskahe gave a "pep talk" to stick with the Indian ways and not worry over the abusive term "Pagan", which is

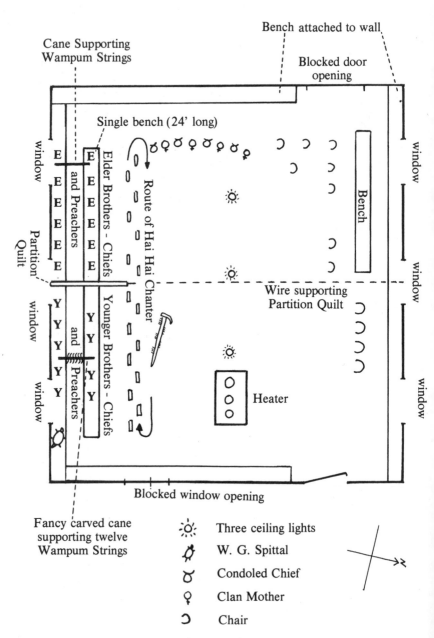

Figure 3: Floor Plan of Condolence Ceremony

so often thrown at the Longhouse People. For the occasion he used Mohawk in his addresses, but most of our Reserve's speakers used Cayuga. Josie followed with an address, then Samson with a brief speech. We were dismissed about 22:30. Calvin's gang went into Solomon's and watched the last game of the Stanley Cup hockey finals – Toronto won; then they left for Six Nations. I am sure they must have been exhausted upon their return, considering their previous all-night drive, today's Condolence and the immediate return trip.

Sunday, April 26, 1964

We were up early again. Solomon told John his wife had given him a very good Indian medicine to cure his back aches. John was interested because he has chronic soreness at hip level. He was obliged to pay a token one cent before Solomon would show the medicine and he reminded him to place an offering of tobacco when he digs it up for use[30]. The medicine was the root of the Crab Grass. He said to make up a bunch of these roots and then boil a tea from them. I believe he said this medicine could only be boiled once; i.e., would not have any strength left for a second boiling. Solomon said the older generation used to tell how Ohsweken people came down to their Reserve "using the night like a canoe to bring them". This meant witches using the cover of darkness to make a quick trip. Between John and Solomon, I was reminded that a person afflicted by witch-induced troubles is more likely to be cured by going to a distant Iroquois reserve and seeking help. They both gave several instances of this. They both likewise agreed that St. Regis was a hot-bed of witchcraft, probably the worst reserve for that evil.

John found it necessary now to set Solomon straight about his unorthodox relationship with Mae and his reasons for this eight-year liaison while still having a wife at home.

Albert was the first to leave, about 10:00; Howard left at 10:30 and we at 11:30. While we were sending Albert off, Howard approached Deskahe and began quietly singing one of the War Dance songs, the one going 'Ganiseda'gã ...'[31]. It had just come to him that this particular song mentioned this Reserve, and he wondered if Deskahe knew how it came to be in the songs down our way. Deskahe had no idea, however. Later, while John and I were talking to Solomon at the rear of his house, we noticed Howard and two others posturing for Wasa'/ zã[32], and could just hear someone singing, so I presume they were illustrating this dance which had memorialized Oka's name ("pile of sand place"). Bunny[33] said Howard sold his copy of BOOK OF RITES to Samson for $5.00 (costs $7.50 in a bookstore).

We took farewell pictures, said we'd like to return in the Fall, and left. We returned by way of the Québec side to Ottawa, then down Hwy. 7 to Peterborough and on to Lindsay and Toronto. About 46 miles longer (392 vs 438), but added variety to the drive. Back in time for a Thunderdance this evening at Onondaga Longhouse for all the Longhouses on the Reserve.

NOTES

1 Vernie Logan, wife of Chief Joseph ('Josie') Logan, Jr. Until their deaths (Joseph - July 3, 1981; Vernie - October 31, 1981) they were a driving force in the Hereditary Council. They supported themselves by making the famous "Logan Special" lacrosse sticks and Indian medicines, among which their cancer and tuberculosis medicines were particularly well-known in the Iroquois world.

2 She subsequently succumbed to this disease.

3 Pronounced conversationally to somewhat rhyme with "buy - buy", but considerably lengthened when being used ceremonially. This term from a specific section of the ritual is used from time to time in English at Six Nations when referring to the entire Grand Condolence Ceremony.

4 Today I would judge the distance to have been closer to 350 feet (see Photo No. 3).

5 At Six Nations it is currently considered inappropriate to light the four local Longhouses electrically, although three of the dining halls have been wired within the last decade or so, and there is now talk of wiring the remaining one at conservative Lower Cayuga Longhouse. In the meantime coal oil lamps provide the necessary illumination.

6 Nawa'ʹhãs – William Johnson, Cayuga Chief, Lower Cayuga Longhouse, almost invariably was referred to in the Longhouse community by his personal Cayuga name, even in English conversations.

The area between Onondaga and Middleport hamlets contains some 700-odd acres of the Six Nations Reserve still remaining on the north side of the Grand River. Direct access from the main body of the Reserve for years was only by way of a summer-operating ferry, docking below Chiefwood, birthplace of the Mohawk poet E. Pauline Johnson. At the end of 1983, it was replaced by a large concrete bridge, the Six Nations Bi-Centennial Bridge.

7 Alexander General, then an 80-ish Upper Cayuga Chief, ritualist and consummate custodian of Iroquois culture from Sour Springs (or "Upper Cayuga") Longhouse; a true gentleman of the old-school. He was a principal informant for F. G. Speck's *MIDWINTER RITES OF THE CAYUGA LONGHOUSE.* In the phoenetic system used by the present writer, his title would be written: 'Deska:ʹhã'. The form given in the text, 'Deskahe' is now so generally used in the Iroquoian literature that it has been perpetuated here also.

8 Oka was settled between 1718 - 1721.

On Page 71 of *WAMPUM BELTS*, Ray Fadden illustrates "Unknown Belts", one of which has three linked human figures and a cross. It would seem this might refer to an alliance of the three northern Mohawk Mission settlements. The flag survives as a relic of a special relationship between those communities. Note the chain linking the two hands on the centre panel, suggestive of the Silver Covenant Chain of Amity, metaphorically linking the Iroquois to their allies in so many of the recorded Council speeches from the seventeenth century onwards. The two Indians in the canoe suggest one of the "words" to be read out of the Two Row Wampum Belt (Dāga'nē dāyōha'dā wadālēwhēssāa hǫ... Mo.; Dāk'nē dāyhōha'tā... Ca.) – that the Indians should paddle their own canoe along side, equal to and undisturbed by the white man's sailing ship. Taken together these two design elements tend to suggest this banner as an emblem of the relationship between the three Mohawk communities (the three coloured panels) and the white man. Whether the Europeans were French or English cannot be certain, but the Covenant Chain was a symbolic concept especially strong between the Confederacy resident below Lake Ontario and the English, so it might be that this flag was produced as a visible manifestation of the new loyalty of the former French-mission Mohawks to the English conquerors of Canada after its fall in 1760. The significance of the "C.L." initials on the lower disc remains problematic.

9 The Ganǫ'hǫnyǫk (Ca.). No gathering of Longhouse people (save certain medicine societies) can begin or end without a brief or long version of this important acknowledgement from those present. Even social dances have been held up until the arrival of someone versed in this address.

10 Omitted from the Journal was the following anecdote, now resurrected for the benefit of those who have read that Iroquois languages are simple dialects of one another, and that if you know one, you know them all without further study: The main breakfast course was bacon and eggs. In Cayuga I asked for "salt" and was given a soup bowl with a spoon in it. I had used tiny glass and silver "salt cellars", but this size seemed excessive and should have tipped me off. While our Mohawk hosts looked on, I sprinkled the "salt" on my eggs. A mouthful told me why they had been watching: 'Odjik'hā'da' may be "salt" in Cayuga, but in Mohawk it is "sugar". Their word for salt is: 'Dayōyō'jēs'.

11 Calvin Miller* (Mohawk), Joseph Logan, Jr.* (Mohawk), Raymond Sprague (Seneca), Oliver Jacobs* (Onondaga), Peter Skye* (Onondaga), Harry Henhawk (Onondaga) and Roy Buck (Cayuga). The asterix indicates those who were, or would become in future years, Hereditary Chiefs at Ohsweken.

12 Unlike inflationary 1984, this bought much more than just a tiny bag of groceries in 1964.

13 Although often used indiscriminately, the former term is more typically used in Canada and the latter in the U.S.A.

14 Now an Onondaga Chief.

15 It was ever Chief Logan's custom, although no ceremonial tyro, to read this address rather than recite it (see Photo No. 3).

16 See Photo No. 4.

17 Gordon Peters, now also an Onondaga Chief (see Photo No. 3).

18 Roy Buck (d. April 17, 1983) a Cayuga, was affiliated with Onondaga Longhouse and had been adopted as a ceremonial speaker on its behalf; thus it was that at this Condolence his impressive command of Iroquois ceremonialism was being exercised for the Elder Brothers.

19 Sprague (Seneca) and Henhawk (Onondaga) on behalf of the Elder Brothers escorted the Condoling Younger Brothers into the Longhouse. Sprague's Indian nick-name "Ma'.mits", is meaningless and arose from sounds made in his early childhood.

20 Herbert Cusick (Cayuga) another master of Iroquois song and ceremony. "Chief" was his English nick-name.

21 These pictographs are shown in W. N. Fenton's *THE ROLL CALL OF THE IROQUOIS CHIEFS*, reprinted by IROQRAFTS, 1983.

22 Fourteen strings are used in condoling a "noble" family; 15 are used in a Grand Condolence such as this. Note: Figure 3 indicates only 12 strings across cane; three were used "at the edge of the woods".

23 Dating ceremonial materials at Six Nations is not an uncommon practice. Among other dated items seen in homes and Longhouses here are the following: water drums; rattles of cow horn, turtle shell, and gourd; and a dancer's beaded vest. It is even rumoured that a framing member in the attic of Seneca Longhouse has a date (said to be in the late 1860's) carved into it, allegedly the year it was built.

24 At Six Nations this would have been a drink of crushed strawberries mixed with cold water and maple syrup, a very delicious refreshment that is also passed about the Longhouse at certain times to be drunk as members softly offer their thanks to the Creator. Some have seen an analogy to the communion in the Christian churches, but there is no hint here of a similar ritual cannibalism.

25 Photo No. 7 shows Moses Gabriel in a beaded, fringed, leather coat, and Samson Gabriel possibly wearing another.

26 This title is 'Dāhana'karē:na', "Dragging Antlers", the first of the three Bear Clan titles.

27 We never did return for this, nor did I hear if it was carried out.

28 At times corn soup among the various "Mission Mohawk" can take on the appearance of a vegetable soup, with such inclusions as carrots, squash, potatoes, and sometimes other vegetables.

29 Mohawk was at one time the lingua-franca of the Confederacy; it is still considered to be **the** language of the Grand Condolence Ceremony, although others are also used.

30 This old practice is almost universal among Iroquois medicine gatherers.

[31] This song can be heard on Record No. 2, *IROQUOIS SOCIAL DANCE SONGS*, published by IROQRAFTS.

[32] The War Dance, the name seems to derive from the name given the Osage Indians.

[33] My wife. Howard Skye was her mother's father's brother, and was married to her father's mother's sister; he was variously addressed by her as "Uncle" and "Grandfather". In later years he would drop the final "e" in his name.

1. The Oka Longhouse, Sunday, April 26, 1964.

2.(a) Solomon Gabriel, wife and four daughters.

2.(b) Two Ohsweken Cayuga "Younger Brothers" (L) Bill Fish, Lower Cayuga Longhouse. The Fish family was one of the last at Six Nations with a tangible degree of Tutelo ancestry. (R) Patterson Davey, Onondaga Longhouse. Davey was a Keeper of the "Good Medicine" (a.k.a. "the Little Water Medicine").

3. "At the Edge of the Woods", view from the Younger Brothers' side. The grieving Elder Brothers greet the Condoling Younger Brothers: the welcoming fire is in the foreground. Unless otherwise noted the following identifications are of persons from Ohsweken, Six Nations Reserve. Left to right: Raymond Sprague, with simple cane. S: Harry Henhawk, in tan jacket, his Condolence Cane can be seen between Miller's legs O: Calvin Miller. M: Gordon ("Goldie") Peters. Onondaga. N.Y. O: Chief Hastawesera'ta (Joseph Logan. Jr.). M: Peter Skye, hands at buckle. O: Roy Buck, wearing cap. C: Samson Gabriel. Oka. M: Coleman Powless. O: Solomon Gabriel. Oka. M. In background are the Solomon Gabriel home and the new Longhouse. M - Mohawk. O - Onondaga. S - Seneca. C - Cayuga.

4. "At the Edge of the Woods", view from the Elder Brothers' side. Eight Younger Brothers are spread in a line beyond the welcoming fire. Note Howard Skye (cap on head, Condolence Cane over arm) consulting a copy of Horatio Hale's *IROQUOIS BOOK OF RITES*.

5.(a) Younger Brothers awaiting return of Elder Brothers to the Longhouse. In the foreground are Eugene Skye, Howard Skye (beyond him), Raymond Sprague, Patterson Davey, Harry Henhawk. Sprague, S, and Henhawk, O, will escort the Younger Brothers into the Longhouse.

5.(b) Younger Brothers waiting to be "Led by the Hand" to the Longhouse. All are Six Nations, Cayuga, and now deceased. Left to right: Bill Fish, Anderson Joseph, Bill ('Nawa'ᶜ hãs') Johnson, Alexander ("Jack") General . . . Chief Deskahe; Eugene Skye, Herbert ('Ha'ᶜ sena') Cusick; and Howard Skye.

6. Social Dancing (Rabbit Dance) in the Longhouse. Guy Spittal dancing with Miss Gabriel (one of the new temporary Clan Mothers shown in Photo 7); behind her is Chauncey Isaacs of Ohsweken.

7. Presentation of the Chiefs and Clan Mothers. Left to right: Mrs. Gabriel, Bear Clan Mother, her son and newly-named Chief, Moses Gabriel; Samson Gabriel, temporary Chief (holding child); Mrs. Samson Gabriel, temporary Clan Mother; Frank Moses, temporary Chief; Roy Buck, in white shirt with Condolence Cane; Chief Joseph Logan, Jr.; all but obscured behind Logan is Frank Gabriel, temporary Chief; and beside him, in white sweater, is his sister, a Miss Gabriel, temporary Clan Mother.

All photos by, or from the collection of, W. G. Spittal

APPENDIX H
MINUTE BOOK OF THE SIX NATIONS HEREDITARY COUNCIL OF CHIEFS
KEPT IN PART FROM OCT 7,1924 TO FEB 4,1941
*copied from the original in the possession of Hereditary Council
Secretary Arthur Anderson, Mohawk
by Wm Guy Spittal, May 22-23, 1964*

Arthur Anderson was Secretary to the Hereditary Chiefs of Ohsweken, Ontario for some three decades. A Christian, fluent in Mohawk and English, he was convinced of the independent status of the Six Nations and was active in working towards the return of the Chiefs to the management of his people's affairs in the Grand River Territory. For years he, Emily General (for whom a large new consolidated school on Onondaga Road at Fourth Line of the Reserve has just been named) and William Smith were a dedicated and formidable trio researching and making presentations in England, the United States, and Canada on behalf of the Chiefs. The discharge of the Hereditary System by the Canadian Government in October, 1924 factionalized many Reserve families. Arthur would later be the Secretary for the Chiefs Council, while his son Arthur, Junior, would become the Secretary of the Elected Council.

I had met "Art" casually in my late teens, but became better acquainted later. He was a gentleman, someone I was fortunate to know. In May of 1964 I visited his home in the Village of Ohsweken and taped a number of his recollections. During that period he showed me the Minute Book of the Chiefs, begun the day of their expulsion from their Ohsweken Council House, just a short way along Fourth Line from his home. He was concerned that this material not be lost and permitted me to take it home to make a typescript copy for possible future publication. He had spent time in archives on behalf of the Chiefs and knew the importance of such documents. It seems entirely appropriate that this edition, our fourth, of the *Constitution* be expanded to preserve this account. It is not the first occasion in which the Chiefs' minute books have been worked. J.A. Noon (*Law and government of the Grand River Iroquois*, Viking Fund Publications in Anthropology, no. 12, 1949) and S.M. Weaver (*Medicine and Politics among the Grand River Iroquois*, publications in Ethnology, no. 4, National Museums of Canada, 1972) have relied upon these documents. This is the first time one has been published. Original spelling, punctuation and grammar have been preserved.

Local residents are guaranteed to find much of interest. Students of the Iroquois will also mine a rich load. The impost of a land tax by the Chiefs (entry for October 21, 1924) is something which, by today's understanding of traditional government through the Chiefs, will seem unbelievable. My appended footnotes may clarify some of the entries, one hopes they do not cloud. I can not pretend to know or understand the niceties of everything recorded. The turmoil unleashed by the coup of 1924 has not abated within Six Nations society. Families are still divided, the conflict over jurisdiction continues.

WGS
Ohsweken, Ontario
October, 1991.

Agricultural Hall
Oct 7th 1924

General Council of the Chiefs of the Six Nations was held at the Agrl Hall,
the Council House being under repairs, opened in due form by Chief Ger.
Davis one of the Fire Keepers.

Present

Col. ~~ED~~ CE Morgan	Supt
Mr HM Hill	Clerk Indian Office
Chief JC Martin	Acting Speaker
" C Garlow	Deputy Speaker
DS HIll	Secretary

and 19 Chiefs with about a score of RCMP accompanying Agent Morgan.

The Agent read a lengthy procleamation desolving the Six Nations Council
of Chiefs and appointing a day for an election day under a clause of the Indian Act.[1]

Re late Wm Johnson's estate,
The Secretary read letter from the Indian Office, Brantford, notifying the
Chiefs of its disaproval of a decision in reference to the disposition of the
estate.

The Council re-affirmed its decision of 2nd Sept last and instructed the Secretary to make out a full report giving reasons upon which the Chiefs decided to dispose of the property.

[4]

The Council decided to approve of a Lease entered into between Jacob
Lewis and Ellen Jamieson Lessors and Sahag Balia Lessee of the 5½ Lot,
No. 29. Con 1 Tuscarora, for five years, rent payable in advance.

Mrs. Susan Hill's application for the guardianship of the infant children of
Ida Gibson, deceased so that she may receive the rents from the property of
the orphan children for their benefit.

The Council decided to appoint the grandmother Susan Hill, guardian of
the infant children of Ida Gibson.

Mrs Wm Maracle, widow, to be notified to pay Mrs Nicholas Maracle within 30 days, otherwise the estate will be held liable according to a former decision and agreement entered into by her husband Wm Maracle, deceased.

Re Alex. Joseph loan
The Council decided to procure a full statement of the loan from the Indian
Office in reference to the loans of Joseph and Wilson Butler for considera-
tion at the next General Council.

The Quit Claim of Chas Green was held over for further consideration.

[5]

The account of H Percy Green $44.76 for extras on his contract repairing
the Doctor's Stables was ordered to be paid.

The Account of Harry Martin $4.00 for putting down a drain from the con-
ductors on the Council House, passed.

The Council decided to pass the account of the Secretary for services for two years at $500.00 per annum as agreed upon at the time of his engagement in October 1922. In the meantime the Council's Treasurer, Chief Chancey Garlow to advance him what money he may have to be refunded by the Secretary when the Department issue a cheque in his favour, as the Chiefs fully understand that the Secretary cannot carry on without some advance.

Repairs to No 9 School
The Council decided to instruct the Inspector of Works to make an inspection and if found necessary to have the repairs made at once.

Will of the late Peter Newhouse
The Council reaffirmed its former decision in approving of the Will.

The Council then adjourned to the 21st inst at the UCL House[2] at 10 AM.

DS Hill Secy.

[6]

UCL House
Oct 21st 1924[3]

In pursuance of an adjournment the Council was opened in due form by Chief Geo. Davis one of the Fire Keepers.
                    Present
Chief JC Martin   Acting Speaker
"   C Garlow   Deputy Speaker & Inspector
David S Hill   Secretary
with 20 Chiefs

Communication of WD Lightfoot KC and AG Chisholm Esq read and filed.[4]

The Council decided to levy a tax[5] of 10 cents per acre upon all lands on the Reserve for the purpose of the redemption of Bonds issued when due in 1928 as arranged for by the Council.

Finding of Exchequer Court in the Case King vs New England Company. The Council decided to file same until such time that the Speaker of the Council[6] returns come when the same will be considered with proper legal advisors.

Re Proposed Election
The Council of Chiefs with a large majority of the Six Nations decided to protest the illegal proposed election as at leat 75% of the Six Nations are in favour of the present Council of Chiefs and

[7]

opposed to the hi jacking tactics of the Indian Office and named the following to prepare a proper protest to be forwarded to the proper authorities. Mr A General, R Froman and Joshua Miller.

The Council decided to authorize the Secretary to deal with the parties who purchased the House thrown upon the Council by Freeman Isaac all sums paid to Secretary to be an advance.

202

The Council then adjourned to the 1st Tuesday in November.

[8]

Onondaga Long House[7]
November 4th 1924

The General Council opened in due form by Chief George Davis one of the Fire Keepers.

Present

Chf C Martin   Acting Speaker
David S Hill   Secretary
with 24 Chiefs

Warrior David Thomas[8], addressed the Council and urged the thorough re-organisation of the Council of Chiefs and the re-introduction of the Wampums by the people, as all the wampums of the Council have been illegally confiscated[9] by the Officials of the Indian Office also urging the Chiefs to carry on as the large majority of the people desire and that all Councils receive their authority from the people, Chiefs Robt David, George Davis and Jos Logan taking part in the descussion. The Council then adjourn for recess.

Re Cayuga Claim[10]-
The Council decided that as the claim only applys to the Cayugas they should have the only say in the matter.

The Council decided to authorize the Secretary to notify the Six Nations' Advisor as to the resolution of the Deleware Council's[11] repudiation of the Speaker Chief Levi General and that the Six

[9]

Nations Council of Chiefs will still continue him on the position accredited to him as representative on behalf of the Six Nations in their fight for right and justice.

Wampum.
The Council decided to leave the matter of the recovery of the Wampums to the people, they to decided upon what action to take.

The Matrons of the Six Nations decided to hold meetings throughout the Reserve and forward their decision to the Woman's party in England as requested.

Chiefs Jesse Lyons and Andrew Gibson of Syracuse NY being present spoke for some time to the Chiefs and people.

A Petition was presented to the Council, asking for the deposing of Chief Dan McNaughton on account of his traitorous actions to the Council.

Council decided to postpone taking any action at present.

Onondaga
November 18th 1924

The Council opened in due form by Chief George Davis, one of the Fire
Keepers.
                    Present
Chief JC Martin   Acting Speaker
DS Hill   Secretary
with 19 other Chiefs

Re Dan McNaughton.
The Council decided to investigate the charges but before taking any action
to lay the matter before the matrons and appointed three Cayuga Chiefs to
lay the same before the Matrons.[12]

Re proposed sale of Mrs May Generals' land by Sherriff of the Country of
Brant for law costs alleged against Chief Levi General.
The Council decided unanimously to protest the threatened sale of land by
the Sheriff of the County of Brant at the Court House on the 6th of Dec
next, for and on the grounds that the lands are the sole property of Mrs
General, she having inherited the same from her late mother Mrs Dan
Bergin.
The Council further authorized the Secretary to forward protest[13] to the
Sheriff at the time of sale.

Mathew Hill addressed the Council re Publicity.
                                                            [11]

The Council decided to authorize Mr Mathew Hill to make all arrangements as to meeting Mr Crowley, as to his desire to aid publicity of the case
of the Six Nations.

Ex Chief Jacob General applys for a reconveyance of his property held by
the Speaker as security for a loan from the funds of the Six Nations as he
has paid of the principle with interest. The Council decided to authorize the
Speaker JmC Martin to execute the Quit Claim on the production of an Official receipt showing the loan with interest has been paid in full.

                                                            [12]

UCLong House
Dec 2nd 1924

Six Nation Council opened in due form by Chief Joseph Logan[14], one of the
Fire Keepers.
                    Present
Chief JmC Martin   Acting Speaker
  "   Chancey Garlow   Deputy Speaker
David S Hill   Secretary
with 21 Chiefs

Re Petition as asked for, by the Women of England in protest as to the illegal action of the Department in introducing an Elective System of Council
contrary to the wishes of a vast majority of the Six Nations. The Council de-

cided to appoint a Committee as follows to assist the Matrons as requested:–
Jm C Martin, Isaac Kick, Joseph Logan, Aug J Hill, Jm A General and Simeon Silver.

Communication of the Editor of the Expositor[15] to the Secretary of the Council read, and after full discussion among the Chiefs, decided that the same to be filed at present, as the Expositor do not feel disposed to insert matter in favor of the Six Nations.

Re Peter Newhouse Will
The Council decided to reaffirm its former decision in approving of

[13]

the will, as it appears from the Official report of CE Morgan, his main grounds for recommending to the Department its disapproval, "that Robt. Henhawk is a member of a faction."

The account of Hilyard Hill for repairs to Schools Nos 3,7, and 8 ammounting to $16.50 be approved of and forwarded to the Supt. General for payment.

[14]

UC Long House
Jany 6th 1925

The General Council of the Six Nations, Chiefs was opened in due form by Chief Jos Logan, one of the Fire Keepers.

Present

Chief JmC Martin	Acting Speaker
" Chancey Garlow	Deputy Speaker
David S Hill	Secretary
with 24 Chiefs.[16]	

The matter of ditching the Glebe lot Brantford.
After a full discussion the Chiefs decided to protest the action of the retiring Council of the City of Brantford and the Indian Office together with 2 or 3 of the members of the so called Six Nations Council in granting from the Indian funds $2500.00[18] towards the relief of unemployment of Brantford whereas no action is taken to releave the distress on the Reserve to whom the funds so to be expended are entitled too. This protest to be laid before the Hon. Wm L McKenzie King and the Hon Chas. Stewart.

Good Roads
The Council decided to protest the proposed route and action of the Indian Department's Council as to the route being to the best interests of the people as the proposed highway three bridges across McKenzie

[15]

Creek would have to be rebuilt whereas the proposed route decided upon by the Chiefs in Council, McKenzie Creek would be crossed but once and in every particular a better route to join the good roads in Brant and Haldimand.

The Council decided to request all Pathmasters[19] appointed last year to again act for 1925.

The Chiefs in Council warned all members of the Six Nations as to enterring cases with the Council appointed by the Department.

The Secretary reports the purchase of stationary amounting to $4.00

In the matter of the Trust Funds as suggested by Wm Johnson, the British Lawyer. The Council decided to give the matter further consideration at a later date.

The Council adjourned to the 20th inst at 10 AM

[16]

Sour Springs Long House
January 20th 1925

The Six Nations Council opened in due form by Chief Jos Logan one of the Fire Keepers.

Present

Chief JmC Martin	Acting Speaker
" C Garlow	Deputy Speaker
David S Hill	Secretary
with	

Dr Svend Ranulf, of the University of Copenhagen, Denmark being a visitor and desires to spend some time on the reserve. Chief Chancey Garlow kindly offered to entertain him and assist him to gather the information desired free of charge.

Quit Claim of Sarah Doctor Patterson to John M Curley approved.

Council decided to approve of the suggestion and arrangement of the Executor Henry K Powless of the estate of the late Jas S Hill, so as to wind and close up the estate by the sale of Nelson Hill's share to his brother Jas S Hill Jr.

The Secretary of the Board of Health Mr C Martin read their report for the year 1924 which was approved of by the Chiefs in Council.

[17]

The matter of a deputation to Ottawa during the coming Session of Parliament to interview private members was endorsed provided the Six Nations' Legal advisor Mr Geo Decker approves of same. and that Mr DS Hill be deputed to ascertain Mr Decker's advice.

The Salaries of the Members of the Board of Health was passed as follows:-

Chief JmC Martin, Secretary	$25.00
" Aug. J. Hill	5.00
" David John	5.00

at this point the Minute Book lapses for eight years to be resumed by the hand of Art Anderson on page 32; he writes primarily in pencil.

Grand River[20], Ont Jan 3 1933

The Six Nations Hereditary Council was held at Sour Springs L House with
a good attendance, where the Council was duly opened by– Firekeeper
James Crawford with the following present[21]
Mohawks Chiefs Chauncey Garlow, J Lewis, Isaac General, Johnson
Sandy, Joshua Miller, Jm Snow
Chiefs A J General[22], Aug J Hill, Jas Johnson, Norman General, Jm
Jamieson, Sam General,
Firekeepers Chiefs Jas Crawford, John Davey, Wm John Jacobs

A letter from JRO Johnson was read & filed when a resolution was passed
to write Johnson a new years letter of Greatful & thanks that we are still
enjoying health & wishing him Gods speed & care.

The report of the Treasurer Chief A J General was unanimously accepted
by the Council showing a bal on hand of $19.18

[33]

Council appointed the following
Hardy Fish for Cayugas[23]
I Smoke for Senecas[24]
Joe Logan " Onondaga
AJ General for Sour Springs to arrange meetings at their several Long
Houses for accumulating funds for nation defence & exp.[25]

Josh Miller   Edw Miller   Henry Farmer also appointed to canvas.

Confirmation of delegation deferred for a month
Earnest Davis & S Silver
Council closed in due form by Crawford to meet here again the first Tues-
day of next Month.
Secy given authority to call special Council if necessary.

[34]

Grand River Feb 14/933

Council met in Sour Springs LH
Firekeeper Crawford opened Council in due form
J Lewis, Geo Johnson, Isaac General, Johnson Sandy, PJ Maracle, Jas S
Hill, Josh. Miller
S Douglas, Jacob Isaac, Alex Thomas, Jas Johnson, Norman General
Jas Crawrford, Wm John, Jm Davey.

Correspondence read by Johnson and placed on file.

Delegation still deferred until enough firekeepers

Douglas's case
Secy to give certificate to say that SN Council of Chiefs never approved
enfranchisement & that we stick strictly to Hal Treaty[26]

[35]

Grand River Mar 7 1932[27] (3)

SN Hereditary Council met in Sour Springs Long House

Chief Wm John (Firekeeper) opened the Council in due form

Mohawk Ger. Johnson, Andy Powlas, Jacob Lewis, Joshua Miller, Jas S Hill, Johnson Sandy
Aug J Hill, AJ General, Jas Johnson, Norman General, Alex Thomas, Simeon Silver, Wm Williams
Firekeepers Jm Davey, Joe Logan, Jesse Lewis, Wm Johnson, Sam Green, Jm Kick

Communication from Lawyer Johnson read & placed on file, also petition to the world.

Council passed a resolution expressing their thanks for his efficient work and great interest shwn towards us Six Nations.

Council passed that Secy. Anderson draft a letter to Johnson expressing the Chiefs' greatfulness in his endeavours.

[36]

Resolution passed asking C Owens to take up collection to make necessary repairs to typewriter & monies given to Treasurer.
Collection 3.20

Deputation deferred

Council disregarded Johnsons' request of a delegation

Council passed unanimously that Mrs Johnson to receive an equivalent of Mr Johnsons agreement in case of death of Mr Johnson as case is fully arranged.
Council closed in due form to meet at Onondagas next Gen. Council

Jacob Skye sec[28] chief to Mc Lean Davey
Chauncey Williams sec chief to Ernie Jamieson
Alex Nanticook[29]

[37]

April 5 1933

Council opened in due form by Firekeeper Geo. Davis with the following present,—
Chief C Garlow, J Lewis, Josh Miller, Isaac General, Jm Snow, Johnson Sandy

A J General, ~~Isaac General~~[30], Chauncey Isaac, Jacob Isaac, Norman General, Alex Thomas, Alex Nanticook, McLain Davey, Simeon Silver, Wm Williams, Jm Jamieson, Earnest Jamieson, Elias Gibson.

Firekeepers Jesse Lewis, Wm John, Jm Davey, Geo Davis, James Crawford

The newly elected Chiefs was duly installed by Chiefs in Council, Namely Alex Nanticook, McLean Davey & Earnest Jamieson

[38]

Grand River May 2 1933

Onondaga Long House
Council opened in due form by Firekeeper Wm Johnson
The newly appointed Chiefs were presented for approval
Freeman Green
Peter Buck
Adam Burning
~~Buck~~
Chiefs C Garlow, J Lewis, Geo Johnson, Isaac General, Johnson Sandy, Jas S Johnson, Joshua Miller, Jm Snow

Norman General, Alex Nanticook, Alex Thomas, Siamon[31] Silver, Aug J Hill, Jm Jamieson, McLean Davey, Elias Gibson

Firekeepers Jas Crawford, Joe Logan, Wm John, Jessie Lewis, Jm Davey.

the question of one Chief Buck was rejected and advised the title holders to agree and bring their decision to Council next month.[32]

[39]

The Council unanimously accepts Johnsons letter and places same on file.

Mrs Eunice Jones asked for to let & rent 4 acres and one room to a Mac. Vandousen[33]. Which was accepted to let according to the agreement as suits Mrs Jones.

Mrs Elias Gibson to be located on W ½ 5Cn of 10 acres formerly owned by her late Father.

Council closed in due form to meet here next general meeting.

[40]

Grand River, Ontario
June 6, 1933

The Six Nations Confederacy Council was held at the Onondaga LongHouse with the following Chiefs present.
Council duly opened by
    Present
Chiefs Chauncey Garlow, Jacob Lewis, Johnson Sandy, Adam Burning, Joshua Miller, Isaac General, Jm Snow

Jm Jamieson, Wm Williams, A J General, Alex Nanticook, Alex Thomas, Seaman Silver, Norman General, Earnest Jamieson

James Crawford, Wm John, Jesse Lewis,

Secy asked for a confirmation of the appointment of the three delegates appointed 3 months ago. Firekeeper Wm John objected while the other two present very in favor of the appointment, while the two other groups of Chiefs were unanimous in their appointment.

[41]

Levi Hill (Warrior) spoke and explained to the Council the dire need of unity and activity and that we should co-operate and send a delegate at once.

Firekeeper Jas Crawford reminded the Council that if the two sides of the House agree the Firekeepers can but confirm resolution, if they can not suggest anything better.[34]

Wm John replied that according to Chief Crawford the resolution is confirmed.

Therefore according to the Hereditary ruling the three delegates are appointed.

[42]

Grand River
Sept 19, 1933

Six Nations Hereditary Chiefs held a special Council[35] at the Onondaga Longhouse with the following Chiefs present:-

Chiefs		Chiefs	
C Garlow			A J General
Geo Johnson			Alex Nanticook
Josh Miller			Jm Jamieson
Johnson Sandy			Aug J Hill
Adam Burning			Wm Williams
Jm Snow			Jm Smoke
	Joe Logan		
	Wm John		
	Jessie Lewis		
	Jm Davey		
	Robt Henhawk		

Council decided to give Johnson a further 5%[36] on other page.

Council decided to meet at Thomas School House for next General Council 1st Tues in Oct.

Council closed in due form.

[43]

Sept 19, 1933
Resolution

At a Special Council of the Six Nations Hereditary Chiefs it was resolved that owing to the conditions of our people and Country it was unanimously passed that we give a further 5% to Mr JRO Johnson making our Lawyer and advisor J R Ockleshaw Johnson a further 5% making 25%. This additional 5% to be in appreciation of his sincerity and to assist in the expense of other Council or expense in connection with our case. It was further agreed that this agreement only to be valid up to Dec 31 1933. But if satisfactory results can be shown at that date the Council agrees to reconsider same.

Done at Onondaga Long House September 19, 1933.

A Anderson[37]
Secy of Confederacy

[44]

Grand River Oct 3/33

A General Council of the Six Nations Hereditary Chiefs was held in Thomas's School House with the following present,-

Chiefs   C Garlow   Aug J Hill

Chiefs	C Garlow	Aug J Hill
	Geo Johnson	A J General
	A Powless	Alex Thomas
	Isaac General	Jm Jamieson
	Jacob Lewis	Seaman Silver
	Joseph Miller	
	Johnson Sandy	
	Jas S Hill	

Jas Crawford
Jm Davey

The Council decided to adjourn the suggestion of Lawyer Johnson for a month, of adopting the Company to be known as St Lawrence Great Lakes Indigenes Rights Company.

The Council decided to hold a special Council here again two weeks today and wire Johnson advising him that his proposal is laid over for reconsideration in 2 weeks.

Adjourned Council

[45]

Grand River October 17, 1933

The Confederacy of the SN Council met in Thomas's School House with the following present,-

Chiefs	C Garlow	A J General
	Geo Johnson	Aug J Hill
	A Powless	Jm Jamieson
	J Lewis	Alex Thomas
	PJ Maracle	Simeon Silver
	I General	Alex Nanticook
	Johnson Sandy	

Joe Logan
Peter Buck   Joe Crawford
Jessie Lewis
Freeman Green   Jm Davey

Cable & letter from JRO Johnson read.
Explanation of Company Act given by Warrior Jerry Maracle & others.

After a long and searching discussion, the Council decided to (_____[38])
The firekeepers deferred the proposition until next Council or until we hear from Lawyer as to how he takes the offer of an extra 5%.

[46]

Nov 7 1933

The Six Nations Council of Hereditary Chiefs met for business & Council at the Onondaga Longhouse with the following present

Chiefs Chauncey Garlow   Aug J Hill
        Geo Johnson   Alex Nanticook
        Jacob Lewis   McLean Davey
        Joshua Miller   Seaman Silver
        Johnson Sandy   Wm Williams
        A Powless   Jm Jamieson
        Adam Burning   Alex Thomas
                 Joe Logan
                 Jas Crawford
                 Robt Henhawk
                 Wm John
                 Geo Davey
                 Jm Davey
                 Peter Buck

The adjourned Council re Johnson proposition which was deferred by firekeepers. The Firekeepers unanimously referred the case back for re-consideration.

Council decided to write Johnson for a further explanation giving reasons in detail.

[47]

Dec 5 1933

The Six Nations Hereditary Council of Chiefs met at the Onondaga Long House with the following present
Chiefs Josh Miller   Alex Thomas
        Adam Burning   "   Nanticook
        Johnson Sandy   McLean Davey
        Adam Burning   Jm Jamieson
        Levi Hill   Earnest Jamieson
                 Joe Logan
                 Jos Crawford
                 Robt Henhawk
                 Wm John
                 Jm Davey
                 Jesse Lewis
                 Peter Buck

Hunting & fishing rights laid over till next month so that more evidence may be gathered.

Major Muir to be given name next months Council.

Council closed in due form.

[48]

Jan 2, 1934

Council opened in due form by Chief Wm John
Mohawks Chauncy Garlow   AJ Hill
         Geo Johnson   Alex Thomas
         Andy Powless   Alex Nanticook

J Lewis	McLean Davey
Johnson Sandy	Jm Jamieson
Adam Burning	Wm Williams
	Ed Doxterday[39]
	Elias Gibson
	S Douglas
	Chan Isaac

Jesse Lewis
Robt Henhawk
Joe Logan
D John
Robt Davey
Wm John
Geo Davey
Jas Crawford
Peter Buck

No letter from Johnson but firekeepers asked that the case adjourned from last Council be taken up re-Hunting & Fishing rights.

Council decided to give Fred Douglas a written statement to say that the Six Nations as a Confederacy has never accepted the Indian Act.

The Council decided to Authorize Secy Anderson to write different Indian nations in the USA and elsewhere re-joining hands for our rights fully explained the condition & difficulties which the Can. Govt has placed us in etc, & that we now adj to meet for next General Council at Thomas School House.

[50]

Jan 9, 1934

An adjourned Council of the Hereditary Chiefs to discuss ways and means of a more effective move to have our case enquired into.

Present

Chiefs	Geo Johnson	Firekeepers	Jm Davey
	J Lewis		Geo Davey
	Jas Hill		Wm John
	Johnson Sandy		Robt Henhawk
			Jesse Lewis

Isaac General
Jm Jamieson
Simeon Davey
Aug J Hill
Alex Thomas
" Nanticook
McLean Davey

Council deferred the prop of warriors delegate.[40]
Propostion of Wm John referred to next gn Council of withdrawing power of attorneys from Johnson & Can Govt.
Secy authorized to be placed on record of objection to the Brit NA Act.
The Council adjourned to met at Onondaga L House for next Gen Council.

Feb 6, 1934

Council duly opened by Firekeeper Chief Logan with the following Chiefs present,-

Chiefs Chan Garlow   Aug J Hill
          Geo Johnson   Alex Thomas
          Josh Miller   Norman General
          Jacob Lewis   Alex Nanticook
          Andy Powless   McLean Davey
          Johnson Sandy   Jm Jamieson
          Adam Burning
              Joe Logan
              Jessie Lewis
              Jm Davey
              Wm John

The Council decided to delegate Chiefs Chauncey Garlow, Norman General, & Secy Anderson to go to Buffalo and wherever necessary for to and search for Documents where the United States have bound themselves to protect the Six Nations.

The Case of C Owens was deferred until next Gen Council and he to bring proper evidence or documents to prove he to be proper owner of said property in question.

page 52 – 53 blank

[54]

Grand River May 1, 1934

The Hereditary Council of the SN Chiefs held their Council in the Onondaga Longhouse which was duly opened by firekeeper Chief Wm John with the following present,-

Chiefs C Garlow   Aug J Hill
          Geo Johnson   Alex Thomas
          J Lewis   Sam General
          Josh Miller   Jacob Isaacs
          Isaac General   Jm Jamieson
          Johnson Sandy   McLean Davey
                            Seaman Silver
                            Earnest Jamieson
                            Wm Williams
                            Jm Alex General
              Joe Logan
              Jm Davey
              Wm John
              Jesse Lewis
              Peter Buck
              David John

Johnsons letter read when a sharp discussion followed

214

on a loose piece of foolscap inserted into the Minute Book is this pencil written document settling the matter of the above Hill Estate

June 1st 1934

One rod wide outlet to the main road on the West side of lot

Settlement of
Isaac Hill Estate

Situated on the south ½ of lot no 33 in the first concession of the township of Tuscarora in the Country of Brant Consisting of 46 acres more or less.

First
Joseph Hill get the House & 7½ acres on the south end. He's to give Abraham Hill a note of $15.00 dollars for one year. And he also pay his sister $15.00 dollars for her share of the property & he pay the loan

Second
Abraham Hill get 10 acres & pay his sister $15.00 dollars for her share of the property

Third
Isaac Hill get 9½ acres & pay his sister $15.00 dollars for her share of the property

Fourth
Alex Hill gets 9½ acres & pay his sister $15.00 dollars for her share of the property

Fifth
Levi Hill get 9½ acres & pay his sister $15.00 dollars for her share of the property

These five brothers above mentioned must make their payment to there sister within one year to the above date.

Arbitrators
Chief George A Johnson

Chief Jacob Lewis

{ Mr. Levi Hill

the settlement appears to be written in the hand of Chief G A Johnson; signatures seem to be by each of the three individuals indicated

[55]

Re-New-House estate Council decided to call all who claim heir to the said estate.

46 acres Hill Estate- Lewis & Johnson report. Joe claims estate is held under loan but is willing to give 7½ acres to Bros but will pay for loan but him to retain house.

Grand Council to meet at Tonawanda.[41]

[56]

Grand River June 5, 1934

The Six Nations Hereditary Chiefs met for Gen Council in the Onondaga Longhouse with the following present,-

Chiefs	C Garlow	Aug J Hill
	Geo Johnson	Isaac General
	J Lewis	Alex Thomas
	Johnson Sandy	" Nanticook
	Adam Burning	Sam General
	Joshua Miller	Jm Jamieson
		Wm Williams
		Seaman Silver

Jas Crawford
Geo Davey
Wm John
Joe Logan
Freeman Green
Jesse Lewis
Robt Henhawk

Council unanimously accepted the Mothers & Warriors gift of the Six Nations (Mase)[42] or emblem of Government Authority
Mohawks leaving out conditions but Council to meet here[43] until the re-establishment of our Government.

[57]

Re-Hills Estate. The Council adopts & confirms the agreement between the Hill Bros. with Chiefs Lewis and Geo Johnson acting arbitrators.

Re-Thomas & Logans acct. the Council passed a resolution that they will pay the balance of the account after July 1st by installments[44]

New House Estate Council gave priviledge to Mrs Frank Staats to take whatever steps she may deem necessary to recover heirship of Estate.

Council closed in due form.

[58]

Onondaga LongHouse July 3, 1934

The Hereditary Council of the Six Nations met at the Onondaga Long House with the following present,-

Chiefs	C Garlow	Jacob General
	HK Powless	Aug J Hill
	J Lewis	Jm Jamieson
	Geo Johnson	Wm Williams
	Isaac General
	Johnson Sandy
	Adam Burning

Wm John
Freeman Green
Jesse Lewis
Robt Henhawk
Jm Davey
Jas Crawford

The proposition of 33 1/3%[45] of Lawyer Johnson was not taken up by Oneidas, Cayugas & Tuscaroras & backed by the Firekeeper. The Mohawks and the Senecas did not agree the Mohawks only agreeable.

[59]

A Visitor from the Oneidas was heard and explained his visit. wishing to unite with us for our common cause.

The Secretary of the Oneidas was also called and gave us a short talk and gave us the names of the persons writing them

The Council decided to hold a Special Council at Thomas' School House two weeks today   ----------

Murray Antone
Southole PO[46]
Ont
Oneida Secy.

[60]

Grand River July 17 1934

A Special Council of the SN Confederacy was held in Thomas's School House with the following present,-

Chiefs	C Garlow	Jacob Isaac
	Geo Johnson	Simeon Snow
	HK Powless	Aug J Hill
	Jacob Lewis	A J General
	Joshua Miller	Alex Nanticook

Joe Logan
Jas Crawford
Robt Henhawk

The Mohawks decided to accept Johnsons proposal of 33 1/3 but to place certain restrictions and limit on agreement or contract. The opposite side the Cayugas Oneidas & Tuscaroras disagreed and case thrown to Firekeepers who deferred the case to next General Council.[47]

Council closed in due form by Firekeeper Logan

Council to meet again at Onondagas first tuesday of next month.

Grand River Aug 7/34

The Hereditary Council of Chiefs met for business at the Onondaga Long House with the following present

Chiefs	C Garlow	A J General
	Geo Johnson	Jacob Isaacs
	Jacob Lewis	Aug J Hill
	H K Powless	Alex Nanticook
	Josh. Miller	Simeon Snow
	Johnson Sandy	Jm Jamieson
	Adam Burning	

Jos Logan
Jesse Lewis
Jas Crawford
Jm Davey

Re Johnsons proposals
Mohawks unan two Senecas objects gives 25% & one for. one Oneida gives while the Cayugas all objects
Johnson given his prop but to limit the time for this agreement.
Com. appointed to draft agreement J Lewis   C Garlow
C Garlow appoints H Martin two Senecas gives to end of year 1 same as Mohawks with one giving 6 months

[62]

Cayugas & Oneidas agree to give him first of Jan with just one giving him 6 months
Choosing Jm Jamieson and A J General to the comm.
Firekeepers confirm the agreement to terminate Jan 1 1935[48]

[63]

Aug 22 1933

A Special Council was called for the purpose to protest the men that are to represent the Six Nations at the Celebration at Niagara on Sept 345&6. With the following present

Chiefs	C Garlow	A J General
	Geo Johnson	Jacob "
	J Lewis	Alex Nanticook
	Josh Miller	" Thomas
	Johnson Sandy	Jm Jamieson

Joe Logan
Jesse Lewis
Wm Jacobs
Jm Davey

The Council unanimously protest against the so called representatives of the Six Nations giving full reasons same to be drafted by men to be appointed.
Mohawks & Senecas appoints Secy, C Garlow J Lewis and Geo Johnson
Cayugas & oneidas & Tuscaroras appoint AJ General
Firekeepers Chief C Garlow, A J General[49], David Thomas

[64]

Warriors allowed to appoint 3 delegates to assist in preparing protest and speech
Jerry Maracle & Harry Martin
speakers for the celebration unanim
Speaker C Garlow & Secy Anderson

Council closed in due form by Firekeeper Joe Logan

Declaration of Independence Proclamation signed by order in Council (refer) Treaty of Ghent article 9 Canada breaking all agreements while Indian Chiefs still relying on treaties.

[65]

Grand River Sept 11 th

The Hereditary Council met in the Onondaga Long House for monthly meeting with the following present

Chiefs	C Garlow	A J General
	J Lewis	Alex Nanticook
	Johnson Sandy	" Thomas
		Jacob Isaac
		Jm Jamieson
		Aug J Hill

(Hepburn)   Joe Logan
Jesse Lewis
Robt Henhawk
Jm Davey
Jas Crawford

The Council decided to have written protest protesting Elliott Moses[50] representing the Mohawks of Grand River or Six Nations

The Council further decided to write Premier of Ontario[51], informing him that the fair society cannot legally give him an Indian name

Re- Grand Council Mohawks suggests to appoint several Chiefs and their expenses paid and leave it open to all others to go at their own exp.

[66]

Mohawks & Senecas appoint Chiefs Lewis and Isaac General Cayugas Oneidas & Tuscaroras appoint A J General Aug J Hill and Secy Anderson[52]
Onondagas appoint Wm John

[67]

Grand River, Nov 6 1934

The Six Nations Hereditary Chiefs met for Council at the Mohawk Long House[53] with the following present,-

Chiefs	C Garlow	Isaac General
	J Lewis	Sam "
	Geo Johnson	Aug J Hill
	HK Powless	Jm Jamieson

Johnson Sandy   Alex Thomas
Adam Burning   "   Nanticook
Isaac General   Chauncey Williams
    Jas Crawford
    Joe Logan

Council appointed Chief C Garlow, Secy Anderson and David Thomas as delegates to go to Washington
Decided to re-confirm Elisabeth Everetts Quit Claim but asks that Wm be allowed to stay during his natural life

[68]

Dec 4 1934

The Hereditary Chiefs met for General Council at the Onondaga Long House with the following present

Chiefs   J Lewis   Aug J Hill
       Johnson Sandy   Alex Nanticook
                   "   Thomas
                  Isaac General
       Wm John
       Jesse Lewis
       Jas Crawford

Mr Johnson letter was read & placed on file
A discussion took place re International Law of Cayuga Arbitration.

page 69 blank

[70]

Grand River Jan 1 1935

The Six Nations Hereditary Chiefs met for Council in the Onondaga Long-House with the following present,-

Chiefs   Chauncy Garlow   A J General
       Geo. Johnson   Sam   "
       J Lewis   Alex Nanticook
       Johnson Sandy   Jm Jamieson
       Adam Burning
            Joe Logan
            Jas Crawford

The Council re-Confirmed the Three appointed two months to go to Washington & interview the President.
The Council left Johnsons agreement alone until we hear further from him & also see what the delegation did at Washington.
W. K Cornelious's suggestion was left as it is until after the trip from Washington
Council closed in due form by Logan
When a special request was made for a spec 1 wk[54]

pages 71, 72, 73 blank

Grand River April 2/35

Council met in Mohawk Long House with the following

Chiefs	C Garlow	Jim Jamieson
	Geo Johnson	Alex Nanticook
	PJ Maracle	" Thomas
	J Lewis	Aug J Hill
	Johnson Sandy	C Isaac
	Adam Burning	
	Isaac General	

Joe Logan
Jas Crawford
Jm Davey

at the bottom of this page is the following entry

Oct 10 1934   The Council passed the will of the late Mrs Eunice Jones to daughter Mrs Jemima Kennedy 4 acres land & contents lot 34 con 1 Tuscarora

Council passed that identification cards be issued to all Chiefs who have not broken Chiefs const-[55]

[75]

[56] Re communication from Basom[57] (Sachem Freeman Johnson) to inform him that communicat. from Chief Jones is all that can be recognized

A visitor from Oneida reservation was called upon for a speech after an address of welcome by Chief Logan.

Mrs Mary Parker's Claim against Alex Hill postponed for a month when both parties may be present for a settlement of her claim.

Resolution passed giving authority to Secy to reply to paper clipping or letters talks on Indian rights.[58]

here was included a paper clipping referring to the revival of a dispute by the Chiefs over the granting of the Reserve lands, and that this dispute had been taken up before, and that white settlement had been legally made upon it

page 76 blank

[77]

Grand River May 7 1935

General Council of the Six Nations Hereditary Chiefs met for business and to hear the reports of the delegates to Washington
With the following present.

Chiefs	C Garlow	Aug J Hill
	J Lewis	Jm Jamieson
	A Powless	Jm Smoke
	PJ Maracle	Alex Nanticook
	Isaac General	Elias Gibson
	Johnson Sandy	
	Adam Burning	
	Isaac Snow	
	Joe Logan	
	Jm Davey	

Secy Anderson first gave verbal report followed by Chief Logan and then David Thomas

The report of the delegates was gladly received & it was urged that case should go forward with greatest possible speed.

[78]

May 21 1935

The Six Nations Hereditary Council held a special Council at the ~~Onondaga~~ Mohawk Long House, which was duly opened by Jas. Crawford with the following present.

Chiefs	C Garlow	A J General
	PJ Maracle	Alex Thomas
	Geo Johnson	" Nanticook
	J Lewis	Jm Jamieson
	A Powless	Norman General
	Jm Snow	Seaman Silver
	Johnson Sandy	
	Isaac General	
	James Crawford	
	John Davey	
	Robt Henhawk	

A discussion of some length regarding Power of Attorney took place & was finally dropped and decided to appoint men to draft memorandum or brief Firekeepers objected on the ground that they would leave the matter to the Grand Council to appoint to show unity

[79]

June 18 1935

Special Council held at Mohawk Long House to discuss ways & means of procedure in presenting our case to US
Council duly opened by John Henhawk with the following Chiefs present

Chiefs	C Garlow	Alex Thomas
	A Powless	" Nanticook
	J Lewis	Norman General
	J Maracle	Aug J Hill
	Isaac General	(Visitor) Alex Elija[59]

Robt Henhawk
John   "   (assisting)

Council asked Secy to give reports on Correspondence (none)

Council decided to have Brief read & translated into the Mohawk Language and Chief Garlow to interpret same, as Brief is in his possession & should now thoroughly understand contents.

Council decided to have Garlow have finished brief by next General Council which will be held at Onondagas July next.

Closed in due form

[80]

Grand River July 2 1935

The Six Nations Council of Chiefs met for business with the following present

Chiefs	C Garlow	Jm Jamieson
	J Lewis	Aug J Hill
	Geo Johnson	Alex Thomas
	Andy Powless	
	Isaac General	
	Joe Logan	
	Jas Crawford	

Council decided to further explain reasons in Brief before presenting.

The Case of William Maracle was dismissed

Council decided to notify other Reservations that we have drawn up a brief and would like to have their approval.

[81]

Grand River, Aug. (___) 1935

The Six Nations Hereditary Council of Chiefs met for business with the following present & the Council duly opened by Chief J Logan

Chiefs	C Garlow	Alex Thomas
	J Lewis	" Nanticook
	Geo Johnson	Aug J Hill
	Andy Powless	Jm Jamieson
	PJ Maracle	
	Joe Logan	
	Freeman Green	

The Council unanimously passed to authorize the Secy to inform all Reservations that we are preparing to go to Washington the Latter part of September & at the same time to ask their moral & financial support. Also to ask Onondagas to arrange the meeting with Senators of US.

Council urges the Support of all workers of our Domain as a trip is proposed in Sept.

Council closed to meet again at the Mohawk LH the first Tuesday in Sept

[82]

Grand River Sept 3rd/35

The Six Nations Hereditary Council of Chiefs met for business with the following present.

Chiefs C Garlow   Aug J Hill
        PJ Maracle   Seaman Silver
        Andy Powless
        Isaac General
        Adam Burning
        Johnson Sandy
                David Thomas
                Harry Martin

The Council unanimously Decided to have a committe to re-draft the Petition inserting our views in the matter.

The Council appoints Chief C Garlow, Chief Isaac General, Secy Anderson & Harry Martin also David Thomas & Levi Hill Chief George Johnson Melvin Johnson or any one who is interested.

page 83 blank

[84]

Grand River Sept 24 1935

The Six Nations Hereditary Chiefs held a special Council to complete the brief and appoint delegates to Washington. The Council was duly opened by Firekeeper Davey with the following present.

Chiefs C Garlow   Aug J Hill
        Geo Johnson   Jm Jamieson
        J Lewis   Alex Nanticook
        Andy Powless
        Johnson Sandy
                Joe Logan
                Jessie Lewis
                Wm Jacobs
                Geo Davey
                Jm Davey
                Jas Crawford

The Council decided to accept the newly drafted petition adding the account of the Oneidas etc also to make mention of the unanimous reunion of all Six Nations of GB & USA

Council decided to authorize Secy to write all Canadian 6 nations & have them endorse our claims as against GB and inform all american 6N as to when we are likely to call on their Reservation to give them ample time to make arrangements.

[85]

Council decided to adjourn their General Council until two weeks today on account of giving time to hear from other reservations for Washington- Garlow, Thomas & Secy Anderson
Council closed in due form to meet here two weeks today.

[86]

Grand River Oct 8, 1935

The Six Nations Hereditary Chiefs met for Special Council for to make further arrangements for the trip to Washington. With the following present
Chiefs   C Garlow   Aug J Hill
         J Lewis
         Geo Johnson
         Andy Powless
         Adam Burning
                    Wm Jacobs
                    Jm Davey

It was unanimously resolved that we accept the proposal of the Nedrow Onondagas to hold another Grand Council a week from Friday & Saturday October 18

Council decided to Authorize Chief Garlow to have petition or brief partly ready for the approval and sanction of Grand Council to be held on Oct 18 & 19/35 and to have all sign at the Grand Council

[87]

Council or Firekeepers could not sanction the appointment of delegates to attend this meeting at Oneida on the 21st inst.

Council closed in due form by Firekeeper Wm Jacobs

[88]

(no date)

Special Council held at Smoke's Corners with the following present,
Chiefs   C Garlow   Alex Thomas
         J Lewis   Geo Jamieson
         Isaac General   Aug J Hill
         Johnson Sandy
         Adam Burning
                    Joe Logan
                    Jesse Lewis
                    Jm Davey

Council decides to appoint the following with full power to act in the way of securing funds to pay expenses of delegation to Washington
Harry Martin   Jm Henhawk
by Mohawks   by Oneidas
—by firekeepers

[89]

Earnest Crow   Rose Neath   Albert Big-Canoe[60] ask for Washingtons pledge

A statement to prove their appointment & to say they uphold the Hereditary rights

Jas A Martin   Oliver & Calvin Hill   Bros twins
John Curley   Howard Jonathan   Sam Jamieson/Gordon Powless
Hiram Skye

Special Council a week today at Onondaga L House
Council closed in due form

[90]

Grand River, Jan 7, 1936

First Council of the year being held at Onondaga Long House and was duly opened by Firekeepers with the following present

Chiefs   Chauncey Garlow   Aug J Hill
          Jacob Lewis   Jacob Isaacs
          P J Maracle   Alex Thomas
          Andy Powless   " Nanticook
          Johnson Sandy   Sam General
                                     Jm Jamieson
                   Joe Logan
                   Jesse Lewis
                   Wm Jacobs
                   Jm Davey

Council decided to pay $15.00 amt due for drafting of petition.

Council decided to give authority to the delegates at Washington

Council decided to send delegates to Washington as soon as possible.

[91]

Sam General, donates $1.00

Council decided to write Oneidas asking forgiveness for disappointing them on the 23rd inst also to ask for financial support.

Council adjourned to have a special council at Herb Martins new Bldg a week today.

pages 92 and 93 blank

[94]

Onondaga LongHouse Tues Sept 21 1936

Special Council to complete arrangements and appoint delegates to the Grand Council to be held on Friday Sept 25, 1936.
Council duly opened by Firekeeper Chief Logan

Joshua Miller   Alex Nanticook
Isaac General   Jm Jamieson
Harry Martin   Jacob Isaac
                  Joe Logan
                  Jesse Lewis
                  Jm Davey
                  Jas Crawford

Council decided to have Ed Walker have M.P.Wood to get the minutes of Council concerning the tender or agreement for grading the road South of Ohsweken in 1921 or 2

Council decided to authorize canvassers to solicit from anyone that will support

Firekeepers appointed Joe Logan as delegate for Grand Council

[95]

Council decided to send Harry Martin as an authorized delegate to Grand Council

Council decided or appointed the following to canvas for expenses of delegation
Chas Johnson   Jerry Maracle   Sanford Bomberry   James General

Decided to hold a special Council to finish of plans for trip to Onondaga or Syracuse. next wednesday a week tomorrow today

Council adjourned till a week tomorrow

[96]

Onondaga Longhouse Saturday Sept 21 1940
120 McNaughty Blvd

25 & 26

Notice

Owing to Bills posted by Major EP Randle[61] that Six Nations are req to register[62] at the Council House Ohsweken on Sept 25 & 26 If not will be subject to penalties. Failure to do so sub to pen.
At a duly called meeting of the Hereditary Chiefs Holders of the Haldimand Treaty. The Six nations are asked not to register Notice is hereby given to members of the Six Nations of Grand River not to register by reason of the following X letter.[63]

Extracts of following—

Done at the Onondaga Long House this 22 day Sept 1940

[97]

Onondaga Long House Sept 21 1940

A Very Special Council was duly called for the purpose of deciding action on the registration, of which notice of complusion is given by EP Randle agent of the Indian Department.
Present[64]
Mohawk Chiefs C Garlow, Jas S Hill, Albert Martin, Johnson Sandy, Adam Burning[65]
Cayugas   Alex Nanticook
Firekeepers   Jessie Lewis, Wm Jacobs, Freeman Green, D Thomas

Council unanimously passed that Secy Anderson get Official letter printed directed to Hon W L M King and that Council confirmed or takes responsibility

Council decided to send Jacob Lewis, Wm Jacobs & Art Anderson to interview Premier[66] King & if possible Gov. General

[98]

Onondaga Longhouse Oct 1 1940

The Council of Chiefs duly assembled at their regular monthly Council unanimously agreed

1 that notice be given the Elective Council that they be no longer respected owing to the many injustices being committed by them and also for their being accepting all the changes brought up by the Dept of Indian Affairs.

2 It was also decided that EP Randles services be dispensed with on account of his imposing registration and threatening (for failure)

3 In the matter of Mrs Joe C Martin (Will) it was decided that Mrs Martin be given the property which was willed to her by her mother, as daughter gave consent that she would pay them the monies mentioned in said will at her own convenience.

4 It was further agreed that EP Randle be arrested for misrepresenting registration & that the Chiefs again take over authority for their people.

pages 99 - 107 blank

[108]

Grand River Domain Feb 4, 1941

The monthly Council of the Confederacy was duly opened by Firekeeper Chief Joe Logan with the following Chiefs present.

Chiefs Chauncey Garlow
Jas S Hill
Lloyd Farmer
Jacob Lewis
Levi Hill
Chas Silversmith
Johnson Sandy

Joe Logan
Alex Nanticook[67]   Jesse Lewis
Thomas Miller
Jm Davey

Council re Affirmed powers given to Chiefs Jas S Hill & others

Council leaves the testing of cattle cattle[68] for a month

pages 109 - 195 blank

[196]

Albert P Martin
Farm Concession 3
33 1/3 to son Hardy
Will all chattels & effects

40 rods long
East ½ lot not 6 Concession 6 east ½ being remainder of farm lot of John Hill allowing Hill road or 16 ft passage to back end of farm
farm being 25 acres South east corner

Reg Martin
Levi Hill
4 horse
3 cows
homes & implements

[197]

Department Legislation of Upper Canada

When Geo III sent out Simcoe as his representative to govern Canada he made a treaty with the Indians at the Bay of Quinte called "the Gunshot Treaty"
Thousands of Indians were present, including the principle Chiefs of the different tribes. The Government stated although the Gov. wanted the lands it was not intended that the fish & game rights be exchanged or that they were to be deprived of their privileges of hunting & fishing as it is a source of their living & sustanance.
These provisions were to hold good as long as the grass grows & water run, & as long as the Brit. Gov. is in existence

~~Eunice hill~~ Jones $8.00 per month
     Joe Hill   reserves
          4 acres shares one room to his wife
                              Mac Vandousen

10 acres belonging Jm Snow Mrs Elias Gibson wishes to be reg[69]

at this point the Minute Book falls silent

Editor's Footnotes

1 Although their Council had just been dissolved by Superintendent Morgan's reading of the Proclamation the Chiefs took no notice and continued in session. Indeed, one might wonder if the full import of their new situation was comprehended. Not only did they continue regular business (approvals of a lease to a non-Indian, a guardianship, an estate settlement, and payment of bills, as well as an order for possible school repairs), they also decided to request the Indian Office for information on loans by two Band members. All this activity was now beyond their authority, that had passed into history. However, the new situation was soon manifest as is reflected in the Minutes. Council business quickly shifts from that of a Government tending to its jurisdiction, to one occupied with little else than matters addressing its reinstatement: petitions, delegations, lawyers.

After 67 years and a complete replacement of individuals, regular Councils continue. Community guidelines on matters of the day are printed in the Reserve newspaper, native rights and interests at both Six Nations and other Iroquois territories are monitored; the Chiefs remain as a shadow government which will not be ignored. A committee established to evaluate community opinion regarding the re-establishment of local control of elementary education recently announced that its final recommendations will "be submitted to both Councils at Six Nations"; this is new behaviour. The 1990 crisis among the Kanesatake Mohawks at Oka, Québec promoted a request for the Chiefs' intervention from Canadian Government officials. This was significant to the Chiefs faction which saw it as an important recognition of their system's survival and authority.

Under the six-year leadership of Chief Councillor Wm Montour (resigned three months before the end of his third two-year term, September 9, 1991) efforts at reconciliation were made by the Elected Council. The Chiefs, however, interpreting various recent signals and approaches to them, anticipate an imminent restoration and an end to the imposed Elected system.

The following item appeared recently in the Reserve newspaper:
OHSWEKEN - Andrew Staats approached Six Nations Band Council with an interesting proposal on Tues. Sept. 17.

As a result of meetings between the confederacy chiefs and elected chiefs held over the past few months, several people from different reserves have questions about the Great Law. Most of these reserves are those without longhouses such as Gibson, Kanestake and Oneida. These people have requested a reading of the Great Law in English.

Staats has proposed a five day conference to be held in middle to late October. According to Staats' proposal to Council, the foremost reason for this conference is Native heritage fostering self-esteem among the Native people. It has been more than twenty-five years since the full contents of the Great Law were heard.

Staats approached Council with a plea for financial assistance. Tyendinaga has agreed to match contributions Staats could raise for the conference. Council has taken the proposal under advisement and will give Staats an answer at the next full council meeting.

Staats says, "We must education ourselves and we have to start somewhere... I think it (the conference) would be a good education process" (*TEKANWENNAKE*, Ohsweken, Ontario, September 25, 1991, p 3).

The Elected Council has since made $3500.00 available towards this project. As this volume was being published replies from other interested reserves were being awaited.

2 UCL House = "Upper Cayuga Longhouse", also known as "Sour Springs Longhouse" (see January 20, 1925).

3 This was also the date of the first Indian Act election at Six Nations, protested further in the entry.

4 Two in a succession of attorneys retained by the Chiefs. Also mentioned are J R O Johnson, and George Decker (an American who worked with the New York State Iroquois); contact with a Wm Johnson in England is also recorded.

5 In my files is the record of a late 19th Century introduction by the Chiefs of dog licensing, no longer in effect. The Chiefs appear to have accepted the concept of raising money in the community through direct and indirect taxation. It would be informative to review the pre-1924 Minute Books to determine to what degree this subject, now a taboo at Six Nations, had been advocated and applied. Weaver has interesting material on the degree to which Council (by then predominantly Christian) was willing to integrate the Reserve into the Canadian system:

> The Conservative Party under Sir John A. Macdonald gave Indians the right to vote in federal elections in 1885. Although council officially urged residents not to exercise their franchise, individual chiefs of the Upper Tribes (Mohawk, Oneida, Tuscarora) became heavily involved in local campaigning.... In 1898 when the Liberals withdrew the franchise, because the Indians had supported the Conservative Party, the council unsuccessfully *petitioned to have it returned* (Sally Weaver: "Six Nations of the Grand River, Ontario", p 532 IN *Handbook of North American Indians*, Vol. 15, 1978, pp 525-536; italics mine, WGS).

A photo of a 1920's Tax Certificate issued by the Six Nations Confederacy (NY) can be seen on page 75 of *The Iroquois and the New Deal*, L M Hauptman, 1981.

6 The position of Permanent Speaker was created by the Chiefs in 1858, it was not established in the *Constitution* (p 33, section 14); with their removal from authority the rôle lapsed. The first incumbent was Chief John Smoke Johnson, grandfather of poet E Pauline Johnson. The Deputy Speaker appeared in the 1870's, and, following proper Iroquois reciprocal ceremonial form, was usually from the side of Council opposite the Speaker. The First Secretary (1880-1915) was Chief Josiah Hill (a Nanticoke) (Weaver, p 528, 533).

The absent Speaker in the Minutes was the Cayuga Chief, Deskahe (Levi General) who was with lawyer Decker in Geneva, Switzerland attempting to lobby the League of Nations against the anticipated coup.

7 This 19th Century frame building has been replaced with a larger log structure. The "Fire" (accrediting wampum) was moved October 19, 1991, the day before hosting the yearly round, known locally as "the Convention", of recitations of the Code of Handsome Lake. See photos.

8 Thomas would later be condoled an Onondaga Chief (Hahĕ: hŏn'), his name first appearing with the Chiefs Aug 22, 1934. His speech from the floor admonishing the Chiefs (June 6, 1933) is one of two by "warriors" in the Minutes. He was a highly qualified ritualist and custodian of his culture. Cayuga Chief Jacob E Thomas continues his father's example. See also fn. 40 for more on "Warriors".

9 Wampum left the Reserve by illicit sale as well as confiscation.

Returns of wampum to the Confederacy at Ohsweken were recently made by the Museum of the American Indian, Heye Foundation, New York City (May 8, 1988), and the Canadian Museum of Civilization, Ottawa (January 5, 1991). Efforts are being made to recover other belts. The Council "Mace" wampum strings (see fn. 42) were returned by Chief Councillor Montour, also May 8, 1988; they had been found in his Council's vault.

10 Cayuga Arbitration Claim: a claim by Ohsweken Cayuga that they were entitled to a share of the interest annually dispersed to the remnant American Cayuga in the matter of lands in New York State sold between 1789 and 1814. A joint British-American commission adjudicated in their favour in 1926 with an award of $100,000 from which per capita payments are now paid biannually. However, the

entitlement has been considerably reduced by the growth in the Cayuga rolls (some in the community contend that many people, suddenly "discovering" Cayuga roots, switched lists solely to partake in the distribution). Canadian policy, dictating enrollment in the father's line, ignores those who are Cayuga within the Iroquois system of matrilineal descent and they receive no benefit whatsoever.

These Minutes illustrate Council's aversion to involvement in internal National affairs. The *Constitution* did not extinguish the Council Fires of member nations (p 55, section 97). The Chiefs, as a defacto municipal government, earlier had had problems with the idea of National Councils at Ohsweken:

> Gradually and sometimes reluctantly the council assumed many of the powers of the tribe, clan, and lineage, thus contributing to the attrition of these units. For example, the council began to settle property and land disputes, to allocate land to families, and to provide relief to the aged and infirm. Tribal councils, infrequent in the 1840's and 1950's, were condemned by leading chiefs as damaging to the unity of the Confederacy council and they soon ceased to figure significantly in reserve politics (Weaver, p 528).

When competing Kahnawake Mohawk factions pressured Council during 1989-90 for intervention in matters it considered internal, they were told to go home and settle these problems among themselves. Council's fruitless 1990 delegation to Oka was an attempt to re-establish Peace, the raison d'être of the League.

The July 17, 1991 issue of *TEKAWENNAKE* carried a unique advertisement on behalf of Mrs Marjorie Skye, Mohawk Turtle Clan Mother of Chief Aionwa:ta' ("Hiawatha"). A list was being made so that important family business might include all the family, as well as to "know who we're kin to" and to arrange a family picnic.

11 Presumably, the "Advisor" was their attorney. Note that at this date the Ohsweken Delaware still maintained a Council. Reserve tradition holds that much of the pressure to "dehorn" (remove) the Chiefs came from this guest Algonquian people — this ignores such early activity as that of a group of Mohawk in 1861 who petitioned the Crown for an elected government (Weaver, p 529).

12 Compare this procedure to that outlined in the *Constitution*, pp 42, 106.

13 The problem here was the impending activity of a County Sheriff against Reserve property; the Indian Act prevents this. The Chiefs' protest also would have been based on sovereignty. What was the new Elected Council's position? The very fact of the sale suggests a relinquishment of Six Nations autonomy in its apparent acquiesence to the intervention.

14 Chief Thadoda-ho; the last at Six Nations (d. December 11, 1961) since the Grand Council decision to return to a single title holder only, and he to be condoled by the New York Onondaga; Leon Shenandoah is the present antler-wearer.

15 *The Brantford Expositor*, the newspaper of nearby Brantford, Ontario.

16 The total of 26 Chiefs attending is the highest shown in these Minutes; a shadow Council attracted only eight Chiefs on October 8, 1935.

17 A tract of some 100 acres, more or less, of Reserve land along the Grand River within the City of Brantford. On it are the Mohawk Chapel (Anglican, 1786) and a former Anglican residential agricultural-educational complex (1831-1970) for Six Nations and other native children known as "The Mohawk Institute", but to the hapless inmates, endurers of insipid meals, it was "The Mush Hole". It is now the site of the Woodland Indian Cultural Education Centre, 184 Mohawk Street. A Band-operated business mall, "The Eagle's Nest", has recently been added to this Reserve enclave.

18 This is reminiscent of the occasions between 1834-1844 when the Crown high-handedly dipped into Band funds to invest in the Grand River Navigation Com-

pany; it foundered in 1861 and the appropriated money was lost. Ottawa refuses to consider redress, holding that it happened before Confederation and therefore the Canadian Government is not accountable. This issue is still being contested.

19 Under the Chiefs neighbourhood roads were maintained by the communal labour of the men who lived along them; they were led by "Pathmasters".

20 "Grand River Territory" and "Grand River Country" are two Reserve designations used by some Six Nations sovereigntists. The final entry in the Minute Book gives "Grand River Domain".

21 Here, Anderson, the new Secretary, breaks with the style of predecessor David S Hill and names the Chiefs, while also separating them into these lines for the Council groupings of Elder and Younger Brothers, and Firekeepers. He maintains this for nine months then re-organizes them into three blocks (September 19, 1934). This blocking presents the Younger Brothers to the right of the Firekeepers, if indeed seating is what is intended by his format. It is, however, this same positioning which Weaver mentions for Councils in Onondaga Longhouse at Middleport on the north side of the Grand River. This was before 1863 when the Council House was erected in the "centre" of the Reserve, around which the Village of Ohsweken soon developed (Weaver, p 529). During the nine-day take-over of the Council House, March 5-13, 1959, I observed the Younger Brothers on the East side of the room. The Fire-Keepers sat just inside the railing facing North, the Elder Brothers to their left (West). This is the same arrangement Anderson shows in the Minutes. Today, the Younger Brothers sit to the left (east) of the Firekeepers, who occupy the North wall of Onondaga Longhouse and face South. This is a break with earlier tradition.

The Minutes of January 9, 1934 inexplicably reverses the positions of the Firekeepers and the Younger Brothers.

22 Alexander "Jack" General, successor to his late (d. June 27, 1925) brother Levi's title, "Deskahe".

23 Lower Cayuga Longhouse. The terminal "s" here, and next with "Senecas", and elsewhere with "Onondagas" (March 7, 1933), is common Six Nations usage when referring to these Longhouses.

24 Seneca Longhouse.

25 The elderly wife of one of the ousted Chiefs was fond of telling how hard their supporters had worked in this period to raise money for legal actions. For her these exercises seemed to have gone on interminably, and eventually she became exasperated by so much work and the want of positive results from the lawyers, but she continued helping. Lack of adequate operating funds remains a problem for the Chiefs.

26 Haldimand Treaty, October 25, 1784.

27 Anderson means 1933.

28 Second Chief = sub-chief = *assistant*; see p 107, paragraph 2. The Cayuga term, Hônda.nôn, translates "He watches the tree" (ie, the Chief).

29 Nanticoke.

30 Scoured out in the Minute Book. Other similar corrections have been included throughout our copy.

31 Name is indistinct here, appears as "Seaman", "Simeon" in other entries.

32 See the *Constitution*, p 44, section 54, and p 107, paragraph 5.

33 Eight and a half years after their removal from office the Chiefs are asked for, and confirm, permission to lease property to an apparent non-Indian. The name appears again at the end of the Minute Book. A "vanDeursen" family is now living some ways past the western end of the Reserve.

34 See the *Constitution*, p 31, section 5, p 33, sections 10, 11, 12, and pp 98-100.

35 Regular Councils normally are the first Tuesday in a month; Special Councils may be called any time, eleven are recorded in the Minutes. This Council was the first minuted since June 6. There are other such gaps in the record as illustrated in the chart with fn. 43.

36 The various references to percentages for Johnson and his wife appear to be conditional financial arrangements by an insolvent Council to be paid out of any award arising from his successful litigation.

37 The first time Anderson's full name appears in the Minute Book, he is mentioned in passing, March 7, 1932.

38 No entry here.

39 Presumably, an attempt at *Doxtador*, or *Doxtater*, or *Doxtator*, or *Doxtdator*, four forms of this surname in use by Six Nations people; *Dockstader* is a version at Oneidatown, Ontario (Oneida of the Thames).

40 The first record here of an approach from the "warriors" as an entity. They are again mentioned August 22, 1933, June 5, 1934, and August 2, 1934. Previously "warrior" had been used as an identifier for individuals: "Warrior David Thomas", November 4, 1924 while D S Hill was Secretary; and an Anderson entry such as "Levi Hill (Warrior)", June 6, 1933. This useage by the two Secretaries indicates the acceptance of the term in this period; it is currently out of favour with the Ohsweken Chiefs. The emphasis is now on the "Peace" aspect of the League. "Warrior" has been discredited locally as a result of its adoption by certain activist St Lawrence River Mohawks, disciples of the elderly Kahnawake Mohawk Louis Hall (Karoniaktajeh) who found authorization in the published *Constitution* (fellow Mohawk Newhouse's version, several times rejected by the Chiefs) for the organization of a militant "Warrior Society" acting outside the authority of the Chiefs.

41 It is normal for Grand Councils to be held at Onondaga, NY; see October 8, 1935. Important meetings relating to the Code of Handsome Lake are usually held at Tonawanda.

42 See the *Constitution*, pp 44-45, section 55, and p 105, paragraph 6. The "elevated place (or pole)" on p 44 became, at Ohsweken's Onondaga Longhouse, the Secretary's small desk along the top of which the strings usually were laid. The "Mase" (mace) noted here was a replacement for the one lost to Council during the coup of 1924 (see also fn. 9). The Cayuga term *Gajēs'ta* ("fire") is the metaphor for the Chiefs' Council Fire, for a Longhouse authorized to conduct Handsome Lake's preaching, and the wampum which validates both. A more complete designation for the "mace" is "the Confederacy Ember", or "the Council Fire"; in Cayuga: "Dāwennaʰgya: dōnʰ Gajē:ʰ sta' Hōnadājēʰsta: en" and in Mohawk: "Tāwennaʰ kāra: tōn Katšе'sta' Rōnatātsēsta: yän".

Wampum is in very short supply at Ohsweken. Many Clan Mothers have only one of the two required strings (one white, one 'black') necessary to authenticate their Chiefs' titles. In 1990 Chief Jacob Thomas offered classes in the making of the traditional quahaug wampum beads. A few men and women soon learned how much work is involved. Techniques have since improved and a trickle of beads is being produced for personal and ceremonial purposes. A second course is planned for the end of 1991.

43 Although the Chiefs decide to light their Council Fire henceforth at Onondaga Longhouse "until the re-instatement of our Government" the Minutes show them continuing their democratic circuit about the Reserve until September, 1935. Even then, the incomplete subsequent record is of only three Councils at "Onondagas", a fourth is not sited.

Thirty-three Regular Councils, four Adjournments, and eleven Special Councils are recorded in seven locations. In most instances of unspecified venues it is possible to place them by referring to the preceding Minutes where the forthcoming location is advanced (see last line, January 2, 1934). The chart and map may help interpret the data.

From October 7, 1924, to February 4, 1941, there are just 33 Regular monthly Councils recorded. Calculating 12 such per year, plus the three ending 1924 and the two to February, 1941 there ought to have been 197 entries, exclusive of Adjournments and Specials. The Minutes are short 163 Regular Councils. The longest gap is the full eight years after January 29, 1925 to January 3, 1933. In the five years after January, 1936, and until February, 1941, there are just two Regular Councils (and two Specials). I did not have the wit to ask Art the reason for these lapses.

44 Yet another example of the shortage of funds besetting the Chiefs during the difficult years of the Great Depression.

45 Lawyer Johnson's contingency fee (if that is what it was then, such fees are currently illegal in the Ontario legal system) originally 20%, then 25% (September 19, 1933), has risen yet another notch.

46 Southwold Post Office, the mailing address for the Oneidas of the Thames Band. There is no explanation for inserting this notation.

In the 1930's Ottawa also forced an Elected System upon the Thames River Oneidas. Their appearance in the Minutes reflects their association with the Ohsweken Chiefs in a mutual contest for re-instatement of traditional government.

47 Another example of traditional Council procedure as cited in fn. 34.

48 Council tables a letter from Johnson, December 4, 1934. On January 1, 1935 it leaves the agreement with him as it was, pending his further communication. Sometime after this his contract must have terminated, or perhaps he did — he is not mentioned again.

49 This duplicate name from the line above was probably a simple recording error as it appears nowhere else in the lists of Firekeepers. A similar duplication occurs in the "Elder Brothers" listing of December 5, 1933 for Adam Burning.

Note that the "warriors" have been "allowed 3 delegates", signifying their continued recognition by Council.

50 Moses was a Delaware, very active in Reserve affairs.

51 "Mitch" Hepburn, the name circled in the margin above this by the Secretary. The Chiefs' position was likely that names belong within traditional families and only they could give them legitimately to outsiders as was sometimes done (see December 5, 1935). Names specifically generated for dignitaries were given out into recent times but the practice has passed from general favour. The "fair society" was the Six Nations Agricultural Society Fairboard (founded in 1867), organizers of the annual Six Nations Fall Fair.

52 "Secy" Anderson had been appointed by his fellow Mohawks to attend a celebration in Niagara Falls August 22. Now the Younger Brothers have appointed this accommodating Mohawk as one of their three representatives to the forthcoming Grand Council.

	1924	1925	1926	1927	1928	1929	1930	1931	1932	1933	1934	1935	1936	1937	1938	1939	1940	1941
January		UCLH-6 -20								UCLH-3	?-2 TS-9	OLH-1	OLH-7 HM-14					?-4
February										UCLH-14	OLH-6							
March										UCLH-7								
April										OLH-5	OLH-1	MLH-2						
May										OLH-2	OLH-5	?-7 MLH-21						
June										OLH-6		MLH-18						
July											OLH-3 TS-17	OLH-2						
August											OLH-7 ?-22	?-?					OLH -21/22	
September	AH-7 UCLH-21									OLH-19	OLH-11	MLH-3 ?-24	OLH-21				OLH-1	
October	OLH-4 -18									TS-3 -17		?-8 / SC- one Council, no date						
November	UCLH-2									OLH-7	MLH-6							
December										OLH-5	OLH-4							
Totals	5	2								11	12	11	3				3	1

Analysis of Hereditary Councils — October 7, 1924 to February 4, 1941, see fn. 43

Abbreviation	Council Location	Number of Councils		Abbreviation	Council Location	Number of Councils
AH	Agricultural Hall	1		MLH	Mohawk L/H	5
UCLH	Upper Cayuga L/H	7		SC	Smoke's Corners	1
OLH	Onondaga L/H	22		HM	Herb Martin's	1
TS	Thomas School	4		?	site not recorded	7

Total of 48 Councils — 33 Regular Councils; 4 Adjournments; 11 Special Councils

53 About this time the establishment of the first of three "Upper End" Mohawk Long-houses was being attempted. All three were vandalized and abandoned, the most recent about 10-15 years ago. According to UCLH Chief Sid General (October 5, 1991) the first two were on the present Mohawk Road between First and Second Lines, the second was on property adjoining the first, just over the fence line; the last was attempted on First Line between Mohawk and Seneca Roads, across the road from the surviving cemetary of the new vanished "Stump Hall" meeting-house (Plymouth Brethren Mission). See map.

54 Possibly: "A Special Council, in one week".

55 This is an intriguing entry, one wishes to know more about the malversation prompting it.

56 1934 or 1935? This would seem a continuation of the April 2, 1935 minutes from which it had been separated by the belated and intrusive October entry.

57 Tonawanda Seneca Reservation, NY.

58 To spare time on Council's agenda Anderson is given a free hand to respond to and set right newspaper accounts about the Six Nations, to answer general mail on Council's behalf (something which I did during the period of the 1959 Uprising), and give talks on Iroquois affairs. With his soft spoken manner and gentlemanly presence he was perfect for the task, and he knew his facts. The clipping inserted at this location, mentioned in the italics, would seem an example of what he would process. There is one record only (June 18, 1935) of Council asking for a report on his correspondence, either monitoring his initial performance or following up regular business.

59 A Chief from the Oneida of the Thames; he sits with the Younger Brothers, not the public. These Oneida recently withdrew from membership in the Confederacy at Ohsweken.

60 These three are not Six Nations surnames. There are "Big-Canoes" on the (Ojibwa) reserve at Christian Island, Ontario, some 130 miles due north of Ohsweken.

61 Col. Morgan had been replaced by another former military officer as Superintendent of the Reserve. The Major's wife was the anthropologist Martha Randle.

62 World War II was a year old. Although Conscription had not come into effect yet (Québec was hostile to the idea), it appears that eligible Indian men already were being required to register for a potential draft. However, Resolution 4 of the Minutes for October 1, 1940, suggests that Randle may have been discovered as less than forthright with his registration notice.

63 The "X letter" was not in the Minutes. A Christian dominated Council was opposed to entering WW I unless requested by the King, but voluntary participation was permitted, and 292 men served (Weaver, p 532). One sometimes hears that Council declared war on the Kaiser and, not being invited to participate in the Verseilles Treaty at war's end, was still at war with Germany when Herr Hitler went on his rampage. I can not vouch for this with my available sources, but Weaver, working with old Minute Books, would seem to contradict such tales. A later Longhouse dominated Council, ex-officio, was opposed on principle to participation in WW II. Longhouse precepts are against bloodletting; this has not, however, prevented men with Longhouse ties from joining various Canadian and US military services. There were also voluntary enlistments in WW II by both Longhouse and Christian "warriors". Agent Randle provided Ray Fadden of the Akwesasne Mohawk Councelor Organization, Hogansburg, NY with the names of 310 individuals from Ohsweken who served in WW II (Six Nations Iroquois Confederacy Record, World War II, no date).

MAP OF SIX NATIONS RESERVE. 1991,
showing locations mentioned in Appendix H.

A   Site of pre-1863 Onondaga Longhouse
B   Arthur Anderson home
C   1863 Council House
D   Agricultural Hall
E   Thomas School
F   First two Mohawk Longhouses
G   Smoke's Corners (now known as
                  "Barney Martin's Corners")
H   Third Mohawk Longhouse

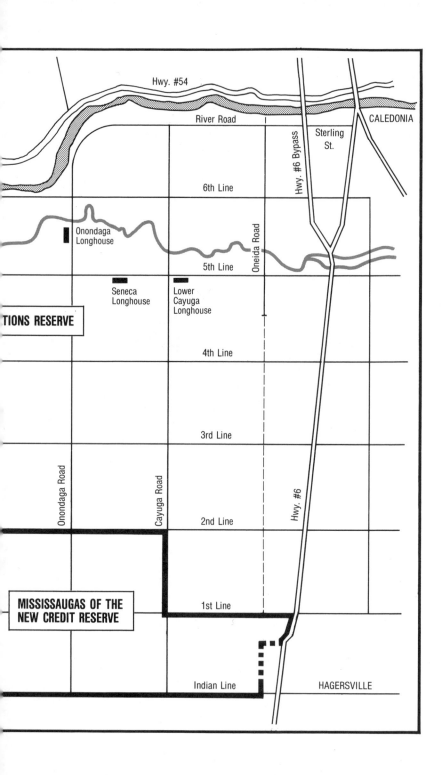

Hwy. #54

River Road

CALEDONIA

Sterling
St.

Hwy. #6 Bypass

6th Line

Onondaga
Longhouse

Oneida Road

5th Line

Seneca
Longhouse

Lower
Cayuga
Longhouse

TIONS RESERVE

4th Line

3rd Line

Onondaga Road

Cayuga Road

Hwy. #6

2nd Line

MISSISSAUGAS OF THE
NEW CREDIT RESERVE

1st Line

Indian Line

HAGERSVILLE

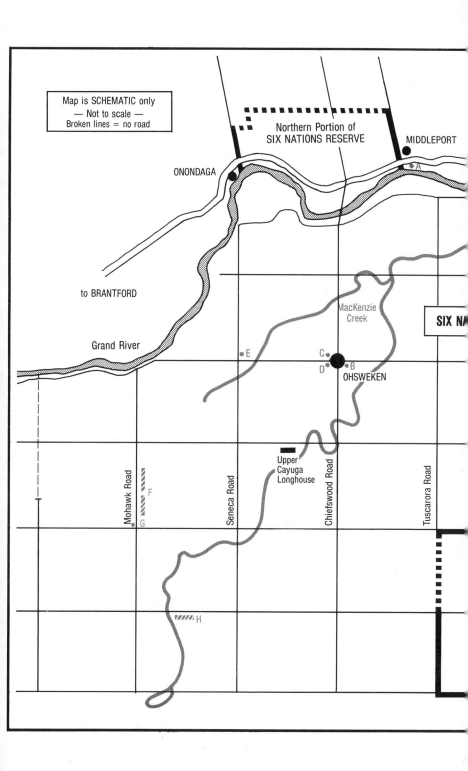

64 Anderson departs from his established format for listing Council in blocks.

65 Sandy and Burning were Seneca Chiefs. Anderson might better have captioned this line of Chiefs as "Elder Brothers", perhaps Mohawk nationalism overcame him here and in two other entries. He does note "Firekeepers" for the Onondagas, and once "Cayuga" but never the inclusive "Younger Brothers".

66 King was Prime Minster of Canada; "Premier" was used then for all Provincial leaders. In striving for its separate identity, Québec has since acquired a "Premier Ministre".

67 For no apparent reason this lone attending Cayuga Younger Brother has been listed below the Elder Brothers.

68 The duplication is in the original.

69 This final entry reveals that, even after 16½ years in a kind of limbo, the Chiefs Council was still being approached to adjudicate such questions at issue as Wills and lands. Yet nothing had changed; the Chiefs' decisions would be useless under the Indian Act, and records in the Indian office would be changed only if the parties were successful with their approaches to the Elected Council, and then often only if the custodial Indian Department gave its final blessing. One interpretation of these events would be that the petitioners sought the sanction of their Government, the one they acknowledged, before approaching the imposed system for a 'legal' confirmation.

WGS

8. ARTHUR ANDERSON, Mohawk, 1975.
(b. June 21, 1888 – d. February 20, 1983)

WGS Collection

10. AKWESASNE LONGHOUSE. New York State. June 28, 1991
In front of the Longhouse is the granite monument shown in the next photo. To the far right is the kitchen-dining hall.

Photo by Larry MacKenzie

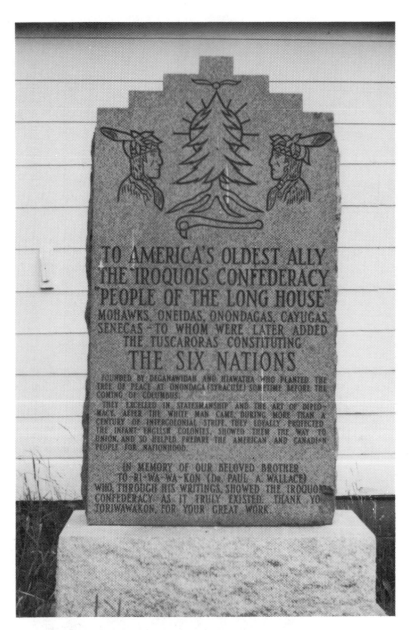

TO AMERICA'S OLDEST ALLY
THE IROQUOIS CONFEDERACY
"PEOPLE OF THE LONG HOUSE"
MOHAWKS, ONEIDAS, ONONDAGAS, CAYUGAS,
SENECAS - TO WHOM WERE LATER ADDED
THE TUSCARORAS CONSTITUTING
THE SIX NATIONS

FOUNDED BY DEGANAWIDAH AND HIAWATHA WHO PLANTED THE
TREE OF PEACE AT ONONDAGA (SYRACUSE) SOMETIME BEFORE THE
COMING OF COLUMBUS.

THEY EXCELLED IN STATESMANSHIP AND THE ART OF DIPLO-
MACY. AFTER THE WHITE MAN CAME, DURING MORE THAN A
CENTURY OF INTERCOLONIAL STRIFE, THEY LOYALLY PROTECTED
THE INFANT ENGLISH COLONIES, SHOWED THEM THE WAY TO
UNION, AND SO HELPED PREPARE THE AMERICAN AND CANADIAN
PEOPLE FOR NATIONHOOD.

IN MEMORY OF OUR BELOVED BROTHER
TO-RI-WA-WA-KON (DR. PAUL A. WALLACE)
WHO, THROUGH HIS WRITINGS, SHOWED THE IROQUOIS
CONFEDERACY AS IT TRULY EXISTED. THANK YOU
TORIWAWAKON, FOR YOUR GREAT WORK.

11. MONUMENT, AKWESASNE LONGHOUSE, 1991.
One of many Iroquois historical monuments erected in Canada and the
USA by the Akwesasne Mohawk Councelor Organization.

Photo by Larry MacKenzie

12. ONONDAGA LONGHOUSE, Friday, June 14, 1991.
The foundation for the new Longhouse has been poured: two rows of cedar logs await assembly by volunteers.
Construction was paid for by donations from within and without the Longhouse community as well as such money raising
functions as meals, sports events, draws, and catering.

WGS Photo

13. ONONDAGA LONGHOUSE. Moving the "Fire". Saturday, October 19, 1991.

Left to right: Women's privy; new log Longhouse; kitchen-dining hall; log cook-house (the old, old Longhouse, long since whittled down to its present size). A hydro pole carries electricity to the dining hall, the new Longhouse remains as its predecessors, illuminated by coal-oil lamps. A much-needed expansion and gravelling of the parking area was completed just in time for the inauguration of the new structure, piles of earth border the east side of the lot. Visitor vehicles lined both sides of Onondaga Road for several hundred feet.

WGS Photo

14. ONONDAGA LONGHOUSE, view from ball field.
Like the building it replaces, and unlike the other three Ohsweken Longhouses, it has but one door, midway along the east wall.

IROQRAFTS Indian Reprint Series